Radio and Television Communication

Radio and Television Communication

Sonia Mahajan

RANDOM PUBLICATIONS
NEW DELHI (INDIA)

Radio and Television Communication

ISBN 978-93-5111-513-7

Published in 2015 in India by

RANDOM PUBLICATIONS

4376-A/4B, Gali Murari Lal, Ansari Road
New Delhi-110 002
Phone : +9111-43580356, 011-23289044, 011-43142548
e-mail: sales@randompublications.com,
info@randompublications.com, randomexports@gmail.com

Reprinted 2024

Type Setting by : Friends Media, Delhi-110089
Digitally Printed at : Replika Press Pvt. Ltd.

Preface

Radio and television are the forms of media that can reach millions of people at a time. They have huge influence on our lives and can be used to educate, inform, entertain, expose us to other people and cultures around the world, and even to babysit our children.

The power of broadcast media is enormous in today's society. It can facilitate public debate and discussion and shape public opinion. Its influence extends to its role in development, setting an agenda it deems relevant to nation building. Media with a capacity and interest to report issues on national strategies, social justice and inclusion, social progress, environmental sustainability, and enabling regulatory environment can create wealth in society, develop people's potential to pursue creative and productive lives, and contribute towards equity and equality for all people.

Strategies differ, from adhering to a free and pluralistic media to imposing a more regulated arrangement. The enormity and complexity of development and its consequences demand a dynamic and sustainable organization, able to adapt to technology and program innovations, creative capacity building approaches, and new delivery platforms to serve both business and development ends.

The present book deals with subject areas related to radio and television communication. It covers issues concerned with broadcast transmission systems, satellites, other carriers and also focuses on technological programming of services. The recent developments of radio and television services, their role in contemporary society are also described. The book is designed to give the student of mass communication a general and comprehensive view of the broadcast media. It will also be useful for media personnel, social scientists, educationists, research scholars and the general audience.

Author

Contents

1

Broadcasting: An Overview

Broadcasting is the distribution of audio and video content to a dispersed audience via any audio or visual mass communications medium, but usually one using electromagnetic radiation (radio waves). The receiving parties may include the general public or a relatively large subset thereof. Broadcasting has been used for purposes of private recreation, non-commercial exchange of messages, experimentation, self-training, and emergency communication such as amateur (ham) radio and amateur television (ATV) in addition to commercial purposes like popular radio or TV stations with advertisements.

History of Broadcasting

The history of broadcasting began with early radio transmissions which only carried the dots and dashes of wireless telegraphy. The history of radio broadcasting (experimentally around 1906, commercially around 1920) starts with audio (sound) broadcasting services which are broadcast through the air as radio waves from a transmitter to an antenna and, thus, to a receiving device. Stations can be linked in radio networks to broadcast common programming, either in syndication or simulcast or both.

United States

One of the first signals of significant power that carried voice and music was accomplished in 1906 by Reginald Fessenden when he made a Christmas Eve broadcast to ships at sea from Massachusetts. He played "O Holy Night" on his violin and read passages from the Bible. However, his financial backers lost interest in the project, leaving others to take the next steps. Early on, the concept of broadcasting was new and unusual—with telegraphs, communication had been one-to-one, not one-to-many. Sending out one-way messages to multiple receivers didn't seem to have much practical use.

Charles Herrold of San Jose, California sent out broadcasts as early as April 1909 from his Herrold School electronics institute in downtown San Jose, using the identification San Jose Calling, and then a variety of different call signs as the Department of Commerce began to regulate radio. His station was first called FN, then SJN (probably illegally). By 1912, the United States government began requiring radio operators to obtain licenses to send out signals. Herrold received licenses for 6XF and 6XE (a mobile transmitter) in 1916.

He was on the air daily for nearly a decade when World War I interrupted operations. After the war, the Herrold operation in San Jose received the callsign KQW in 1923. Today, the lineage of that continues as KCBS, a CBS-owned station in San Francisco.

Herrold, the son of a farmer who patented a seed spreader, coined the terms broadcasting and narrowcasting, based on the ideas of spreading crop seed far and wide, rather than only in rows. While Herrold never claimed the invention of radio itself, he did claim the invention of broadcasting to a wide audience, through the use of antennas designed to radiate signals in all directions.

By comparison, David Sarnoff has been considered by some, arguably and perhaps mistakenly, as "the prescient prophet of broadcasting who predicted the medium's rise in 1915", referring to his radio music box concept.

A few organizations were allowed to keep working on radio during the war. Westinghouse was the most well-known of these. Frank Conrad, a Westinghouse engineer, had been making transmissions from 8XK since 1916 that included music programming.

However, a team at the University of Wisconsin–Madison headed by Professor Earle M. Terry also had permission to be on the air. They operated 9XM, originally licensed by Professor Edward Bennett in 1914, and usually sent Morse code weather reports to ships on the Great Lakes, but they also experimented with voice broadcasts starting in 1917. They reportedly had difficulties with audio distortion, so the next couple of years were spent making transmissions distortion-free.

Following the war, Herrold and other radio pioneers across the country resumed transmissions. The early stations gained new call signs. 8XK became KDKA in 1920. Herrold received a license for KQW in 1921 (later to become KCBS). 9XM became WHA in 1922.

The National Broadcasting Company began regular broadcasting in 1926, with telephone links between New York and other Eastern cities. NBC became the dominant radio network, splitting into Red and Blue networks.

The Columbia Broadcasting System began in 1927 under the guidance of William S. Paley.

Radio in education soon followed and colleges across the U.S. began adding radio broadcasting courses to their curricula. Curry College, first in Boston and then in Milton, Massachusetts, introduced one of the first broadcasting majors in 1932 when the college teamed up with WLOE in Boston to have students broadcast programs.

Several independent stations formed the Mutual Broadcasting System to exchange syndicated programming, including The Lone Ranger and Amos 'n' Andy.

A Federal Communnications Commission decision in 1939 required NBC to divest itself of its Blue Network. That decision was sustained by the Supreme Court in a 1943 decision, National Broadcasting Co. v. United States, which established the framework that the "scarcity" of radio-frequency meant that broadcasting was subject to greater regulation than other media. This Blue Network network became the American Broadcasting Company (ABC). Around 1946, ABC, NBC, and CBS began regular television broadcasts. Another TV network, the DuMont Television Network, was founded earlier, but was disbanded in 1956.

Britain

The first experimental broadcasts, from Marconi's factory in Chelmsford, began in 1920.

Two years later, a consortium of radio manufacturers formed the British Broadcasting Company (BBC). This broadcast continued until its licence expired at the end of 1926. The company then became the British Broadcasting Corporation, a non-commercial organisation. Its governors are appointed by the government but they do not answer to it.

Lord Reith took a formative role in developing the BBC, especially in radio. Working as its first manager and Director-General, he promoted the philosophy of public service broadcasting, firmly grounded in the moral benefits of education and of uplifting entertainment, eschewing commercial influence and maintaining a maximum of independence from political control.

Commercial stations such as Radio Normandie and Radio Luxembourg broadcast into the UK from other European countries. This provided a very popular alternative to the rather austere BBC. These stations were closed during the War, and only Radio Luxembourg returned afterward.

BBC television broadcasts in Britain began on November 2, 1936, and continued until wartime conditions closed the service in 1939.

Germany

Before the Nazi assumption of power in 1933, the use of radio broadcasting was supervised by the Post Office. A listening fee of 2 Reichsmark per receiver paid most subsidies.

Immediately following Hitler's assumption of power, Joseph Goebbels became head of the Ministry for Propaganda and Public Enlightenment. Non-Nazis were removed from broadcasting and editorial positions. Jews were fired from all positions.

The Reichsrundfunk programming began to decline in popularity as the theme of Kampfzeit was continually played. Germany was easily served by a number of European mediumwave stations, including the BBC and domestic stations in France, the Low Countries, Denmark and Sweden, and Poland. It became illegal for Germans to listen to foreign broadcasts. (Foreign correspondents and key officials were exempt from this rule).

During the war, German stations broadcast not only war propaganda and entertainment for German forces dispersed through Europe and the Atlantic, but provided air raid alerts.

Germany experimented with television broadcasting before the Second World War, using a 180-line raster system beginning before 1935. German propaganda claimed the system was superior to the British mechanical scanning system, but this was subject to debate by persons who saw the broadcasts.

Sri Lanka

Sri Lanka has the oldest radio station in Asia (world's second oldest). The station was known as Radio Ceylon. It developed into one of the finest broadcasting institutions in the world. It is now known as the Sri Lanka Broadcasting Corporation.

Sri Lanka created broadcasting history in Asia when broadcasting was started in Ceylon by the Telegraph Department in 1923 on an experimental footing, just three years after the inauguration of broadcasting in Europe.

Gramophone music was broadcast from a tiny room in the Central Telegraph Office with the aid of a small transmitter built by the Telegraph Department engineers from the radio equipment of a captured German submarine.

This broadcasting experiment was a huge success and barely three years later, on December 16, 1925, a regular broadcasting service came to be instituted. Edward Harper who came to Ceylon as Chief Engineer of the Telegraph Office in 1921, was the first person to actively promote broadcasting in Ceylon. Sri Lanka occupies an important place in the history of broadcasting with broadcasting services inaugurated just three years after the launch of the BBC in the United Kingdom.

Edward Harper launched the first experimental broadcast as well as founding the Ceylon Wireless Club, together with British and Ceylonese radio enthusiasts on the island. Edward Harper has been dubbed ' the Father of Broadcasting in Ceylon,' because of his pioneering efforts, his skill and his determination to succeed. Edward Harper and his fellow Ceylonese radio enthusiasts, made it happen.

The 1950s and 1960s

Television began to replace radio as the chief source of revenue for broadcasting networks. Although many radio programs continued through this decade, including Gunsmoke and The Guiding Light, by 1960 networks had ceased producing entertainment programs.

As radio stopped producing formal fifteen-minute to hourly programs, a new format developed. "Top 40" was based on a continuous rotation of short pop songs presented by a "disc jockey." Famous disc jockeys in the era included Alan Freed, Dick Clark, Don Imus and Wolfman Jack. Top 40 playlists were theoretically based on record sales; however, record companies began to bribe disc jockeys to play selected artists, in what was called payola.

In the 1950s, American television networks introduced broadcasts in color. (The Federal Communications Commission approved the world's first monochrome-compatible color television standard in Dec., 1953. The first network colorcast followed on January 1, 1954, with NBC transmitting the annual Tournament of Roses Parade in Pasadena, Calif. to over 20 stations across the country.) An educational television network, National Educational Television (NET), predecessor to PBS, was founded.

Shortwave broadcasting played an important part of fighting the cold war with Voice of America and the BBC World Service argumented with Radio Free Europe and Radio Liberty transmitting through the "Iron Curtain", and Radio Moscow and others broadcasting back, as well as jamming (transmitting to cause intentional interference) the western voices.

Radio Luxembourg remained popular during the 1950s but saw its audience decline as commercial television and pirate radio, combined with a switch to a less clear frequency, began to erode its influence.

BBC television resumed on June 7, 1946, and commercial television began on September 22, 1955. Both used the pre-war 405-line standard.

BBC2 came on the air on April 20, 1964, using the 625-line standard, and began PAL colour transmissions on July 1, 1967, the first in Europe. The two older networks transmitted in 625-line colour from 1969.

During the 1960s there was still no UK-based commercial radio. A number of 'pirate' radio ships, located in international waters just outside the jurisdiction of English law, came on the air between 1964 and 1967. The most famous of these was Radio Caroline, which was the only station to continue broadcasting after the offshore pirates were effectively outlawed on August 14, 1967 by the Marine Broadcasting Offences Act. It was finally forced off air due to a dispute over tendering payments, but returned in 1972 and continued on and off until 1990. The station still broadcasts, nowadays using satellite carriers and internet.

When the Federal Republic of Germany was organized in 1949, its Enabling Act established strong state government powers. Broadcasting was organized on a state, rather than a national, basis. Nine regional radio networks were established. A technical coordinating organization, the Arbeitsgemeinschaft der offentlich-rechtlichen Rundfunkanstalten der Bundesrepublik Deutschland (ARD), came into being in 1950 to lessen technical conflicts.

The Allied forces in Europe developed their own radio networks, including the U.S. American Forces Network (AFN). Inside Berlin, Radio in the American Sector (RIAS) became a key source of news in the German Democratic Republic.

Germany began developing a network of VHF FM broadcast stations in 1955 because of the excessive crowding of the mediumwave and shortwave broadcast bands.

Radio Ceylon ruled the airwaves in the 1950s and 1960s in the Indian sub-continent. The station developed into the most popular radio network in South Asia. Millions of listeners in India for example tuned into Radio Ceylon.

Announcers like Livy Wijemanne, Vernon Corea, Pearl Ondaatje, Tim Horshington, Greg Roskowski, Jimmy Bharucha, Mil Sansoni, Eardley Peiris, Shirley Perera, Bob Harvie, Christopher Greet, Prosper Fernando, Ameen Sayani (of Binaca Geetmala fame),Karunaratne Abeysekera, S.P.Mylvaganam (the first Tamil Announcer on the Commercial Service) were hugely popular across South Asia.

The Hindi Service also helped build Radio Ceylon's reputation as the market leader in the Indian sub-continent. Gopal Sharma, Sunil Dutt Ameen Sayani, Hamid Sayani, were among the Indian announcers of the station.

The Commercial Service of Radio Ceylon was hugely successful under the leadership of Clifford Dodd, the Australian administrator and broadcasting expert who was sent to Ceylon under the Colombo Plan. Dodd hand picked some of the most talented radio presenters in South Asia. They went on to enjoy star status in the Indian sub-continent. This was Radio Ceylon's golden era.

The 1970s, 1980s, and 1990s

The introduction of FM changed the listening habits of younger Americans. Many stations such as WNEW-FM in New York City began to play whole sides of record albums, as opposed to the "Top 40" model of two decades earlier.

In the 1980s, the Federal Communications Commission, under Reagan Administration and Congressional pressure, changed the rules limiting the number of radio and television stations a business entity could own in one metropolitan area. This deregulation led to several groups, such as Infinity Broadcasting and Clear Channel to buy many stations in major cities. The cost of these stations' purchases led to a conservative approach to broadcasting, including limited playlists and avoiding controversial subjects to not offend listeners, and increased commercials to increase revenue.

AM Radio declined throughout the 1970s and 1980s due to various reasons including: Lower cost of FM receivers, narrow AM audio bandwidth, and poor sound in the AM section of automobile receivers (to combat the crowding of stations in the AM band and a "loudness war" conducted by AM broadcasters), and increased radio noise in homes caused by fluorescent lighting and introduction of electronic devices in homes. AM radio's decline flattened out in the mid 1990s due to the introduction of niche formats and over commercialization of many FM stations.

A new Pirate station, Swiss-owned Radio Nordsee International, broadcast to Britain and the Netherlands from 1970 until outlawed by Dutch legislation in 1974 (which meant it could no longer be supplied from the European mainland). The English service was heavily jammed by both Labour and Conservative Governments in 1970 amid suggestions that the ship was actually being used for espionage. Radio Caroline returned in 1972 and continued until its ship sank in 1980 (the crew were rescued). A Belgian station, Radio Atlantis, operated an English service for a few months before the Dutch act came into force in 1974.

Land-based commercial radio finally came on air in 1973 with London's LBC and Capital Radio.

Channel 4 television started in November 1982. Britain's UHF system was originally designed to carry only four networks.

Pirate radio enjoyed another brief resurgence with a literal re-launch of Radio Caroline in 1983, and the arrival of American-owned Laser 558 in 1985. Both stations were harassed by the British authorities; Laser closed in 1987 and Caroline in 1989, since then it has pursued legal methods of broadcasting, such as temporary FM licences and satellite.

Two rival satellite television systems came on the air at the end of the 1980s: Sky Television and British Satellite Broadcasting. Huge losses forced a rapid merger, although in many respects it was a takeover of BSB (Britain's official, Government-sanctioned satellite company) by Sky.

Radio Luxembourg launched a 24-hour English channel on satellite, but closed its AM service in 1989 and its satellite service in 1991.

The Broadcasting Act 1990 in UK law marked the establishment of two licencing authorities - the Radio Authority and the Independent Television Commission - to facilitate the licencing of non-BBC broadcast services, especially short-term broadcasts.

Channel 5 went on the air on March 30, 1997, using "spare" frequencies between the existing channels.

The Government of Sri Lanka opened up the market in the late 1970s and 1980s allowing private companies to set up radio and television stations.

Sri Lanka's public services broadcasters are the Sri Lanka Broadcasting Corporation (SLBC), Independent Television Net Work (ITN) and the affiliated radio station called Lak-handa. They had stiff competition on their hands with the private sector.

Broadcasting in Sri Lanka went through a transformation resulting in private broadcasting institutions being set up on the island among them Telshan Network (Pvt) Ltd, (TNL, Maharaja Television -TV, Sirasa TV and Shakthi TV, and EAP Network (Pvt) Ltd - known as Swarnawahini - these private channels all have radio stations as well.

The 1990s saw a new generation of radio stations being established in Sri Lanka among them the 'Hiru' radio station. In the 1980s public service broadcasters like the Sri Lanka Broadcasting Corporation set up their own FM arm.

Sri Lanka celebrated 80 years of broadcasting in December 2005. In January 2007 the Sri Lanka Broadcasting Corporation celebrated 40 years as a public corporation.

In 1987, stations in the European Broadcasting Union began offering Radio Data System (RDS), which provides written text information about programs that were being broadcast, as well as traffic alerts, accurate time, and other teletext services.

The 2000s

The 2000s (decade) saw the introduction of digital radio and direct broadcasting by satellite (DBS) in the USA.

Digital radio services, except in the United States, were allocated a new frequency band in the range of 1,400 MHz. In the United States, this band was deemed to be vital to national defense, so an alternate band in the range of 2,300 MHz was introduced for satellite broadcasting. Two American companies, XM and Sirius, introduced DBS systems, which are funded by direct subscription, as in cable television. The XM and Sirius systems provide approximately 100 channels each, in exchange for monthly payments.

In addition, a consortium of companies received FCC approval for In-Band On-Channel digital broadcasts in the United States, which use the existing mediumwave and FM bands to provide CD-quality sound. However, early IBOC tests showed interference problems with adjacent channels, which has slowed adoption of the system.

In Canada, the Canadian Radio-television and Telecommunications Commission plans to move all Canadian broadcasting to the digital band and close all mediumwave and FM stations.

European and Australian stations have begun digital broadcasting (DAB). Digital radios began to be sold in the United Kingdom in 1998.

Regular Shortwave broadcasts using Digital Radio Mondiale (DRM), a digital broadcasting scheme for short and medium wave broadcasts have begun. This system makes the normally scratchy international broadcasts clear and nearly FM quality, and much lower transmitter power. This is much better to listen to and has more languages.

In Sri Lanka in 2005 when Sri Lanka celebrated 80 years in Broadcasting, the former Director-General of the Sri Lanka Broadcasting Corporation, Eric Fernando called for the station to take full advantage of the digital age - this included looking at the archives of Radio Ceylon.

Ivan Corea asked the President of Sri Lanka, Mahinda Rajapakse to invest in the future of the SLBC.

Types of Broadcasting

Historically, there have been several types of electronic media broadcasting:

— Telephone broadcasting (1881–1932): the earliest form of electronic broadcasting (not counting data services offered by stock telegraph companies from 1867, if ticker-tapes are excluded from the definition). Telephone broadcasting began with the advent of Théâtrophone ("Theatre Phone") systems, which were telephone-based distribution systems allowing subscribers to listen to live opera and theatre performances over telephone lines, created by French inventor Clément Ader in 1881. Telephone broadcasting also grew to include telephone newspaper services for news and entertainment programming which were introduced in the 1890s, primarily located in large European cities. These telephone-based subscription services were the first examples of electrical/electronic broadcasting and offered a wide variety of programming.

— Radio broadcasting (experimentally from 1906, commercially from 1920): radio broadcasting is an audio (sound) broadcasting service, broadcast through the air as radio waves from a transmitter to a radio antenna and, thus, to a receiver. Stations can be linked in radio networks to broadcast common radio programs, either in broadcast syndication, simulcast or subchannels.

— History of television broadcasting (telecast), experimentally from 1925, commercial television from the 1930s: this television programming medium was long-awaited by the general public and rapidly rose to compete with its older radio-broadcasting sibling.

— Cable radio (also called "cable FM", from 1928) and cable television (from 1932): both via coaxial cable, serving principally as transmission mediums for programming produced at either radio or television stations, with limited production of cable-dedicated programming.

— Direct-broadcast satellite (DBS) (from circa 1974) and satellite radio (from circa 1990): meant for direct-to-home broadcast programming (as opposed to studio network uplinks and downlinks), provides a mix of traditional radio or television broadcast programming, or both, with dedicated satellite radio programming.

— Webcasting of video/television (from circa 1993) and audio/radio (from circa 1994) streams: offers a mix of traditional radio and television station broadcast programming with dedicated internet radio-webcast programming.

Economic Models

Economically there are a few ways in which stations are able to broadcast continually. Each differs in the method by which stations are funded:

— in-kind donations of time and skills by volunteers (common with community radio broadcasters)

— direct government payments or operation of public broadcasters
— indirect government payments, such as radio and television licenses
— grants from foundations or business entities
— selling advertising or sponsorships
— public subscription or membership

Broadcasters may rely on a combination of these business models. For example, National Public Radio (NPR), a non-commercial educational (NCE) public radio media organization within the U.S., receives grants from the Corporation for Public Broadcasting (CPB) (which, in turn, receives funding from the U.S. government), by public membership and by selling "extended credits" to corporations.

Underwriting spots vs. commercials

In contrast with commercial broadcasting, NPR does not carry traditional radio commercials or television commercial. It offers major donors brief statements that are called underwriting spots and unlike commercials, are governed by specific FCC restrictions in addition to the truth-in-advertising laws; they cannot advocate a product or contain any "call to action"

Recorded Broadcasts and Live Broadcasts

The first regular television broadcasts started in 1937. Broadcasts can be classified as "recorded" or "live". The former allows correcting errors, and removing superfluous or undesired material, rearranging it, applying slow-motion and repetitions, and other techniques to enhance the program. However, some live events like sports television can include some of the aspects including slow-motion clips of important goals/hits, etc., in between the live television telecast.

American radio-network broadcasters habitually forbade prerecorded broadcasts in the 1930s and 1940s requiring radio programs played for the Eastern and Central time zones to be repeated three hours later for the Pacific time zone (See: Effects of time on North American broadcasting). This restriction was dropped for special occasions, as in the case of the German dirigible airship Hindenburg disaster at Lakehurst, New Jersey, in 1937. During World War II, prerecorded broadcasts from war correspondents were allowed on U.S. radio. In addition, American radio programs were recorded for playback by Armed Forces Radio radio stations around the world.

A disadvantage of recording first is that the public may know the outcome of an event from another source, which may be a "spoiler". In addition, prerecording prevents live radio announcers from deviating from an officially approved script, as occurred with propaganda broadcasts from Germany in the 1940s and with Radio Moscow in the 1980s.

Many events are advertised as being live, although they are often "recorded live" (sometimes called "live-to-tape"). This is particularly true of performances of musical artists on radio when they visit for an in-studio concert performance. Similar situations have occurred in television production ("The Cosby Show is recorded in front of a live television studio audience") and news broadcasting.

A broadcast may be distributed through several physical means. If coming directly from the radio studio at a single station or television station, it is simply sent through the studio/transmitter link to the transmitter and hence from the television antenna located on the radio masts and towers out to the world. Programming may also come through a communications satellite, played either live or recorded for later transmission. Networks of stations may simulcast the same programming at the same time, originally via microwave link, now usually by satellite.

Distribution to stations or networks may also be through physical media, such as magnetic tape, compact disc (CD), DVD, and sometimes other formats. Usually these are included in another broadcast, such as when electronic news gathering (ENG) returns a story to the station for inclusion on a news programme.

The final leg of broadcast distribution is how the signal gets to the listener or viewer. It may come over the air as with a radio station or television station to an antenna and radio receiver, or may come through cable television or cable radio (or "wireless cable") via the station or directly from a network. The Internet may also bring either internet radio or streaming media television to the recipient, especially with multicasting allowing the signal and bandwidth to be shared.

The term "broadcast network" is often used to distinguish networks that broadcast an over-the-air television signals that can be received using a tuner (television) inside a television set with a television antenna from so-called networks that are broadcast only via cable television (cablecast) or satellite television that uses a dish antenna. The term "broadcast television" can refer to the television programs of such networks.

Social Impact

The sequencing of content in a broadcast is called a schedule. As with all technological endeavors, a number of technical terms and slang have developed. A list of these terms can be found at List of broadcasting terms. Television and radio programs are distributed through radio broadcasting or cable, often both simultaneously. By coding signals and having a cable converter box with decoding equipment in homes, the latter also enables subscription-based channels, pay-tv and pay-per-view services.

In his essay, John Durham Peters wrote that communication is a tool used for dissemination. Durham stated, "Dissemination is a lens—sometimes a usefully distorting one—that helps us tackle basic issues such as interaction, presence, and space and time…on the agenda of any future communication theory in general". Dissemination focuses on the message being relayed from one main source to one large audience without the exchange of dialogue in between. There's chance for the message to be tweaked or corrupted once the main source releases it. There is really no way to predetermine how the larger population or audience will absorb the message. They can choose to listen, analyze, or simply ignore it. Dissemination in communication is widely used in the world of broadcasting.

Broadcasting focuses on getting one message out and it is up to the general public to do what they wish with it. Durham also states that broadcasting is used to address an open ended destination. There are many forms of broadcast, but they all aim to distribute a signal that will reach the target audience. Broadcasting can arrange audiences into entire assemblies.

In terms of media broadcasting, a radio show can gather a large number of followers who tune in every day to specifically listen to that specific disc jockey. The disc jockey follows the script for his or her radio show and just talks into the microphone. He or she does not expect immediate feedback from any listeners. The message is broadcast across airwaves throughout the community, but there the listeners cannot always respond immediately, especially since many radio shows are recorded prior to the actual air time.

References

Briggs Asa. *The History of Broadcasting in the United Kingdom*, Oxford University Press, 1961.

Ceylon, Radio. - *Standards of Broadcasting Practice* - Commercial Broadcasting Division. - Radio Ceylon, 1950.

Crisell, Andrew *An Introductory History of British Broadcasting.* 2nd ed. London: Routledge. 2002.

John Dunning, *On The Air: The Encyclopedia of Old-Time Radio*, Oxford University Press, 1998. ISBN 0-19-507678-8

Scannell, Paddy, and Cardiff, David. *A Social History of British Broadcasting, Volume One, 1922-1939*, Basil Blackwell, 1991.

Sterling Christopher, and Kittross John M. *Stay Tuned: A Concise History of American Broadcasting*, Wadsworth, 1978.

Tim Crook; *International Radio Journalism: History, Theory and Practice* Routledge, 1998.

2

Radio Broadcasting

Radio is the transmission of signals through free space by electromagnetic radiation of a frequency significantly below that of visible light, in the radio frequency range, from about 30 kHz to 300 GHz. These waves are called radio waves. Electromagnetic radiation travels by means of oscillating electromagnetic fields that pass through the air and the vacuum of space.

Information, such as sound, is carried by systematically changing (modulating) some property of the radiated waves, such as their amplitude, frequency, phase, or pulse width. When radio waves strike an electrical conductor, the oscillating fields induce an alternating current in the conductor. The information in the waves can be extracted and transformed back into its original form.

The word "radio" also appears in a 1907 article by Lee De Forest. It was adopted by the United States Navy in 1912, to distinguish radio from several other "wireless" communication technologies in use at the time, such as the photophone. The term became common by the time of the first commercial broadcasts in the United States in the 1920s. The term was adopted by other languages in Europe and Asia. British Commonwealth countries continued to commonly use the term "wireless" until the mid-20th century, though the magazine of the BBC in the UK has been called Radio Times ever since it was first published in the early 1920s.

In recent years the term "wireless" has gained renewed popularity through the rapid growth of short-range computer networking, e.g., Wireless Local Area Network (WLAN), Wi-Fi, and Bluetooth, as well as mobile telephony, e.g., GSM and UMTS. Today, the term "radio" often refers to the actual transceiver device or chip, whereas "wireless" refers to the system and/or method used for radio communication; hence one talks about radio transceivers and Radio Frequency Identification (RFID), but about wireless devices and wireless sensor networks.

Radio Technology

Radio systems used for communications will have the following elements. With more than 100 years of development, each process is implemented by a wide range of methods, specialized for different communications purposes.

Transmitter and Modulation

Each system contains a transmitter. This consists of a source of electrical energy, producing alternating current of a desired frequency of oscillation. The transmitter contains a system to modulate (change) some property of the energy produced to impress a signal on it. This modulation might be as simple as turning the energy on and off, or altering more subtle properties such as amplitude, frequency, phase, or combinations of these properties. The transmitter sends the modulated electrical energy to a tuned resonant antenna; this structure converts the rapidly changing alternating current into an electromagnetic wave that can move through free space (sometimes with a particular polarization).

Amplitude modulation of a carrier wave works by varying the strength of the transmitted signal in proportion to the information being sent. For example, changes in the signal strength can be used to reflect the sounds to be reproduced by a speaker, or to specify the light intensity of television pixels. It was the method used for the first audio radio transmissions, and remains in use today. "AM" is often used to refer to the mediumwave broadcast band.

Frequency modulation varies the frequency of the carrier. The instantaneous frequency of the carrier is directly proportional to the instantaneous value of the input signal. Digital data can be sent by shifting the carrier's frequency among a set of discrete values, a technique known as frequency-shift keying.

FM is commonly used at VHF radio frequencies for high-fidelity broadcasts of music and speech. Normal (analog) TV sound is also broadcast using FM.

Angle modulation alters the instantaneous phase of a carrier wave to transmit a signal. It is another term for Phase modulation.

Antenna

An antenna (or aerial) is an electrical device which converts electric currents into radio waves, and vice versa. It is usually used with a radio transmitter or radio receiver. In transmission, a radio transmitter applies an oscillating radio frequency electric current to the antenna's terminals, and the antenna radiates the energy from the current as electromagnetic waves (radio waves). In reception, an antenna intercepts some of the power of an electromagnetic wave in order to produce a tiny voltage at its terminals, that is applied to a receiver to be amplified. An antenna can be used for both transmitting and receiving.

Propagation

Once generated, electromagnetic waves travel through space either directly, or have their path altered by reflection, refraction or diffraction. The intensity of the waves diminishes due to geometric dispersion (the inverse-square law); some energy may also be absorbed by the intervening medium in some cases. Noise will generally alter the desired signal; this electromagnetic interference comes from natural sources, as well as from artificial sources such as other transmitters and accidental radiators. Noise is also produced at every step due to the inherent properties of the devices used. If the magnitude of the noise is large enough, the desired signal will no longer be discernible; this is the fundamental limit to the range of radio communications.

Resonance

Electrical resonance of tuned circuits in radios allow individual stations to be selected. A resonant circuit will respond strongly to a particular frequency, and much less so to differing frequencies. This allows the radio receiver to discriminate between multiple signals differing in frequency.

Receiver and Demodulation

The electromagnetic wave is intercepted by a tuned receiving antenna; this structure captures some of the energy of the wave and returns it to the form of oscillating electrical currents. At the receiver, these currents are demodulated, which is conversion to a usable signal form by a detector sub-system. The receiver is "tuned" to respond preferentially to the desired signals, and reject undesired signals.

Early radio systems relied entirely on the energy collected by an antenna to produce signals for the operator. Radio became more useful after the invention of electronic devices such as the vacuum tube and later the transistor, which made it possible to amplify weak signals. Today radio systems are used for applications from walkie-talkie children's toys to the control of space vehicles, as well as for broadcasting, and many other applications.

A radio receiver receives its input from an antenna, uses electronic filters to separate a wanted radio signal from all other signals picked up by this antenna, amplifies it to a level suitable for further processing, and finally converts through demodulation and decoding the signal into a form usable for the consumer, such as sound, pictures, digital data, measurement values, navigational positions, etc.

Radio Band

Radio frequencies occupy the range from a few hertz to 300 GHz, although commercially important uses of radio use only a small part of this spectrum. Other types of electromagnetic radiation, with frequencies above the RF range, are infrared, visible light, ultraviolet, X-rays and gamma rays. Since the energy of an individual photon of radio frequency is too low to remove an electron from an atom, radio waves are classified as non-ionizing radiation.

Radio Communication System

A radio communication system sends signals by radio. Types of radio communication systems deployed depend on technology, standards, regulations, radio spectrum allocation, user requirements, service positioning, and investment.

The radio equipment involved in communication systems includes a transmitter and a receiver, each having an antenna and appropriate terminal equipment such as a microphone at the transmitter and a loudspeaker at the receiver in the case of a voice-communication system.

The power consumed in a transmitting station varies depending on the distance of communication and the transmission conditions. The power received at the receiving station is usually only a tiny fraction of the transmitter's output, since communication depends on receiving the information, not the energy, that was transmitted.

Classical radio communications systems use frequency-division multiplexing (FDM) as a strategy to split up and share the available radio-frequency bandwidth for use by different parties communications concurrently. Modern radio communication systems include those that divide up a radio-frequency band by time-division multiplexing (TDM) and code-division multiplexing (CDM) as alternatives to the classical FDM strategy. These systems offer different tradeoffs in supporting multiple users, beyond the FDM strategy that was ideal for broadcast radio but less so for applications such as mobile telephony.

A radio communication system may send information only one way. For example, in broadcasting a single transmitter sends signals to many receivers. Two stations may take turns sending and receiving, using a single radio frequency; this is called "simplex." By using two radio frequencies, two stations may continuously and concurrently send and receive signals - this is called "duplex" operation.

Invention of Radio

The identity of the original inventor of radio, at the time called wireless telegraphy, is contentious. Early radios ran the entire power of the transmitter through a carbon microphone. While some early radios used some type of amplification through electric current or battery, until the mid 1920s the most common type of receiver was the crystal set. In the 1920s, amplifying vacuum tube radio receivers and transmitters came into use.

The theoretical basis of the propagation of electromagnetic waves was first described in 1873 by James Clerk Maxwell in his paper to the Royal Society, A dynamical theory of the electromagnetic field, which followed his work between 1861 and 1865. Towards the end of 1875, while experimenting with the telegraph, Thomas Edison noted a phenomenon that he termed "etheric force", announcing it the press on November 28. He abandoned this research when Elihu Thomson, among others, ridiculed the idea.

In 1878 David E. Hughes was the first to transmit and receive radio waves when he noticed that his induction balance caused noise in the receiver of his homemade telephone. He demonstrated his discovery to the Royal Society in 1880 but was told it was merely induction. Between 1886 and 1888 Heinrich Rudolf Hertz first validated Maxwell's theory through experiment, demonstrating that radio radiation had all the properties of waves (now called Hertzian waves), and discovering that the electromagnetic equations could be reformulated into a partial differential equation called the wave equation.

Mahlon Loomis was issued U.S. Patent 129971 on July 30, 1872. Roberto Landell de Moura, a Brazilian priest and scientist, conducted experiments in 1893/1894. He did not publicize his achievement until 1900. Claims have been made that Nathan Stubblefield invented radio before either Tesla or Marconi, but his device seems to have worked by induction transmission rather than radio transmission.

In 1893 in St. Louis, Missouri, Tesla made devices for his experiments with the electricity. Addressing the Franklin Institute in Philadelphia and the National Electric Light Association, he described and demonstrated in detail the principles of his work. The descriptions contained all the elements that were later incorporated into radio systems before the development of the vacuum tube. He initially experimented with magnetic receivers, unlike the coherers used by Marconi and other early experimenters. Tesla is usually considered the first to apply the mechanism of electrical conduction to wireless practices.

On 19 August 1894, British physicist Sir Oliver Lodge demonstrated the reception of Morse code signalling using radio waves, using a coherer. Edouard Branly of France and Popov of Russia later produced improved versions of the coherer.

Alexander Popov, who was the first to develop a practical communication system based on the coherer, is sometimes considered to have been the inventor of radio. In 1894 he built a coherer and presented it to the Russian Physical and Chemical Society on May 7, 1895. In March 1896, he transmitted radio waves between different campus buildings in Saint Petersburg, but did not apply for a patent.

Between 1894 and 1900 the Indian physicist Jagdish Chandra Bose performed pioneering research on radio waves and created waves as short as 5 mm. In November 1894, Bose ignited gunpowder and rang a bell at a distance using electromagnetic waves, confirming that communication signals could be sent without using wires, but he too did not patent his work.

The New Zealander Ernest Rutherford, 1st Baron Rutherford of Nelson was instrumental in the development of radio. In 1895 he was awarded an Exhibition of 1851 Science Research Scholarship to Cambridge. He arrived in England with a reputation as an innovator and inventor, and distinguished himself in several fields, initially by working out the electrical properties of solids and then using wireless waves as a method of signalling.

Rutherford was encouraged in his work by Sir Robert Ball, who had been scientific adviser to the body maintaining lighthouses on the Irish coast; he wished to solve the difficult problem of a ship's inability to detect a lighthouse in fog. Sensing fame and fortune, Rutherford increased the sensitivity of his apparatus until he could detect electromagnetic waves over a distance of several hundred metres. Thomson quickly realised that Rutherford was a researcher of exceptional ability and invited him to join in a study of the electrical conduction of gases. The commercial development of wireless technology was thus left for Guglielmo Marconi.

In 1896 Marconi was awarded what is sometimes recognised as the world's first patent for radio with British Patent 12039, Improvements in transmitting electrical impulses and signals and in apparatus there-for. In 1897 he established the world's first radio station on the Isle of Wight, England. The same year in the U.S., some key developments in radio's early history were made and patented by Tesla. The U.S. Patent Office reversed its decision in 1904, awarding Marconi a patent for the invention of radio, possibly influenced by Marconi's financial backers in the States, who included Thomas Edison and Andrew Carnegie. Some believe this was made for financial reasons, allowing the U.S. government to avoid having to pay the royalties that were being claimed by Tesla for use of his patents.

In 1909, Marconi, with Karl Ferdinand Braun, was awarded the Nobel Prize in Physics for "contributions to the development of wireless telegraphy". However, Tesla's patent was reinstated in 1943 by the U.S. Supreme Court, shortly after his death. This decision was based on the fact that prior art existed before the establishment of Marconi's patent. Some believe the decision was also made for financial reasons, to allow the U.S. government to avoid having to pay damages that were being claimed by the Marconi Company for use of its patents during World War I.

"Wireless" Factories and Vacuum Tubes

Marconi opened the world's first "wireless" factory in Hall Street,

Chelmsford, England in 1898, employing around 50 people. Around 1900, Tesla opened the Wardenclyffe Tower facility and advertised services. By 1903, the tower structure neared completion. Various theories exist on how Tesla intended to achieve the goals of this wireless system. Tesla claimed that Wardenclyffe, as part of a world system of transmitters, would have allowed secure multichannel transceiving of information, universal navigation, time synchronization, and a global location system.

The next great invention was the vacuum tube detector, invented by a team of Westinghouse engineers. On Christmas Eve, 1906, Reginald Fessenden used a synchronous rotary-spark transmitter for the first radio program broadcast, from Brant Rock, Massachusetts. Ships at sea heard a broadcast that included Fessenden playing O Holy Night on the violin and reading a passage from the Bible. The first radio news program was broadcast August 31, 1920 by station 8MK in Detroit, Michigan. The first regular entertainment broadcasts commenced in 1922 from the Marconi Research Centre at Writtle, near Chelmsford, England.

Developments in Early 20th Century

Aircraft used commercial AM radio stations for navigation. This continued until the early 1960s when VOR systems finally became widespread. In the early 1930s, single sideband and frequency modulation were invented by amateur radio operators. By the end of the decade, they were established commercial modes.

Radio was used to transmit pictures visible as television as early as the 1920s. Standard analog transmissions started in North America and Europe in the 1940s. In 1954, Regency introduced a pocket transistor radio, the TR-1, powered by a "standard 22.5 V Battery".

Developments in Latter half of the 20th Century

In 1960, Sony introduced their first transistorized radio, small enough to fit in a vest pocket, and able to be powered by a small battery. It was durable, because there were no tubes to burn out. Over the next 20 years, transistors replaced tubes almost completely except for very high-power uses.

In 1963 color television was commercially transmitted, and the first (radio) communication satellite, TELSTAR, was launched.

In the late 1960s, the U.S. long-distance telephone network began to convert to a digital network, employing digital radios for many of its links.

In the 1970s, LORAN became the premier radio navigation system. Soon, the U.S. Navy experimented with satellite navigation, culminating in the invention and launch of the GPS constellation in 1987.

In the early 1990s, amateur radio experimenters began to use personal computers with audio cards to process radio signals. In 1994, the U.S. Army and DARPA launched an aggressive, successful project to construct a software radio that could become a different radio on the fly by changing software. Digital transmissions began to be applied to broadcasting in the late 1990s.

Characteristics of Radio

Radio is a fascinating medium among the various mass communication media because of its special characteristics. It continues to be as relevant and potent as it was in the early years despite the emergence of more glamourous media. It is a truism that in the first phase of broadcasting spanning three decades from the early twenties, radio reigned alone or was the dominant player. However, over a period of time, the media scene has changed drastically. Television with its inherent strength of audio-visual component has captured the imagination of the people. The advent of satellite television, the Internet and the convergence of technology have added further dimensions in media utilisation patterns. However, despite the presence of a plethora of media, there is room and scope for each medium. Experience has revealed that 'new technologies add things on but they don't replace'. One medium is not displaced by another—each medium reinvents itself in the context of changes in the communication environment. In the changed media scenario, radio is reorienting itself with more innovative programmes and formats.

Unlike the live medium of the stage, where there are live performers (speaker, actor, etc.) and live audience, radio is a 'sightless' or a viewless' medium. In radio, the performer does not see his/her audience (called listener) and the listeners cannot see the performer, the talker, the actor, etc. That is why radio is sometimes called the blind medium. Since it is a blind or sightless medium, the performer (announcer, newsreader, discussant, narrator, etc.) has to creatively conjure up images of his/her listeners. The listeners too have to imagine the performance creatively. But the performer must spark off the imagination of the listeners with expressive performance or communication.

Here are some important characteristics of radio:

Medium of Sound

Radio is an exclusive medium of the sound. It is an aural or auditory medium, a medium of the ear. There are three major elements of a radio broadcast: spoken-word, music and sound effects. They are all sounds carried on the air waves to the listener. To be acceptable, all these sounds must be pleasant and expressive for the ears. They must be artistically integrated or mixed to provoke the imagination of the listener, otherwise, the intention of the broadcast would be defeated.

Radio is a medium of the voice. The performer can use only his/her voice in a broadcast. The producer mixes voice with music and sound effects, but it does not mean that a broadcaster, say, an actor, has only to learn a few tricks of the voice. An actor, using only vocal tricks, would soon start sounding untruthful to the listener as a radio listener has a highly developed sound sense. It has been correctly said that an actor or any other performer must broadcast with his/her mind. For example, an actor is not wearing any costume or make-up; there is no scenery or properties. Neither s/he nor the co-actors are seen by the listener. So s/he must imaginatively give cues or intimations only through his/her expressive voice. This s/he will be able to do only if s/he mentally gets under the skin of the character and dialogues or speeches.

Vocal tricks will fail a broadcaster because voice does not exist autonomously or independently. It is a part of the total person of the performer. A truthful vocal expression will come only if a person's mind, soul, psyche, imagination and body all are in tune with one another.

Microphone is the instrument through which a radio broadcaster speaks to the listeners. And, microphone is a devilish precision instrument. It is a hi-fi (high fidelity or faithful) instrument that catches the softest sigh, the minutest shade of the voice, the tiniest rustle of the paper. It exposes all vocal lies or untruthful expressions. It amplifies even the feeblest hiss or a sob. Microphone will tell all, the truth from a lie hence only truthful vocal expressions can go well with the ear of the listeners.

Because of these characteristics of the microphone, broadcaster must speak into the mike as if the listeners are sitting by his/her side. S/he must not speak like a stage performer who has to reach out to the last man in the last row. The stage performer has to project oneself because the auditorium diminishes the voice and body. But the radio performer must project 'inwards' because the microphone amplifies or magnifies the voice.

Intimate Medium

Radio is an intimate medium. The broadcaster must imagine the listeners sitting by his/her side, shoulder to shoulder. To the listeners, it sounds as if the broadcaster is speaking from within the sound box, the radio set or the transistor for each listener individually. Radio being an intimate medium, the best subjects for radio broadcasts are those which intimately concern the listener like the personal, the private and the innermost feelings. Intimate subjects are especially relevant to good radio drama and intimate style of acting is especially relevant to the radio. The manner of expressing or articulating the words must also be intimate because the condition in which broadcasts are received are very informal. May be one or two or three listeners are sitting by the fireside or in bed or moving about the house, or engaged in some activities. The communication must be informal and intimate.

The broadcaster must build an instant equation or rapport with the listener. If s/he does not find the show or the broadcast interesting enough for die first two or three minutes, s/he will switch off the broadcast. The rule of the oil industry applies here: if you cannot drill in the first two minutes, stop boring. Hence, a talk, a discussion, a documentary, a feature, or a docu-drama, etc., must get into the subject informally, intimately and interestingly right at the start.

Mobile Medium

Radio is a mobile medium. You can have it at home, take it to the picnic resort, listen to it while driving, have it on land or under the sea, in public or in private, hence, it is a convenient medium. It can accompany you and entertain you anywhere as a never-failing companion.

It does not follow the three unities of time, place and action as prescribed by Aristotle, more than two thousand years ago, for dramatic communication. Stage drama may, even now, respect these unities because of the obvious limitations of the stage medium. But radio drama, which is drama of the mind, may hop from any period or place to any other period or place. Because the radio player performs on the canvas of the listener's mind and the mind, truthfully sparked off by the player, can construct any period, any place. The subjects that the stage can never dream of dramatising (for example, going centuries back and, then, suddenly switching over to die present, tasting the atmosphere of, say, hell or heaven, going under the ground or the sea or to remote corners of the globe etc.) can be very well dramatised on the radio.

Quick and Inexpensive Medium

Radio is a medium of immediacy. It can report the events almost instantly, as they are happening, hence, it is a medium of the "here and now". It is the radio which can be the first to report the happenings while TV crew would take some time to reach the spot.

From the production angle also, radio is a quicker medium than television. For example, it requires a performer and a producer who may also be a recordist and an 'effects' person. As against this, a TV production (tele-production) would require a costumes person, a make-up person, two or three cameras and cameramen, a dolly man to assist the cameraman in moving the cameras, a scene designer, a carpenter, several lights and lightmen, several monitoring sets, engineers, a producer, a performer, etc. The cost of radio production is much less than that of TV production. Since the cost and time required to produce a programme are much less, radio can produce a wide variety of programmes. It can also afford to experiment with new and innovative programmes.

It costs much less to set up a radio station as compared to a TV station. Not only the capital cost, but recurring expenses to run a radio service are far less. A large number of people can afford a radio set but not a TV set.

Medium with Limitations

Radio has a plethora of limitations as well. The foremost limitation of radio is that it entirely depends on the sense of hearing. Broadcast is not reinforced by the powerful medium of sight. Comprehension and assimilation, therefore, require more efforts. For instance, it is almost impossible to convey the beauty or finer points of works of art such as paintings, sculptures or intricate handicrafts merely by trying to describe them.

Then, suppose there has been a major disaster somewhere - say an earthquake or a war, the extent of damage, the hardship being faced by the people are instantly clear on television. On radio, one has to use one's imagination after listening to other accounts. By the same token, take a cricket, football or a tennis match. On TV, one does not even need a commentator, whereas on radio a commentator and a few sound effects are essential for the listener to follow the game. The same is true of colour, sense of space, a situation, or appearances. A listener can only use his/her imagination, which may or may not give a true picture. There can be gaps between illusion and reality.

At times, a facial expression or body language can communicate unuttered messages. Both, the broadcaster and the listener, have to constantly keep in mind that what is being conveyed will have to be heard, understood and remembered instantly. It is an ephemeral medium, unless one has access to a recording or a repeat broadcast, the message can be lost for ever. This puts immense limitations on the broadcaster and demands a great deal of concentration and involvement on the part of the listener. Radio has little value for the hearing-challenged just as television is of little use to the visually-challenged.

Uses of Radio

Many of radio's early uses were maritime, for sending telegraphic messages using Morse code between ships and land. The earliest users included the Japanese Navy scouting the Russian fleet during the Battle of Tsushima in 1905. One of the most memorable uses of marine telegraphy was during the sinking of the RMS Titanic in 1912, including communications between operators on the sinking ship and nearby vessels, and communications to shore stations listing the survivors.

Radio was used to pass on orders and communications between armies and navies on both sides in World War I; Germany used radio communications for diplomatic messages once its submarine cables were cut by the British. The United States passed on President Woodrow Wilson's Fourteen Points to Germany via radio during the war.

Broadcasting began to become feasible in the 1920s, with the widespread introduction of radio receivers, particularly in Europe and the United States. Besides broadcasting, point-to-point broadcasting, including telephone messages and relays of radio programs, became widespread in the 1920s and 1930s.

Another use of radio in the pre-war years was the development of detecting and locating aircraft and ships by the use of radar (RAdio Detection And Ranging).

Today, radio takes many forms, including wireless networks, mobile communications of all types, as well as radio broadcasting. Read more about radio's history.

Before the advent of television, commercial radio broadcasts included not only news and music, but dramas, comedies, variety shows, and many other forms of entertainment. Radio was unique among dramatic presentation that it used only sound.

There are a number of uses of radio:

Audio

AM broadcast radio sends music and voice in the Medium Frequency (MF—0.300 MHz to 3 MHz) radio spectrum. AM radio uses amplitude modulation, in which louder sounds at the microphone causes wider fluctuations in the transmitter power while the transmitter frequency remains unchanged. Transmissions are affected by static because lightning and other sources of radio add their radio waves to the ones from the transmitter.

FM broadcast radio sends music and voice, with higher fidelity than AM radio. In frequency modulation, louder sounds at the microphone cause the transmitter frequency to fluctuate farther, the transmitter power stays constant. FM is transmitted in the Very High Frequency (VHF—30 MHz to 300 MHz) radio spectrum. FM requires more radio frequency space than AM and there are more frequencies available at higher frequencies, so there can be more stations, each sending more information. Another effect is that shorter VHF radio waves act more like light, travelling in straight lines, hence the reception range is generally limited to about 50-100 miles. During unusual upper atmospheric conditions, FM signals are occasionally reflected back towards the Earth by the ionosphere, resulting in Long distance FM reception. FM receivers are subject to the capture effect, which causes the radio to only receive the strongest signal when multiple signals appear on the same frequency. FM receivers are relatively immune to lightning and spark interference.

FM Subcarrier services are secondary signals transmitted "piggyback" along with the main program. Special receivers are required to utilize these services. Analog channels may contain alternative programming, such as reading services for the blind, background music or stereo sound signals. In some extremely crowded metropolitan areas, the subchannel program might be an alternate foreign language radio program for various ethnic groups. Subcarriers can also transmit digital data, such as station identification, the current song's name, web addresses, or stock quotes. In some countries, FM radios automatically retune themselves to the same channel in a different district by using sub-bands.

Aviation voice radios use VHF AM. AM is used so that multiple stations on the same channel can be received. (Use of FM would result in stronger stations blocking out reception of weaker stations due to FM's capture effect). Aircraft fly high enough that their transmitters can be received hundreds of miles (kilometres) away, even though they are using VHF.

Marine voice radios can use AM in the shortwave High Frequency (HF—3 MHz to 30 MHz) radio spectrum for very long ranges or narrowband FM in the VHF spectrum for much shorter ranges.

Government, police, fire and commercial voice services use narrowband FM on special frequencies. Fidelity is sacrificed to use a smaller range of radio frequencies, usually five kHz of deviation, rather than the 75 kHz used by FM broadcasts and 25 kHz used by TV sound.

Civil and military HF (high frequency) voice services use shortwave radio to contact ships at sea, aircraft and isolated settlements. Most use single sideband voice (SSB), which uses less bandwidth than AM. On an AM radio SSB sounds like ducks quacking. Viewed as a graph of frequency versus power, an AM signal shows power where the frequencies of the voice add and subtract with the main radio frequency. SSB cuts the bandwidth in half by suppressing the carrier and (usually) lower sideband.

TETRA, Terrestrial Trunked Radio is a digital cell phone system for military, police and ambulances. Commercial services such as XM, WorldSpace and Sirius offer encrypted digital Satellite radio.

Telephony

Cell phones transmit to a local cell transmitter/receiver site, which connects to the public service telephone network through an optic fiber or microwave radio. When the phone leaves the cell radio's area, the central computer switches the phone to a new cell. Cell phones originally used FM, but now most use various digital encodings.

Satellite phones come in two types: INMARSAT and Iridium. Both types provide world-wide coverage. INMARSAT uses geosynchronous satellites, with aimed high-gain antennas on the vehicles. Iridium provides cell phones, with the cells being satellites in orbit.

Navigation

All satellite navigation systems use satellites with precision clocks. The satellite transmits its position, and the time of the transmission. The receiver listens to four satellites, and can figure its position as being on a line that is tangent to a spherical shell around each satellite, determined by the time-of-flight of the radio signals from the satellite. A computer in the receiver does the math. Loran systems also used time-of-flight radio signals, but from radio stations on the ground.

VOR systems (used by aircraft), have an antenna array that transmits two signals simultaneously. A directional signal rotates like a lighthouse at a fixed rate. When the directional signal is facing north, an omnidirectional signal pulses. By measuring the difference in phase of these two signals, an aircraft can determine its bearing from the station. An aircraft can get readings from two VORs, and locate its position at the intersection of the two beams. Radio direction-finding is the oldest form of radio navigation. Before 1960 navigators used movable loop antennas to locate commercial AM stations near cities. In some cases they used marine radiolocation beacons, which share a range of frequencies just above AM radio with amateur radio operators.

Radar

Radar detects things at a distance by bouncing radio waves off them. The delay caused by the echo measures the distance. The direction of the beam determines the direction of the reflection. The polarization and frequency of the return can sense the type of surface.

Navigational radars scan a wide area two to four times per minute. They use very short waves that reflect from earth and stone. They are common on commercial ships and long-distance commercial aircraft. General purpose radars generally use navigational radar frequencies, but modulate and polarize the pulse so the receiver can determine the type of surface of the reflector. The best general-purpose radars distinguish the rain of heavy storms, as well as land and vehicles. Some can superimpose sonar data and map data from GPS position.

Search radars scan a wide area with pulses of short radio waves. They usually scan the area two to four times a minute. Sometimes search radars use the doppler effect to separate moving vehicles from clutter.

Targeting radars use the same principle as search radar but scan a much smaller area far more often, usually several times a second or more.

Weather radars resemble search radars, but use radio waves with circular polarization and a wavelength to reflect from water droplets. Some weather radar use the doppler to measure wind speeds.

Emergency Services

Emergency position-indicating rescue beacons (EPIRBs), emergency locating transmitters or personal locator beacons are small radio transmitters that satellites can use to locate a person or vehicle needing rescue. Their purpose is to help rescue people in the first day, when survival is most likely. There are several types, with widely-varying performance.

Digital Radio

The oldest form of digital broadcast was spark gap telegraphy, used by pioneers such as Marconi. By pressing the key, the operator could send messages in Morse code by energizing a rotating commutating spark gap. The rotating commutator produced a tone in the receiver, where a simple spark gap would produce a hiss, indistinguishable from static. Spark gap transmitters are now illegal, because their transmissions span several hundred megahertz. This is very wasteful of both radio frequencies and power.

The next advance was continuous wave telegraphy, or CW (Continuous Wave), in which a pure radio frequency, produced by a vacuum tube electronic oscillator was switched on and off by a key. A receiver with a local oscillator would "heterodyne" with the pure radio frequency, creating a whistle-like audio tone. CW uses less than 100 Hz of bandwidth. CW is still used, these days primarily by amateur radio operators (hams). Strictly, on-off keying of a carrier should be known as "Interrupted Continuous Wave" or ICW.

Radio teletypes usually operate on short-wave (HF) and are much loved by the military because they create written information without a skilled operator. They send a bit as one of two tones. Groups of five or seven bits become a character printed by a teletype. From about 1925 to 1975, radio teletype was how most commercial messages were sent to less developed countries. These are still used by the military and weather services.

Aircraft use a 1200 Baud radioteletype service over VHF to send their ID, altitude and position, and get gate and connecting-flight data.

Microwave dishes on satellites, telephone exchanges and TV stations usually use quadrature amplitude modulation (QAM). QAM sends data by changing both the phase and the amplitude of the radio signal. Engineers like QAM because it packs the most bits into a radio signal. Usually the bits are sent in "frames" that repeat. A special bit pattern is used to locate the beginning of a frame.

Systems that need reliability, or that share their frequency with other services, may use "corrected orthogonal frequency-division multiplexing" or COFDM. COFDM breaks a digital signal into as many as several hundred slower subchannels. The digital signal is often sent as QAM on the subchannels. Modern COFDM systems use a small computer to make and decode the signal with digital signal processing, which is more flexible and far less expensive than older systems that implemented separate electronic channels. COFDM resists fading and ghosting because the narrow-channel QAM signals can be sent slowly. An adaptive system, or one that sends error-correction codes can also resist interference, because most interference can affect only a few of the QAM channels. COFDM is used for WiFi, some cell phones, Digital Radio Mondiale, Eureka 147, and many other local area network, digital TV and radio standards.

Radio-frequency Energy for Heating

Radio-frequency energy generated for heating of objects is generally not intended to radiate outside of the generating equipment, to prevent interference with other radio signals. Microwave ovens use intense radio waves to heat food. Diathermy equipment is used in surgery for sealing of blood vessels. Induction furnaces are used for melting metal for casting.

Mechanical Force

Tractor beams: Radio waves exert small electrostatic and magnetic forces. These are enough to perform station-keeping in microgravity environments.

Conceptually, spacecraft propulsion: Radiation pressure from intense radio waves has been proposed as a propulsion method for an interstellar probe called Starwisp. Since the waves are long, the probe could be a very light metal mesh, and thus achieve higher accelerations than if it were a solar sail.

Other Uses of Radio

Amateur radio is a hobby in which enthusiasts purchase or build their own equipment and use radio for their own enjoyment. They may also provide an emergency and public-service radio service. This has been of great use, saving lives in many instances. Radio amateurs are able to use frequencies in a large number of narrow bands throughout the radio spectrum. They use all forms of encoding, including obsolete and experimental ones. Several forms of radio were pioneered by radio amateurs and later became commercially important, including FM, single-sideband AM, digital packet radio and satellite repeaters.

Personal radio services such as Citizens' Band Radio, Family Radio Service, Multi-Use Radio Service and others exist in North America to provide simple, (usually) short range communication for individuals and small groups, without the overhead of licensing. Similar services exist in other parts of the world.

Wireless energy transfer: A number of schemes have been proposed that transmit power using microwaves, and the technique has been demonstrated. These schemes include, for example, solar power stations in orbit beaming energy down to terrestrial users.

Radio remote control: Use of radio waves to transmit control data to a remote object as in some early forms of guided missile, some early TV remotes and a range of model boats, cars and aeroplanes. Large industrial remote-controlled equipment such as cranes and switching locomotives now usually use digital radio techniques to ensure safety and reliability.

Energy autarkic radio technology consists of a small radio transmitter powered by environmental energy (push of a button, temperature differences, light, vibrations, etc.).

Radio as a Mass Medium

Radio has its own strengths and weaknesses. Understanding the medium, which capitalizes mainly on sound, will act as a guide to using radio effectively for development and education.

1. *Radio, a medium for hearing*. The most striking attribute of radio is that it is an auditory medium. It has no visuals. It is blind. Listeners

cannot see its messages. With radio, they can only hear and imagine objects, actions and ideas.

2. *Radio is a mass medium.* It addresses a many at the same time. With distance the contact becomes less personal than in face-toface communication. The chance of being misunderstood is great. Also, feedback is not immediate.

3. *Radio lacks permanence.* The audience may not read and re-read messages as in the print press. Radio is transient.

4. *Radio has no visuals.* There is no image and no text. The receivers cannot see the sender or broadcaster as they do on television or film. Radio's codes are purely auditory - speech, music, sounds, and silence. The occasion of being misunderstood, or of complete communication failure, is high. To use radio effectively much effort must be expended in order to compensate for the lack of visuals.

5. *Radio stimulates imagination.* The listeners of radio supply the visual data for themselves. They picture the messages suggested by voices, words and sound effects. When one school was asked about television drama the response was "I prefer radio, the scenery is so much better."

6. *Radio is personal and intimate.* Real voices, insinuating personalities and emotions are passed on through radio impulses. Warmth, compassion, anger, pain, and laughter are conveyed more adequately in an audio medium. With accent, inflection, hesitation, pause, and a variety of emphasis and speed the voice report is able to convey far more than the printed speech. The fact that radio often reaches the listener during his/her situation of solitude and privacy adds to the intimate character of radio.

7. *Radio listeners do other things.* They can be plowing in the field, traveling, driving, washing clothes or mending fishing nets. One drawback of this is that the audience may be only half listening, and much of the message could be missed, ignored or misunderstood. The radio speaker cannot command full attention from a housemaker who is attending to her children going to school, or who may be chatting with a neighbor.

8. *Radio appeals to disadvantaged groups.* Being portable and inexpensive it is affordable to the common people, especially to farmers, fishermen and rural audiences. Those who have little access

to newspapers can get news and information through radio. The less educated, such as those who have difficulty reading, are easily attracted to radio.

9. *Radio negates geographical and physical barriers.* Radio reaches the radio listener who could be anywhere, in the sea, on a mountain or on a bus. Radio can bring a commonality to people separated by geography, culture, learning or status.

10. *Radio gets messages to the listeners instantly.* The words spoken by an announcer in the radio studio are sent to thousands of listeners at the speed of light. The speed and reach of radio should also apply to situations whereby the availability of piglets or rambutan seedlings in a nearby farm could be made known to the rest of the community. Such local items are too numerous and minor for big networks and newspapers. They are, however, vital to small communities and can be publicized far more cheaply and quickly through community radio.

11. *Radio is selective.* Program materials have been chosen previously. The radio presenter selects exactly what is to be received by his/ her listener. With radio the selection process takes place in the studio. The listener is presented with a single thread of material. Choice for the listener exists only in the mental switching off and switching on, such as when the news or program material fails to maintain the listener's interest. He/she might tune to another station.

12. *Radio has music.* Radio provides the enjoyment of listening to a guitar or to the ballad of a songbird. Music on radio can serve as a background or can be the focus of total absorption. Music relaxes, induces pleasure, nostalgia, excitement or curiosity.

13. *Radio can suffer from interference.* While the printed page is received in exactly the form in which it left the press, radio is always subject to interference. What leaves the studio is not necessarily what is heard in the possibly noisy environment of the listener. Intrusion of other station's signals, atmospheric noise, distortions of sound, a fading signal all add to the infidelity of message.

14. *Radio is an entertainment medium.* A majority of listeners accept radio as a means of entertainment rather than as a source of education. Therefore, when one looks to radio as a means to serve development and education, the design of enjoyable and stimulating programs is

essential. Heavily laden development programs fail to attract the desired number of listeners, which is waste of effort and the chance to change people's lives.

With the knowledge of the basic characteristics of the medium comes the realization of the possibility of how radio can be used effectively to affect the lives of individuals or society.

Role of Radio

The role of the mass media is to provide the audience information, education or entertainment or all the three balanced in different proportions. The role of radio, as a medium of mass communication varies from country to country. There are radio networks which devote themselves exclusively to entertainment. They are commercial enterprises which are run with profit motive serving trade interests. They carry a large number of advertisements along with progra-mmes. There are radio networks operated by educational institutions, which specialise in educational programming. The third category of radio broadcasts are community broadcasters. The local communities or NGOs serving them operate radio service for the benefits of the local community. The most important and universally recognised category of broadcasting is often referred to as Public Service Broadcasting which uses radio for public service by providing a blend of programmes of information, education and entertainment in accordance with the communication needs of the people it serves.

Alfred Srnerdits, noted communicator after a survey of broadcasting in Europe, observed that the public service media must perform the "democratic task of providing independent, free and pluralistic information and promoting cultural development." Pierre Juneau, of the World Radio & TV Council visualised a larger role encompassing not only information, education and entertainment, but also cultural enlightenment. It would be interesting to note that in the US, the need for a public service broadcasting was felt long after private broadcasting took firm roots in that country. In the UK, it was public service broadcasting which was established first and private commercial broadcasting followed.

In communication, there are certain things which the people want and some other things which they need. Radio can bring about the convergence between the two through appropriate programming mix. To Lord Reith who helped the BBC to develop as a public service broadcasting organisation, information and education were its predominant components. Merlya Rees, Privy Councillor, United Kingdom setting out the parameters of public service broadcasting observed that the public service broadcasting must be the one which is available to the entire population. It must be universally attractive. In other words, it must be concerned with as many interests and tastes as possible. Minorities and disadvantaged groups who suffer discrimination must receive special attention. Broadcasting must be distanced from vested interests.

In developing countries, the radio is looked upon as catalytic agent for development. The Vidyalankar Committee constituted by the Indian Planning Commission in 1963 envisaged an active role for radio when it observed "our development task is so great and our population so large that only by the most efficient possible programmes of public information can we hope to reach our people often enough and effectively enough to activate on the needed scale, discussion processes and subsequent actions in the cities, towns and villages". According to a policy document of the Government of India, "radio should become an input in the nation-building tasks and must strengthen the confidence of the people, promote the concept of self-reliance and encourage forces of unity and national harmony."

In tune with various policy guidelines, the educational and information programmes of radio aim at preparing the people to receive and assimilate the new opportunities created for their advancement and well-being. They seek to strengthen the confidence of the people, promote the concept of self-reliance, encourage forces of unity and national harmony and help in the establishment of an egalitarian society. In the preparation of software to realise these objectives, the programme planners constantly bear in mind of what Pandit Jawaharlal Nehru said while addressing the Constituent Assembly (Legislative) on March 15, 1948. Referring to the approach in broadcasting programmes he said "If anybody is going to sermonise, I am not going to listen to that sermon.., you must do it in an entertaining way."

Bertolt Brecht, renowned playwright warned that the 'one-way' nature of radio would condemn it to sterility. The organisation of Charcha Mandate in the early phase of farm broadcasting facilttafed participatory programming. Akashvani Qaon se, the Farm-school-on-the-Air, the rural science gatherings, the science sammelans, the People's Forum Programmes are some of the later-day innovations to make radio a two-way communication medium constantly striving to "reach the people effectively enough to activate on the needed scale, discussions, processes and actions." The Phone-in programme, Voice Mail Programmes, the People's Forum Programmes (which while voicing the grievances of the people bring the administration and the audiences on a common platform in the exercise for resolving problems) and the radio-bridge programmes connecting experts and the listeners situated in different places are all aimed at strengthening the two-way communication system. Various educational programme projects have an in-built provision for listeners' participation.

Radio's primary role as a public service broadcaster is crucial for a developing society. However, a new programming orientation is urgently needed to avoid 'unimaginative' and 'heavy' broadcasts. All programming should be meaningful, interesting, entertaining, relevant and imaginative. In the words of P. C. Joshi "we have to ensure that communication media does not widen the hiatus between the rich and poor, town and village, elite and the mass, men and women, centre and periphery".

Radio for the Individual

— Provides relaxation and entertainment. It moves people away from their problems and anxieties.

— Helps to solve problems by providing information and advice.

— Widens the horizons of people by stimulating interest in previously unknown topics.

— Promotes creativity.

— Contributes to self-knowledge and awareness, enabling the listeners to see themselves in relation to others.

— Guides social behavior by setting standards and offering role models.

— Provides topics of conversation through shared experience and hence facilitates personal contacts.

— Allow individuals to exercise choice, make decisions and act as responsible citizens.

— Inspires the individual and can move him/her into action.

Radio for the Community

— Speeds up the process of informing the community and therefore acts as a catalyst of change.

— Serves as a watchdog on power holders, affording active relationships between leaders and the citizens.
— Helps to approach consensus and to develop common objectives by providing debate and discussing issues.
— Exposes options for community action.
— Enhances artistic and intellectual culture.
— Brings out and disseminates ideas promoting diversity and change.
— Reinforces values to help maintain social order through the status quo.
— Offers chance for individuals and groups to speak to each other, thus developing awareness of a common membership of community.
— Mobilizes both private and collective resources for personal or community needs.

The radio producer may aim to achieve program objectives along any of the impacts outlined above or by some other community and individual purpose. He/she should be able to state his/her program purpose clearly.

Radio Programming

Radio programming is undergoing intense metamorphosis these days keeping in view the challenge thrown by 24 hour television programming. In the recent years, there is a quantum jump in the media channels, particularly TV channels. Most of them are commercial channels dishing out entertainment programmes. Since television offers multifaceted and multifarious fare on national networks, in a commercialised media-environment, radio receives less attention. However, some positive developments have taken place which hold great future for radio broadcasting. One such major development in the field of radio in this country is the end of government's monopoly of the airwaves. The demand for permission to establish private channels has been made from time to time, but the Supreme Court gave the landmark judgment, that the airwaves cannot be controlled solely by the government. With the setting up of the Prasar Bharati Broadcasting Corporation, there is a change in the situation. The advent of private radio broadcasting has become a reality.

The introduction of Frequency Modulation (FM) channels in metro cities is another development which has brought in a breath of fresh air in their content and style of presentation. More than 70 per cent radio, listening in the U.S. today is on the F.M. stations and the same trend is catching up in India as well'. While 50 per cent radio stations in U.S. are commercial, in India, the trend towards commercialisation is limited but is catching on. A number of private operators have been given licences to operate FM channels. The FM channels that have come up recently are at major centres addressing the modern, urban youth. However, FM channels mean much more than mere pop and film music for the entertainment of a privileged few.

The Gyan Vani network allotted to IGNOU has started broadcasting programmes on education and development from several cities. The number of such channels is bound to increase in the years to come. Under a scheme devised by the Ministry of Information and Broadcasting, educational institutions can get licences to operate radio stations for educational purposes.

Yet another significant development in radio broadcasting all over the world is the concept of Community radio. It has come to be known as the 'narrow casting' as opposed to 'broadcasting'. The introduction of the community radio is a milestone not only in reaching out to the remotest area but also persuading the citizen to share in the vision and excitement of development. With the avowed objective of developing itself as community broadcasting, the local radio strives to demolish the division between the broadcaster and the audience and serve as a link between the citizen and the extension agencies. In course of time, these community radio stations would act as a catalytic agent in galvanising the local community into action for their own development.

In India, this concept can be effectively harnessed keeping in view the variety in region, background, culture, language, education and economic status. Community radio stations can be used to project and reflect the needs, desires, problems, joys and sorrows of a society clearly defined within a limited area. For example, the need to construct a new road, remove stagnant water, put down gang warfare or whatever problem is being faced by the people in a specific area, could be dealt with in a meaningful way. Fruitful negotiations could be held by the affected people with area development workers, local authorities and voluntary agencies. Similar background of the people facilitates problem solving, and imparting instructions on various development related issues.

Technological Developments are taking place at a meteoric pace globally. The advent of internet and the convergence of technology is opening up new possibilities. Radio is increasingly becoming an integral part of the multimedia concept. Technology has brought in innovations in the hardware aspects of broadcasting. Satellite technology has rendered it possible to have digital broadcasting on Direct Broadcast Receivers. This has triggered the need for innovations in the software generation. In shaping the radio of tomorrow conscious efforts are made by all those involved in conceiving, planning and producing to make radio programmes absorbing, relevant, topical and need-based. Concerted efforts are made to identify those programming areas which are radio's forte and innovations encouraged for fully exploiting the medium's potential. Increasing attention is paid to 'leisure time' listening. Formats like entertaining contests, competitions, quiz shows and family serials are ingeniously exploited for enhancing listenership. Radio stations in the West have developed innovating styles and features, for example, 'contemporary hit radio' (CHR) is a recent popular category targeting the younger audiences. Creative formats, modes, styles of presentation and publicity, are being used. Play-by-play sports, talks, interview and children's programmes with a mix of education and entertainment are some popular formats. Motivation services devoted to health and nutrition, stress reduction, and personal improvement programmes are popular.

In the changes scenario, outmoded, impersonal approaches are being discarded away for a more personalised, informal and direct style, in which the listener plays an active role. Music is the backbone or mainstay of the overall radio fare. Thematic presentations, fea'turised formats or personalised treatment go a long way in making these programmes popular among the diverse radio audiences.

International hook-ups for sharing and exchange of ideas among specialists, political and other personalities are also being explored. All India Radio may swap airtime with Voice of America (VoA) and British Broadcasting Corporation (BBC). AIR may get an equal amount of air time on BBC's local channels in Britain, VoA cannot offer that since it has no domestic service. Both broadcasters may be given half hour weekly slots for entertainment and lifestyle programmes. Other broaidcasting organisations are also likely to follow.

With the expansion of technology, the possibilities of making radio programmes exciting and alluring are limitless. Widening the scope of a programme also opens up fresh opportunities for building up radio personalities, presenters, and anchor persons. As future radio professionals, you need to prepare yourselves to meet these challenges. Your role in making radio an interesting, creative and relevant medium of mass communication in the era of multi-channel communication is crucial.

Selection of Broadcast Materials

The events and personalities that the station choose to put on air, including the amount of time that it devotes to them, will reflect the station's bias. If it broadcasts the entire proceedings of a beauty contest listeners get the impression that it condones, or gives social significance to, the event. If it puts a ten-minute interview on air with a gambling lord who doled out a P1,000 donation to a charity ball the station puts aside the adverse impact of gambling. On the other hand, if the station gives more importance to those who strive to achieve than to less motivated personalities it can send an inspirational message to young people. Science contests, in lieu of pure movie gossip, can demonstrate the serious educational thrust of the station.

If it concentrates on playing American rock music and fails to give adequate time for local and community developed renditions, the station does not promote patronage of native talent and products. Similarly, if an event of one political party is covered, and not the other, the station can be seen as taking sides in an electoral contest. The station is expected to always strive for balance in presentation of material, particularly in cases of diversity of ideas and conflicts. While the perfect balance is unattainable the broadcaster must bear in mind that audiences can readily discern the bias and prejudices of a broadcaster or the station.

In general, the station should project a positive image by opting for materials that educate the listeners. Program material must present facts and depth. The presentation should be geared towards uplifting the community. Education, motivation, intellectual deliberation, opinion formation based on reason should be developed. Even as community broadcasters are urged to "join the building gang rather than the wrecking crew," malpractice and wrongdoing of leaders and public officials must be pointed out. These exposes, however, should be a product of meticulous research and establish unimpeachable data rather than conjecture or speculation.

Views and Opinions

Interpretation, analysis, editorials and opinions have to be well thought out.

Better still, they must be the output of careful deliberation by a group of responsible people in the radio station who have access to adequate facts. The community radio council, or a special editorial board mandated by the CMC, might handle the station editorials on such issues as forest denudation, child rights, cooperativism, education on family relationships.

Personal attacks should give way to logical analysis and presentation of facts. The oft repeated phrase "walang personalan' [nothing personal] might well find its application as a policy for opinion slots. Opinions expressed by community members on tape, telephone or live interviews must always be divested of slanderous remarks or name-calling. Nothing defamatory or libelous must be allowed to go on the air.

Vox pops

The voice of the people (voz populi) is important in community radio. Views coming from a wide social spectrum depict the conscience of the citizenry. A mobile tape recorder that picks up speech, from the one sentence to three-minute interview, will develop the authenticity of public opinion. Again, the station must endeavor to achieve balance of views.

Vox pops can either be aired at random during whole program hours or aired in specific slots devoted solely to public opinion. They can also be accommodated in a public affairs, news or documentary program.

Documentary Programs

Considered as the highest form of radio programs, documentaries usually take more time, effort and perhaps money to prepare. Documentaries take an intense look at an issue and present the findings in as balanced and comprehensive a manner as possible. The feature usually starts from originally compiled information, voice clips and lowdowns gathered in normal news activities and interviews accomplished by the station. Other information, actualities and materials are sought to paint a thorough picture of a problem. The documentary can have a short dramatization of the situation, interviews, vox pops, voice clips, relevant music as well as live commentaries. While it is easy to tilt balance in documentary presentation the noble aim is to paint an impartial picture of a question. Integrity is put on line every time the station presents a documentary.

Side Remarks

Most of the strong and hard-hitting comments do not come during a commentary or editorial program. They are off-the-cuff remarks delivered, either wittingly or unwittingly, by the station personalities or guests.

In one instance a TV newscaster, who scorned the interview done by the station with a notorious couple, was asked to resign when she wryly commented, "why does television have to glorify thieves?" The author of this manuscript used to give out news and receive live field reports in a radio magazine program. At the end of one field report about a statement coming from the President the technician played one of the many voice clips done by a seven year old girl, "Tito Louie, isn't it a sin to tell lies?" Consequently a letter was received from the Information Minister pleading for the program not be too harsh on the President.

Some radio personalities are adept at employing these short quips. The impact could be truly stinging but unless done on purpose, and as part of the general picture painting, they must be used sparingly. The seemingly off-the-cuff remarks can be repulsive, amusing, and derisive or simply arise out of bad taste. People who use the station microphone should be advised to doubly watch their tongue. When the tongue slips it is sometimes worse than the foot.

Interviews and Panel Discussion

The very choice of interviewees and panelist often indicates the partiality or impartiality of the station. The length of the interview, together with the manner of questioning, reveals the leanings of the producer, host and/or the station. Leading questions reveal the interviewers positions. The way guests are addressed gives away the disposition of the program host.

Radio Broadcasting in India

All India Radio (AIR), officially known as Akashwani is the radio broadcaster of India and a division of Prasar Bharati (Broadcasting Corporation of India), an autonomous corporation of the Ministry of Information and Broadcasting, Government of India. It is the sister service of Prasar Bharati's Doordarshan, the national television broadcaster.

All India Radio is one of the largest radio networks in the world. The headquarters is at Akashwani Bhavan, on the Parliament Street next to the Indian parliament. Akashwani Bhavan houses the drama section, the FM section and the National service. The Doordarshan Kendra (Delhi) is also located on the 6th floor of Akashwani Bhavan. Broadcasting house is an old building next to Akashwani Bhavan. The New Service Division of All India Radio under the Director General (New functions) from this building. Built during the British rule, it is a very popular location and easily recognised building in New Delhi.

History of AIR

Radio broadcasting began in India in 1927, with two privately-owned transmitters at Mumbai and Calcutta. These were nationalised in 1930 and operated under the name Indian Broadcasting Service until 1936, when it was renamed All India Radio (AIR). Although officially renamed again to Akashwani in 1957, it is still popularly known as All India Radio

Coverage

AIR covers 99.37% of India's populace, the largest democracy in the world with over one billion inhabitants. AIR maintains approximately 200 broadcasting centres around the country and transmits in 24 different languages. In spite of recent penetration by other media such as Cable TV, AIR remains the most common means of gaining access to information and entertainment, as the radio receivers are relatively cheap and affordable.

AIR Services

AIR has many different services each catering to different regions/languages across India. One of the most famous services of the AIR is the Vividh Bharati Seva (roughly translating to "Multi-Indian service"). This service is the most commercial of all and is popular in Mumbai and other cities of India. This service offers a wide range of programmes including news, film music, comedy shows, etc. The Vividh Bharti service operates on different MW band frequencies for each city as shown below.

Some programs broadcast on the Vividh Bharti:

— Binaca geet mala (later renamed to Cibaca geet mala) - Featuring Hindi film songs.

— Hawa-mahal - Skit based on some novels/plays.

— Santogen ki mehfil - Jokes & humour.

The following is a partial list of AIR services.

North Regional Service

— Agra 1530 kHz

— Allahabad 1026 kHz
— Delhi 'Indraprastha' 819 kHz
— Delhi 'Rajdhani' 666 kHz
— Delhi 'D' 1017 kHz
— Jaipur 'A' 1476 kHz
— Jalandhar 'A' 873 kHz
— Jammu 'A' 990 kHz
— Jodhpur 'A' 531 kHz
— Lucknow 'A' 747 kHz
— Srinagar 'A' 1116 kHz
— Varanasi 'A' 1242 kHz

East Regional Service

— Bhagalpur 1458 kHz
— Cuttack 'A' 972 kHz
— Darbhanga 1296 kHz
— Jamshedpur 1584 kHz
— Kolkata 'A' 657 kHz
— Patna 'A' 621 kHz
— Ranchi 'A' 549 kHz

North-east Regional Service

Agartala 1269 kHz
— Guwahati 'A' 729 kHz
— Shillong 864 kHz

West regional Service

— Ahmedabad 'A' 846 kHz
— Aurangabad 1521 kHz
— Bhopal 'A' 1593 kHz
— Gwalior 1386 kHz
— Indore 'A' 648 kHz
— Jalgaon 963 kHz

— Mumbai ‘A’ 1044 kHz
— Mumbai ‘B’ 558 kHz
— Nagpur ‘A’ 585 kHz
— Panaji ‘A’ 1287 kHz
— Pune ‘A’ 792 kHz
— Rajkot ‘A’ 810 kHz
— Ratnagiri 1143 kHz
— Sholapur 1602 kHz

South Regional Service

— Adilabad 1485 kHz
— Bangalore ‘A’ 612 kHz
— Chennai ‘A’ 720 kHz
— Gulbarga 1107 kHz
— Hyderabad ‘A’ 738 kHz
— Kozhikode ‘A’ 684 kHz
— Madurai 1269 kHz
— Ootakamund 1602 kHz
— Pondicherry 1215 kHz
— Port Blair 684 kHz
— Thiruvananthapuram ‘A’ 1161 kHz
— Tiruchirapalli ‘A’ 936 kHz
— Vijayawada ‘A’ 837 kHz
— Visakhapatnam 927 kHz

Vividh Bharati Service

— Chennai ‘C’ 783 kHz
— Cuttack ‘B’ 1314 kHz
— Delhi ‘C’ 1368 kHz
— Jalandhar ‘C’ 1350 kHz
— Kanpur 1449 kHz
— Kolkata ‘C’ 1323 kHz
— Lucknow ‘C’ 1278 kHz

— Mumbai 'C' 1188 kHz
— Panaji 'B' 1539 kHz
— Vijayawada 'B' 1503 kHz
— Varanasi 'B' 1602 kHz
— Varanasi FM' 100.6MHz

The Voice of Youth

The Yuv-vani service of AIR provides an enriching and novel radio-experience by encouraging youth participation and experimenting with varied script ideas. With shows like "Mehfil", "In the groove" and "The Roving Microphone" which have been around for more than three decades, Yuv-vani still holds a firm ground of its own.

Some of the big names on the Indian media scene began their journey with Yuv-vani. Comments Praful Thakkar, a well known documentary maker - "Yuv-vani came as a breath of fresh air in our reckless college days. It was a great learning experience for me and it made me realize that radio is not all about goofy quotes and PJs."

Some of the other names that have been associated with Yuv-vani in the past include Celebrity game show host Roshan Abbas, VJ Gaurav Kapoor, DJ Kaushal Khanna, and DJ Pratham among others.

News-on-phone Service

All India Radio, after launching the news-on-phone service on 25th February 1998 from New Delhi, is running the service from Chennai, Mumbai, Hyderabad, Patna and Bangalore also. The service is accessible through STD, ISD and local telephone calls. The service is going to be started from 9 more cities — Ahmedabad, Guwahati, Imphal, Jaipur, Kolkata, Lucknow, Raipur, Simla and Thiruvanthapuram shortly.

References

Aitkin Hugh G. J. *The Continuous Wave: Technology and the American Radio, 1900-1932*. Princeton University Press, 1985.

Douglas B. Craig. *Fireside Politics: Radio and Political Culture in the United States, 1920-1940*, 2005.

Ewbank Henry and Lawton Sherman P. *Broadcasting: Radio and Television*, Harper & Brothers, 1952.

Maclaurin W. Rupert. *Invention and Innovation in the Radio Industry*. The Macmillan Company, 1949.

Gwenyth L. Jackaway; *Media at War: Radio's Challenge to the Newspapers, 1924-1939* Praeger Publishers, 1995.

Lazarsfeld Paul F. *The People Look at Radio*, University of North Carolina Press, 1946.

Rosen Philip T. *The Modern Stentors; Radio Broadcasting and the Federal Government 1920-1934*, Greenwood Press, 1980.

Wavell, Stuart. - *The Art of Radio* - Training Manual written by the Director Training of the CBC. - Ceylon Broadcasting Corporation, 1969.

White Llewellyn. *The American Radio*, University of Chicago Press, 1947.

3

FM Radio Services

FM broadcasting is a broadcasting technology pioneered by Edwin Howard Armstrong which uses frequency modulation (FM) to provide high-fidelity sound over broadcast radio. The term "FM band" describes the "frequency band in which FM is used for broadcasting". This term is slightly misleading, since it equates a modulation method with a range of frequencies.

FM Broadcast Band

The FM broadcast band, used for FM broadcast radio by radio stations, differs between different parts of the world. In Europe and Africa (ITU region 1), it spans from 87.5 to 108.0 megahertz (MHz), while in America (ITU region 2) it goes only from 87.7 to 108.0 MHz. The FM broadcast band in Japan uses 76.0 to 90 MHz. The OIRT band in Eastern Europe is from 65.8 to 74.0 MHz, although these countries now primarily use the 87.5 to 108 MHz band, as in the case of Russia. Some other countries have already discontinued the OIRT band and have changed to the 87.5 to 108 MHz band.

Frequency modulation radio originated in the United States of America during the 1930s; the system was developed by the American electrical engineer Edwin H. Armstrong. However, FM broadcasting did not become widespread even in North America until the 1960s.

Frequency-modulated radio waves can be generated at any frequency. All the bands mentioned in this article are in the Very High Frequency (VHF) band, which extends from 30 to 300 MHz.

CCIR Bandplan

Center frequencies

While all countries use FM channel center frequencies ending in 0.1, 0.3, 0.5, 0.7, and 0.9 MHz, some countries also use center frequencies ending in 0.0, 0.2, 0.4, 0.6, and 0.8 MHz. A few others also use 0.05, 0.15, 0.25, 0.35, 0.45, 0.55, 0.65, 0.75, 0.85, and 0.95 MHz.

An ITU conference in Geneva, Switzerland, on December 7, 1984, resolved to discontinue the use of 50 kHz channel spacings throughout Europe.

Most countries have used 100 kHz or 200 kHz channel spacings for FM broadcasting since this ITU conference in 1984.

Some digitally-tuned FM radios are unable to tune using 50 kHz increments. Therefore when traveling abroad, stations that broadcast on certain frequencies using such increments may not be heard clearly. This problem will not affect reception on an analog-tuned radio.

A few countries, such as Italy, which have heavily-congested FM bands, still allow a station on any multiple of 50 kHz wherever one can be squeezed in.

The 50 kHz channel spacings help prevent co-channel interference, and these take advantage of FM's capture effect and receiver selectivity.

ITU Region II Bandplan and Channel Numbering

The original frequency allocation in North America used by Edwin Armstrong used the frequency band from 42 through 50 MHz, but this allocation was changed to a higher band beginning in 1945. In Canada, the United States, Mexico, the Bahamas, etc., there are 101 FM channels numbered from 200 (center frequency 87.9 MHz) to 300 (center frequency 107.9 MHz), though these numbers are rarely used outside the fields of radio engineering and government.

The center frequencies of the FM channels are spaced in increments of 200 kHz. The frequency of 87.9 MHz, while technically part of TV channel 6 (82 to 88 MHz), is used by just two FM class-D stations in the United States. Portable radio tuners often tune down to 87.5 MHz, so that the same radios can be made and sold worldwide. Automobiles usually have FM radios that can tune down to 87.7 MHz, so that TV channel 6's audio at 87.75 MHz (±10 kHz) could be received, such as in Birmingham,

Alabama, and Denver, Colorado. With the advent of universal digital television in the United States and southern Canada, this ability is irrelevant—but there are still analog television stations in Mexico and in the sparsely-populated regions of northern Canada. There are also analog TV stations on the other continents and on scores of different islands.

In the United States, the twenty-one channels with center frequencies of 87.9–91.9 MHz (channels 200 through 220) constitute the reserved band, exclusively for non-commercial educational (NCE) stations. The other channels (92.1 MHz through 107.9 MHz (Channels 221–300) may be used by both commercial and non-commercial stations. (Note that in Canada and in Mexico this reservation does not apply.)

Originally, the American Federal Communications Commission (FCC) devised a bandplan in which FM radio stations would be assigned at intervals of four channels (800 kHz separation) for any one geographic area. Thus, in one area, stations might be at 88.1, 88.9, 89.7, etc., while in an adjacent area, stations might be at 88.3, 89.1, 89.9, 90.7 etc. Certain frequencies were designated for Class A only (see FM broadcasting), which had a limit of three kilowatts of effective radiated power (ERP) and an antenna height limit for the center of radiation of 300 feet (91.4 m) height above average terrain (HAAT). These frequencies were 92.1, 92.7, 93.5, 94.3, 95.3, 95.9, 96.7, 97.7, 98.3, 99.3, 100.1, 100.9, 101.7, 102.3, 103.1, 103.9, 104.9, 105.5, 106.3 and 107.1. On other frequencies, a station could be Class B (50 kW, 500 feet) or Class C (100 kW, 2000 feet), depending on which zone it was in.

In the late 1980s, the FCC switched to a bandplan based on a distance separation table using currently operating stations, and subdivided the class table to create extra classes and change antenna height limits to meters. Class A power was doubled to six kilowatts, and the frequency restrictions noted above were removed. As of late 2004, a station can be "squeezed in" anywhere as long as the location and class conform to the rules in the FCC separation table. The rules for second-adjacent-channel spacing do not apply for stations licensed before 1964.

Deviation and bandpass

Normally each channel is 200 kHz (0.2 MHz) wide, and can pass audio and subcarrier frequencies up to 100 kHz. Deviation is typically limited to 150 kHz total (±75 kHz) in order to prevent adjacent channel interference on the band. Stations in the U.S. may go up to 10% over this limit if they use non-stereo subcarriers, increasing total modulation by 0.5% for each 1% used by the subcarriers.

OIRT Bandplan

The OIRT FM broadcast band covers 65.8 to 74 MHz. It was used in the Union of Soviet Socialist Republics and most of the other socialist member countries of the International Radio and Television Organisation in Eastern Europe (OIRT), with the exception of East Germany, which always used the 87.5 to 100 (later 104) MHz broadcast band in line with Western Europe. Note that Yugoslavia, although a socialist country, was not a member of OIRT.

The lower portion of the VHF band behaves a bit like Short Wave in that it has a longer reach than the upper portion of the VHF band. It was ideally suited for reaching vast and remote areas, that would otherwise lack FM radio reception. In a way, FM suited this band because the capture effect of FM could mitigate interference from skip.

Following the collapse of the communist governments in Eastern Europe, the 87.5 to 108 MHz band began to be adopted and is now in use in all those countries. This was prompted by the expansion of broadcasting and the modernisation of existing transmission networks, using new or second-hand transmitters from western countries, together with a general desire for standardization with the West.

Many countries have completely ceased broadcasting on the OIRT FM band, although declining use continues in others, mainly the former republics of the USSR. The future of broadcasting on the OIRT FM band is limited, due to the lack of new consumer receivers for that band.

Countries which still use the OIRT band include at least Russia, Belarus, Moldova, and Ukraine.

Hungary closed down its remaining broadcast transmitters in 2007, and for thirty days in July of that year, several Hungarian amateur radio operators received a temporary experimental permit to perform propagation and interference experiments in the 70–70.5 MHz band.

Unlike Western practice, OIRT FM frequencies are based on 10 kHz rather than 50 or 100 kHz multiples. This may have been to reduce co-channel interference caused by Sporadic E propagation and other atmospheric effects, which occur more often at these frequencies. However, multipath distortion effects are less annoying than on the CCIR band.

Stereo is generally achieved by sending the stereo difference signal, using a process called polar modulation.

The 4-meter band (70–70.5 MHz) amateur radio allocation used in many European countries is entirely within the OIRT FM band. Operators on this band and the 6-meter band (50–54 MHz) use the presence of broadcast stations as an indication that there is an "opening" into Eastern Europe or Russia. This can be a mixed blessing because the 4 meter amateur allocation is only 0.5 MHz or less, and a single broadcast station causes considerable interference to a large part of the band.

The System D television channels R4 and R5 lie wholly or partly within the 87.5–108 MHz FM audio broadcast band. Countries which still use System D therefore have to consider the re-organisation of TV broadcasting in order to make full use of this band for audio broadcasting.

Japanese Bandplan

The FM band in Japan is 76–90 MHz. The 90–108 MHz section was used for analog VHF TV Channels 1, 2 and 3 (each NTSC television channel was 6 MHz wide). The narrowness of the Japanese band (14 MHz compared to slightly more than 20 MHz for the CCIR band) limits the number of FM stations that can be accommodated on the dial with the result that many commercial radio stations are forced to use AM. However, as the NTSC channels cease analog operations, it is possible that the CCIR FM band might expand to Japan.

Many Japanese radios are capable of receiving both the Japanese FM band and the CCIR FM band, so that the same model can be sold within Japan or exported. The radio may cover 76 to 108 MHz, the frequency coverage may be selectable by the user, or during assembly the radio may be set to operate on one band by means of a specially-placed diode or other internal component.

Conventional analog-tuned (dial & pointer) radios may be marked with "TV Sound" in the 90–108 section. If these radios were sold in the USA, for example, the 76–88 section would be marked TV sound for VHF channels 5 and 6 (as two 6 MHz-wide NTSC TV channels), with the 88–108 section band as normal FM.

Second-hand automobiles imported from Japan contain a radio designed for the Japanese FM band, and importers often fit a "converter" to down-convert the 87.5 to 107.9 MHz band to the frequencies that the radio can accept. In addition to showing an incorrect frequency, there are two other disadvantages that can result in undesired performance; the converter cannot downconvert in full the regular international FM band (up to 20.5 MHz wide) to the only 14 MHz-wide Japanese band (unless the converter incorporates two user-switchable downconvert modes), and the car's antenna may perform poorly on the higher FM band. Some converters simply down-convert the FM band by 12 MHz, leading to logical frequencies (e.g. 78.9 for 90.9, 82.3 for 94.3, etc), but leaving off the 102–108 MHz band. Also, RDS is not used in Japan, whereas most modern car radios available in Europe have this system. Also the converter may not allow pass-through of the MW band, which is used for AM broadcasting. A better solution is to replace the radio and antenna with ones designed for the country where the car will be used.

Australia had a similar situation with Australian TV channels 3, 4 and 5 that are between 88 and 108 MHz, and was intending to follow Japan, but in the end opted for the western bandplan, due to CCIR radios that entered the country. There were some radios sold in Australia for 76 to 90 MHz.

Historic US Bandplan

Early FM broadcasting in North America originally used the 42–50 MHz band (this range was also used by a class of experimental wideband AM stations known as apex broadcasters). Shortly after World War II the United States FCC decided to move FM broadcasters to the 88.1–105.9 MHz band (later extended to 107.9 MHz). Only non-commercial stations can use the 88–92 MHz range.In March 2008, the FCC requested public comment on turning the bandwidth currently occupied by analog television channels 5 and 6 (76–88 MHz) over to extending the FM broadcast band when the digital television transition was to be completed in February 2009 (ultimately delayed to June 2009). This proposed allocation would effectively assign frequencies corresponding to the existing Japanese FM radio service (which begins at 76 MHz) for use as an extension to the existing North American FM broadcast band.

Modulation Characteristics

Frequency modulation (FM) is a form of modulation which conveys information over a carrier wave by varying its frequency (contrast this with amplitude modulation, in which the amplitude of the carrier is varied while its frequency remains constant). In analog applications, the instantaneous frequency of the carrier is directly proportional to the instantaneous value of the input signal. This form of modulation is commonly used in the FM broadcast band.

Pre-emphasis and De-emphasis

Random noise has a triangular spectral distribution in an FM system, with the effect that noise occurs predominantly at the highest frequencies within the baseband. This can be offset, to a limited extent, by boosting the high frequencies before transmission and reducing them by a corresponding amount in the receiver. Reducing the high frequencies in the receiver also reduces the high-frequency noise. These processes of boosting and then reducing certain frequencies are known as pre-emphasis and de-emphasis, respectively.

The amount of pre-emphasis and de-emphasis used is defined by the time constant of a simple RC filter circuit. In most of the world a 50 μs time constant is used. In North America and South Korea, 75 μs is used. This applies to both mono and stereo transmissions. For stereo, pre-emphasis is applied to the left and right channels before multiplexing.

The amount of pre-emphasis that can be applied is limited by the fact that many forms of contemporary music contain more high-frequency energy than the musical styles which prevailed at the birth of FM broadcasting. They cannot be pre-emphasized as much because it would cause excessive deviation of the FM carrier. Systems more modern than FM broadcasting tend to use either programme-dependent variable pre-emphasis; e.g., dbx in the BTSC TV sound system, or none at all.

Stereo FM

In the late 1950s, several systems to add stereo to FM radio were considered by the FCC. Included were systems from 14 proponents including Crosley, Halstead, Electrical and Musical Industries, Ltd (EMI), Zenith, and General Electric. The individual systems were evaluated for their strengths and weaknesses during field tests in Uniontown, Pennsylvania using KDKA-FM in Pittsburgh as the originating station. The Crosley system was rejected by the FCC because it degraded the signal-to-noise ratio of the main channel and did not perform well under multipath conditions. In addition, it did not allow for SCA services because of its wide FM subcarrier bandwidth. The Halstead system was rejected due to lack of high frequency stereo separation and reduction in the main channel signal-to-noise ratio. The GE and Zenith systems, so similar that they were considered theoretically identical, were formally approved by the FCC in April 1961 as the standard stereo FM broadcasting method in the USA and later adopted by most other countries.

It is important that stereo broadcasts be compatible with mono receivers. For this reason, the left (L) and right (R) channels are algebraically encoded into sum (L+R) and difference (L-R) signals. A mono receiver will use just the L+R signal so the listener will hear both channels through the single loudspeaker. A stereo receiver will add the difference signal to the sum signal to recover the left channel, and subtract the difference signal from the sum to recover the right channel.

The (L+R) Main channel signal is transmitted as baseband audio in the range of 30 Hz to 15 kHz. The (L-R) signal is modulated onto a 38 kHz double-sideband suppressed carrier (DSBSC) signal occupying the baseband range of 23 to 53 kHz.

A 19 kHz pilot tone, at exactly half the 38 kHz sub-carrier frequency and with a precise phase relationship to it, as defined by the formula below, is also generated. This is transmitted at 8–10% of overall modulation level and used by the receiver to regenerate the 38 kHz sub-carrier with the correct phase.

The final multiplex signal from the stereo generator contains the Main Channel (L+R), the pilot tone, and the sub-channel (L-R). This composite signal, along with any other sub-carriers, modulates the FM transmitter.

Converting the multiplex signal back into left and right audio signals is performed by a decoder, built into stereo receivers.

In order to preserve stereo separation and signal-to-noise parameters, it is normal practice to apply pre-emphasis to the left and right channels before encoding, and to apply de-emphasis at the receiver after decoding.

Stereo FM signals are more susceptible to noise and multipath distortion than are mono FM signals.

In addition, for a given RF level at the receiver, the signal-to-noise ratio for the stereo signal will be worse than for the mono receiver. For this reason many stereo FM receivers include a stereo/mono switch to allow listening in mono when reception conditions are less than ideal, and most car radios are arranged to reduce the separation as the signal-to-noise ratio worsens, eventually going to mono while still indicating a stereo signal is being received.

Quadraphonic FM

In 1969 Louis Dorren invented the Quadraplex system of single station, discrete, compatible four-channel FM broadcasting. There are two additional subcarriers in the Quadraplex system, supplementing the single one used in standard stereo FM. The baseband layout is as follows:

— 50 Hz to 15 kHz Main Channel (sum of all 4 channels) (LF+LR+RF+RR) signal, for mono FM listening compatibility.

— 23 to 53 kHz (cosine quadrature subcarrier) (LF+LR) - (RF+RR) Left minus Right difference signal. This signal's modulation in algebraic sum and difference with the Main channel was used for 2 channel stereo listener compatibility.

— 23 to 53 kHz (sine quadrature 38 kHz subcarrier) (LF+RF) - (LR+RR) Front minus Back difference signal. This signal's modulation in algebraic sum and difference with the Main channel and all the other subcarriers is used for the Quadraphonic listener.

— 61 to 91 kHz (cosine quadrature 76 kHz subcarrier) (LF+RR) - (LR+RF) Diagonal difference signal. This signal's modulation in algebraic sum and difference with the main channel and all the other subcarriers is also used for the Quadraphonic listener.

— 95 kHz SCA subcarrier, phase-locked to 19 kHz pilot, for reading services for the blind, background music, etc.

There were several variations on this system submitted by GE, Zenith, RCA, and Denon for testing and consideration during the National Quadraphonic Radio Committee field trials for the FCC. The original Dorren Quadraplex System outperformed all the others and was chosen as the national standard for Quadraphonic FM broadcasting in the United States. The first commercial FM station to broadcast quadraphonic program content was WIQB (now called WWWW-FM) in Ann Arbor/Saline, Michigan under the guidance of Chief Engineer Brian Brown.

Other Subcarrier Services

The subcarrier system has been further extended to add other services. Initially these were private analog audio channels which could be used internally or rented out. Radio reading services for the blind are also still common, and there were experiments with quadraphonic sound. If stereo is not on a station, everything from 23 kHz on up can be used for other services. The guard band around 19 kHz (±4 kHz) must still be maintained, so as not to trigger stereo decoders on receivers. If there is stereo, there will typically be a guard band between the upper limit of the DSBSC stereo signal (53 kHz) and the lower limit of any other subcarrier.

Digital services are now also available. A 57 kHz subcarrier (phase locked to the third harmonic of the stereo pilot tone) is used to carry a low-bandwidth digital Radio Data System signal, providing extra features such as Alternative Frequency (AF) and Network (NN). This narrowband signal runs at only 1187.5 bits per second, thus is only suitable for text. A few proprietary systems are used for private communications. A variant of RDS is the North American RBDS or "smart radio" system. In Germany the analog ARI system was used prior to RDS for broadcasting traffic announcements to motorists (without disturbing other listeners). Plans to use ARI for other European countries led to the development of RDS as a more powerful system. RDS is designed to be capable of being used alongside ARI despite using identical subcarrier frequencies.

In the United States, digital radio services are being deployed within the FM band rather than using Eureka 147 or the Japanese standard ISDB. This in-band on-channel approach, as do all digital radio techniques, makes use of advanced compressed audio. The proprietary iBiquity system, branded as "HD Radio", currently is authorized for "hybrid" mode operation, wherein both the conventional analog FM carrier and digital sideband subcarriers are transmitted. Eventually, presuming widespread deployment of HD Radio receivers, the analog services could theoretically be discontinued and the FM band become all digital.

In the USA services (other than stereo, quad and RDS) using subcarriers are sometimes referred to as subsidiary communications authorization (SCA) services. Uses for such subcarriers include book/newspaper reading services for blind listeners, private data transmission services (for example sending stock market information to stockbrokers or stolen credit card number blacklists to stores) subscription commercial-free background music services for shops, paging ("beeper") services and providing a program feed for AM transmitters of AM/FM stations. SCA subcarriers are typically 67 kHz and 92 kHz.

Dolby FM

A commercially unsuccessful noise reduction system used with FM radio in some countries during the late 1970s, Dolby FM was similar to Dolby B but used a modified 25 μs pre-emphasis time constant and a frequency selective companding arrangement to reduce noise.

A similar system named High?Com FM was tested in Germany between July 1979 and December 1981 by IRT. It was based on the Telefunken High?Com broadband compander system, but never introduced commercially in FM broadcasting.

Distance Covered by Stereo FM Transmission

The range of mono FM transmission is related to the transmitter's RF power, the antenna gain, and antenna height. The FCC (USA) publishes curves that aid in calculation of this maximum distance as a function of signal strength at the receiving location.

For stereo FM, the range is significantly reduced. This is due to the need to lower the modulation index of the main (sum) signal to accommodate the presence of the 38 kHz DSBSC subcarrier and 19 kHz pilot tone. Many stations use extreme audio compression to keep the sound above the background noise for "distant" listeners, at the expense of degrading the sound quality.

Adoption of FM Broadcasting Worldwide

Despite FM having been patented in 1933, commercial FM broadcasting did not begin until 1939, when it was initiated by WRVE, the FM station of General Electric's main factory in Schenectady, NY. In countries outside of Europe it took many years for FM to be adopted by the majority of radio listeners.

The first commercial FM broadcasting stations were in the United States, but initially they were primarily used to broadcast classical music to an upmarket listenership in urban areas, and for educational programming. By the late 1960s FM had been adopted by fans of "Alternative Rock" music ("A.O.R. - 'Album Oriented Rock' Format"), but it wasn't until 1978 that listenership to FM stations exceeded that of AM stations in North America. During the 1980s and 1990s, Top 40 music stations and later even country music stations largely abandoned AM for FM. Today AM is mainly the preserve of talk radio, news, sports, religious programming, ethnic (minority language) broadcasting and some types of minority interest music. This shift has transformed AM into the "alternative band" that FM once was. (Some AM stations have begun to simulcast on, or switch to, FM signals to attract younger listeners and aid reception problems in buildings, during thunderstorms, and near high tension wires. Some of these stations now emphasize their presence on the FM dial.)

Europe

The medium wave band (known as the AMband because most stations using it employ amplitude modulation in North America) is overcrowded in Western Europe, leading to interference problems and, as a result, many MW frequencies are suitable only for speech broadcasting.

Belgium, the Netherlands, Denmark and particularly Germany were among the first countries to adopt FM on a widespread scale. Among the reasons for this were:

1. The medium wave band in Western Europe became overcrowded after World War II, mainly due to the best available medium wave frequencies being used at high power levels by the Allied Occupation Forces, both for broadcasting entertainment to their troops and for broadcasting cold war propaganda across the Iron curtain.
2. After World War II, broadcasting frequencies were reorganized and reallocated by delegates of the victorious countries in the Copenhagen Frequency Plan. German broadcasters were left with only two remaining AM frequencies, and were forced to look to FM for expansion.

Public service broadcasters in Ireland and Australia were far slower at adopting FM radio than those in either North America or continental Europe.

Australia

FM started in Australia in 1947 but did not catch on and was shut down in 1961 to expand the television band. It was not reopened until 1975. Subsequently, it developed steadily until in the 1980s many AM stations transferred to FM because of its superior sound quality. Today, as elsewhere in the developed world, most urban Australian broadcasting is on FM, although AM talk stations are still very popular. Regional broadcasters still commonly operate AM stations due to the additional range the broadcasting method offers. Some stations in major regional centres simulcast on AM and FM bands.

New Zealand

Like Australia, New Zealand adopted the FM format relatively late. As was the case with privately-owned AM radio in the late 1960s, it took a spate of 'pirate' broadcasters to persuade a control-oriented, technology adverse government to allow FM to be introduced after at least five years of consumer campaigning starting in the mid-1970s, particularly in Auckland.

An experimental FM station, FM 90.7, was broadcast in Whakatane in early 1982. Later that year, Victoria University of Wellington's Radio Active began full-time FM transmissions. Commercial FM licences were finally approved in 1983, with Auckland-based 91FM and 89FM being the first to take up the offer.

United Kingdom

In the United Kingdom, the BBC began FM broadcasting in 1955, with three national networks carrying the Light Programme, Third Programme and Home Service (renamed Radio 2, Radio 3 and Radio 4 respectively in 1967). These three networks used the sub-band 88.0–94.6 MHz. The sub-band 94.6–97.6 MHz was later used for BBC and local commercial services. Only when commercial broadcasting was introduced to the UK in 1973 did the use of FM pick up in Britain.

With the gradual clearance of other users (notably Public Services such as police, fire and ambulance) and the extension of the FM band to 108.0 MHz between 1980 and 1995, FM expanded rapidly throughout the British Isles and effectively took over from LW and MW as the delivery platform of choice for fixed and portable domestic and vehicle-based receivers.

In addition, Ofcom (previously the Radio Authority) in the UK issues on demand Restricted Service Licences on FM and also on AM (MW) for short-term local-coverage broadcasting which is open to anyone who does not carry a prohibition and can put up the appropriate licensing and royalty fees. In 2010 around 450 such licences were issued.

Independent Local Radio

Legal commercial broadcasting began in the United Kingdom in 1973, with the launch of LBC, though offshore pirate radio stations operated in the 1960s to 1990s, usually from ships anchored off the coast of Britain.

Early licenses were granted to wide-area stations, such as Capital Radio which served London and the home counties. Later more local stations were introduced. There is also one national commercial radio station, Classic FM.Commercial radio stations simulcasted on both FM and medium wave from the beginning until 1989–1990, when the IBA asked radio stations to end the practice. Typically another service, often a Gold format, was introduced on AM and the original service continued on FM.

Frequency allocation

From 1955 the band 88.0 - 94.6 MHz was used for three BBC national networks. Over the next 40 years, the band grew piecemeal to 87.5 - 108.0 MHz, allowing for five national networks and many local stations.

Until 1995, parts of the band had been used in the United Kingdom for mobile communications by police, fire brigades and the fuel and power industries. These parts were reallocated to broadcasting gradually over many years as the communications services were transferred to new equipment in other parts of the spectrum.

The current frequency plan is based on an ITU agreement made in Geneva in 1984. In some areas there is some commercial usage of the 'BBC local' sub bands while in Scotland, Wales and Northern Ireland the 'Radio 4' and 'BBC Local' ranges are used interchangeably. Community radio stations and RSLs tend to be fitted into any locally-available position.

Future switch off

The final report (written by Digital Radio Working Group) says FM should be switched off between 2017 and 2022. And this switch off is recommended to boost digital radio and improve profit of United Kingdom digital radio IC suppliers. No further details about alternative use were provided. This report is only a recommendation and successive Governments have admitted that FM VHF Band II analogue radio would not cease until the "majority" use "digital", so no actual date has ever been agreed.

Digital listening figures however consistently include Satellite, DTT and online streaming, not just DAB. In any case there is a commitment to maintain community FM Radio. This means that as long as there are significant numbers of listeners on FM in the United Kingdom no government is likely to take the politically unpopular decision to turn off analogue.

United States

FM broadcasting in the United States began in the 1930s at engineer and inventor Edwin Howard Armstrong's experimental station, W2XMN. The use of FM radio has been associated with higher sound quality in music radio.

In the United States FM radio stations broadcast at frequencies of 87.8–108 MHz. FM radio was developed in the United States by Edwin Armstrong.

During the 1930s there were a small number of experimental (known as "Apex") stations attempting to broadcast high fidelity audio using wide-bandwidth AM on VHF frequencies. In 1937 W1XOJ was the first FM radio station, granted a construction permit by the FCC. On June 17, 1936, FM radio was demonstrated to the FCC for the first time. On January 5, 1940, Edwin H. Armstrong demonstrated FM broadcasting in a long-distance relay network, via five stations in five States. FM radio was assigned the 42 to 50 MHz band of the spectrum in 1940.

After World War II, the FCC moved FM to the frequencies between 88 and 108 MHz on June 27, 1945. The change in frequency was said to be for avoiding possible interference problems between stations in nearby cities and to make "room" for more FM radio channels. However, the FCC was influenced by RCA chairman David Sarnoff, who had the covert goal of disrupting the successful FM network that Edwin Armstrong had established on the old band. The 500,000 receivers built for the original FM radio band could be retrofitted with converters, but many were just replaced. The greater expense was to the radio stations themselves that had to rebuild their stations for the new FM radio band.

The move of the FM band, an organized campaign of misinformation by RCA (a company that competed with FM radio by focusing on AM radio and the emerging technology of television), and adverse rulings by the FCC severely set back the development of FM radio.

As late as 1947, in Detroit, there were only 3,000 FM receivers in use for the new band, and 21,000 obsolete ones for the old band. On March 1, 1941 W47NV began operations in Nashville, Tennessee, becoming the first modern commercial FM radio station. However, FM radio did not recover from the setback until the upsurge in high fidelity equipment in the late 1950s.

During the 1970s, FM radio experienced a golden age of integrity programming, with disc jockeys playing what they wanted, including album cuts not designated as "singles" and lengthy progressive rock tracks.

In the United States, frequency-modulated broadcasting stations operate in a frequency band extending from 87.8 MHz to 108.0 MHz, for a total of 20.2 MHz. It is divided into 101 channels, each 0.2 MHz wide, designated "channel 200" through "channel 300." In actual practice, no one (except the FCC) uses these channel numbers; the frequencies are used instead.

To receive a station, an FM receiver is tuned to the center frequency of the station's channel. The lowest channel, channel 200, extends from 87.8 MHz to 88.0 MHz; thus its center frequency is 87.9 MHz. Channel 201 has a center frequency of 88.1 MHz, and so on, up to channel 300, which extends from 107.8 to 108.0 MHz and has a center frequency of 107.9 MHz.

Because each channel is 0.2 MHz wide, the center frequencies of adjacent channels differ by 0.2 MHz. Because the lowest channel is centered on 87.9 MHz, the tenths digit (in MHz) of the center frequency of any FM station in the United States is always an odd number. FM audio for television channel 6 is broadcast at a carrier frequency of 87.75 MHz, and many radios can tune down this low; a few low-power television stations licensed for channel 6 are operated solely for their right to use this frequency and broadcast only nominal video programming. For the same reason, assignment restrictions between TV stations on channel 6 and nearby FM stations are stringent: there are only two stations in the United States (KSFH and translator K200AA) licensed to operate on 87.9 MHz, both due to being forced off of another channel. Therefore, in effect, the FM broadcast band comprises only FM channels 201 (88.1 MHz) through 300 (107.9 MHz).

Originally, FM stations in a market were generally spaced four channels (800 kHz) apart. This spacing was developed in response to problems perceived on the original FM band, mostly due to deficiencies in receiver technology of the time. With modern equipment, this is widely understood to be unnecessary, and in many countries shorter spacings are used. Other spacing restrictions relate to mixing products with nearby television, air-traffic control, and two-way radio systems as well as other FM broadcast stations. The most significant such taboo restricts the allocation of stations 10.6 and 10.8 MHz apart, to protect against mixing products which will interfere with an FM receiver's standard 10.7 MHz intermediate frequency stage.

Commercial broadcasting is licensed only on channels 221 through 300 (the upper 80 channels, frequencies between 92 and 108 MHz), with 200 through 220 (the lower 21 channels, frequencies between 88 and 92 MHz) being reserved for non-commercial educational (NCE) broadcasting. In some "Twin city" markets close to the Canadian or Mexican border, such as Detroit, Michigan and Windsor, Ontario, or San Diego, California and Tijuana, Baja California, commercial stations operating from those countries target U.S. audiences on "reserved band" channels, as neither Canada nor Mexico has such a reservation. Because of this necessary sharing, the FCC reserves a few other channels for such NCE stations.

FM stations in the U.S. are now assigned based on a table of separation distance values from currently licensed stations, based on station "class" (power output, antenna height, and geographical location). These regulations (see Docket 80-90) have resulted in approximately double the number of possible stations, and increases in allowable power levels, over the original bandplan scheme described above. All powers are specified as effective radiated power (ERP), which takes into account the magnifying effect (gain) of multiple antenna elements.

The U.S. is divided into Zone I (roughly the northeastern quarter of the U.S. mainland, excluding the far northern areas), Zone I-A (California south of 40 degrees latitude, U.S. Virgin Islands, Puerto Rico), and Zone II (all other locations). The highest-power stations are class C in zone II, and class B in the others. There are no B stations in zone II, nor any C stations in the others. (See the list of broadcast station classes.) Canada is also divided in this manner, based on the most highly-populated regions.

High power is useful in penetrating buildings, diffracting around hills, and refracting for some distance beyond the horizon. 100,000 watt FM stations can regularly be heard up to 100 miles (160 km) away, and farther (e.g., 150 miles, 240 km) if there are no competing signals.

A few old "grandfathered" stations do not conform to these power rules. WBCT (93.7) in Grand Rapids, Michigan, runs 320,000 watts ERP, and can increase to 500,000 watts ERP by the terms of its original license. This huge power level does not usually help to increase range as much as one might expect, because VHF frequencies travel in nearly straight lines over the horizon and off into space. Nevertheless, when there were fewer FM stations competing, this station could be heard near Bloomington, Illinois, almost 300 miles (480 km) distant.

India

The first FM broadcasting in India was in the year 1977 at Madras. In the mid-nineties, when India first experimented with private FM broadcasts, the small tourist destination of Goa was the fifth place in this country of one billion where private players got FM slots. The other four centres were the big metro cities: Delhi, Mumbai, Kolkata and Chennai. These were followed by stations in Bangalore, Hyderabad, Jaipur and Lucknow.

Times FM (now Radio Mirchi) began operations in 1993 in Ahmedabad. Until 1993, All India Radio or AIR, a government undertaking, was the only radio broadcaster in India. The government then took the initiative to privatize the radio broadcasting sector. It sold airtime blocks on its FM channels in Indore, Hyderabad, Mumbai, Delhi, Kolkata, Vizag and Goa to private operators, who developed their own program content. The Times Group operated its brand, Times FM, till June 1998. After that, the government decided not to renew contracts given to private operators. In 2000, the government announced the auction of 108 FM frequencies across India.

Radio City Bangalore is India's first private FM radio station and was started on July 3, 2001. It launched with presenters such as Rohit Barker, Darius Sunawala, Jonzie Kurian and Suresh Venkat.

Indian policy currently states that these broadcasters are assessed a One-Time Entry Fee (OTEF), for the entire license period of 10 years. Under the Indian accounting system, this amount is amortised over the 10 year period at 10% per annum. Annual license fee for private players is either 4% of revenue share or 10% of Reserve Price, whichever is higher.

Earlier, India's attempts to privatise its FM channels ran into rough weather when private players bid heavily and most could not meet their commitments to pay the government the amounts they owed.

Japan

The frequency modulation radio broadcast band in Japan is 76-90 MHz. The 90-108 MHz section was used for television for VHF Channels 1,2 and 3 until the analog shutdown occurred on July 24, 2011. The narrowness of the Japanese band (14 MHz compared to slightly more than 20 MHz for the CCIR band) limits the number of FM stations that can be accommodated on the dial.

Many Japanese radios are designed to be capable of receiving both the Japanese FM band and the CCIR FM band, so that the same model can be sold within Japan or exported. The radio may cover 76 to 108 MHz, the frequency coverage may be selectable by the user, or during assembly the radio may be set to operate on one band by means of a specially-placed diode or other internal component.

Conventional analog-tuned (dial & pointer) radios may be marked with "TV Sound" in the 90-108 section. If these radios were sold in the USA, for example, the 76-88 section would be marked TV sound for VHF channels 5 and 6, with the 88-108 section band as audio FM.

Second-hand automobiles imported from Japan contain a radio designed for the Japanese FM band, and importers often fit a "converter" to down-convert the 87.5 to 107.9 MHz band to the frequencies that the radio can accept. In addition to showing an incorrect frequency, there are two other disadvantages that can result in undesired performance; the converter cannot downconvert in full the regular international FM band (up to 20.5 MHz wide) to the only 14MHz wide Japanese band (unless the converter incorporates two user-switchable downconvert modes), and the original antenna may perform poorly on the higher FM band. Also, RDS is not used in Japan, whereas most modern car radios available in Europe avail of this system. Also the converter may not allow pass-through of the MW band (if desired). A better solution is to replace the radio and antenna with ones designed for the country where the car will be used.

Small-scale Use of the FM Broadcast Band

Consumer use of FM transmitters

In some countries, small-scale (Part 15 in United States terms) transmitters are available that can transmit a signal from an audio device (usually an MP3 player or similar) to a standard FM radio receiver; such devices range from small units built to carry audio to a car radio with no audio-in capability (often formerly provided by special adapters for audio cassette decks, which are becoming less common on car radio designs) up to full-sized, near-professional-grade broadcasting systems that can be used to transmit audio throughout a property. Most such units transmit in full stereo, though some models designed for beginner hobbyists may not. Similar transmitters are often included in satellite radio receivers and some toys.

Legality of these devices varies by country. The U.S. Federal Communications Commission and Industry Canada allow them. Starting on 1 October 2006 these devices became legal in most countries in the European Union. Devices made to the harmonised European specification became legal in the UK on 8 December 2006.

FM radio microphones

The FM broadcast band can also be used by some inexpensive wireless microphones, but professional-grade wireless microphones generally use bands in the UHF region so they can run on dedicated equipment without broadcast interference. Such inexpensive wireless microphones are generally sold as toys for karaoke or similar purposes, allowing the user to use an FM radio as an output rather than a dedicated amplifier and speaker.

Microbroadcasting

Low-power transmitters such as those mentioned above are also sometimes used for neighborhood or campus radio stations, though campus radio stations are often run over carrier current. This is generally considered a form of microbroadcasting. As a general rule, enforcement towards low-power FM stations is stricter than AM stations due to issues such as the capture effect, and as a result, FM microbroadcasters generally do not reach as far as their AM competitors.

Clandestine use of FM transmitters

FM transmitters have been used to construct miniature wireless microphones for espionage and surveillance purposes (covert listening devices or so-called "bugs"); the advantage to using the FM broadcast band for such operations is that the receiving equipment would not be considered particularly suspect. Common practice is to tune the bug's transmitter off the ends of the broadcast band, into what in the United States would be TV channel 6 (<87.9 MHz) or aviation navigation frequencies (>107.9); most FM radios with analog tuners have sufficient overcoverage to pick up these slightly-beyond-outermost frequencies, although many digitally tuned radios do not.

Constructing a "bug" is a common early project for electronics hobbyists, and project kits to do so are available from a wide variety of sources. The devices constructed, however, are often too large and poorly shielded for use in clandestine activity.

In addition, much pirate radio activity is broadcast in the FM range, because of the band's greater clarity and listenership, the smaller size and lower cost of equipment.

Value Added FM Services

The convergence of telecommunication, radio, television, cable, Internet and digital technology has brought in a new media situation often referred to as 'information super highway'. An information society is a reality now. The shift to the digital domain has erased the distinctions between a television set, personal computer and radio. Therefore, the boundaries separating broadcasting, telecommunications and computer industry are diminishing. The media market of the future is going to be multi-channel, highly competitive, catering to the increasingly fragmented audiences. Retaining a competitive edge in the new market environment will mean examining all possible avenues of business growth, both traditional and non-traditional. Technologies that can offer business expansion opportunities in the emerging communication markets are constantly being explored.

Today, there are over two billion radio receivers in use. The power of sound radio to inform, educate and entertain at home and while on the move at a very low cost is unmatched. Digital technology is now capable of modernising this grand old medium. One of the significant developments is that it has now become possible to transmit additional information in the form of text or graphics on the same radio transmitter. An additional sound signal or a radio programme (music and or spoken word) can also be carried on the same transmitter. Since the 1970's broadcasters have been adding data signals to the normal television transmission. These signals are transmitted in such a way that they do not interfere with the programme signals and can also be received only by the special receiver/decoder. This has been done in radio transmissions, though on an experimental basis. These are known as Value Added Services.

Value Added Service means any additional programme or information broadcast over the transmitting system (transmitter), on a frequency different from that of the frequency of the normal programme without affecting it by utilising the spare capacity.

The International Telecommunication Union (ITU) allots certain frequency ranges to each country for purpose of broadcasting on Amplitude Modulation (AM) and Frequency Modulation (FM) transmitters. Therefore, broadcasters are required to utilise this frequency allocation most effectively so that broadcasting requirements are met. Technological advancements have enabled broadcasters to provide value additions to the listeners over the existing transmitting network by piggy-riding over the normal programme. The additional expenditure on providing the value-added services is rather negligible as compared to the cost of setting up a separate transmitting network.

Radio broadcasting plays a dominant role in information and entertainment delivery to urban and rural communities. These communities rely on broadcasters for public weather forecasts and predictions, economic information, as well as public safety and service announcements. These services have been provided using technology that was developed decades ago. The longevity of these technologies is due to the fact that they are based on standardised, reliable, and relatively inexpensive receivers. Several technologies are currently poised to deliver additional voice as well as data services using the broadcast frequency allocations available on any type of terrestrial broadcast (or land-based) radio transmitter, be it Frequency Modulated (FM), Amplitude Modulated (AM), or Digital Audio Broadcasting (DAB) transmitter. Thus, we have three types of value additions on radio, these are:

— Value additions on FM transmitters;

— Value additions on AM transmitters; and

— Value additions on DAB transmitters.

Let us discuss each of them in some detail.

Value Additions on FM Transmitters

FM broadcasting has enormous potential of becoming a rich source of additional information along with regular radio programmes to distant locations. A conventional FM broadcast system has a spare capacity to accommodate more than one programme at a time. The system has unutilised frequency slots, which can be utilised by inserting sub-carriers for providing additional services without affecting the quality of the main programme. This has resulted in the following value added services on FM transmitters

Radio Data System (RDS)

The Radio Data System (RDS), also known as Radio Broadcast Data System (RBDS) has emerged as the International Standard for data broadcasting using the spare capacity of FM broadcast service. Formulation of RDS is the result of extensive work carried out under the auspices of the European Broadcasting Union (EBU). Some of the applications of RDS are:

— RDS for basic tuning and another functions;

— RDS radio text information service; and

— RDS radio paging.

Basic Tuning and Other Functions

The RDS developed in Europe was maiily intended to transmit codes. These codes were intended to assist receivers, particularly car receivers tuning in crowded reception conditions and to display certain messages, such as programme service name, clock-time and date in the RDS receiver.

The other functions, which are transmitted as codes for assisting automatic tuning of broadcasting receivers, are:

1. *Programme Identification (PI):* This code is transmitted to enable the receiver to search automatically for an alternative frequency in case of bad reception of the programme to which the receiver is tuned.
2. *Programme Service (PS) name:* To indicate the name of the radio station in not more than eight characters.
3. *Programme Type (PTY):* This is an identification number to be transmitted with each programme item, to specify the programme type, e.g., news, current affairs, sports, education, alarm, etc.
4. *Traffic Programme Identification (TP):* This is an on/off switching signal to indicate, by means of a special lamp on the receiver, that this is a programme on which announcements are usually made for the motorists.
5. *List of Alternative Frequencies (AF):* To give the information on other transmitters broadcasting, the same programme in the same or adjacent areas. This is particularly useful in car/portable receivers.
6. *Enhanced Other Networks Information (EON):* This infor-mation like AF, PS, TP and PTY on other network programme services helps the receivers to get tuned to other network services carrying same PI code.

The signals for other functions, which are transmitted in RDS, are:

1. *Traffic Announcement Identification (TA):* This is an on/off-switching signal to indicate whether an announcement for the motorists is on the

air. This could be used to switch automatically from cassette listening to a traffic announcement, and vice-versa.

2. Decoder Identification (DI): This is a switching signal indicating which of the possible operating modes is appropriate for use with broadcast signals.
3. *Music/Speech Switch (M/S):* This is a two-state signal to provide information on whether Music or Speech is being broadcast. This is helpful in receivers fitted with separate volume controls one for music and the other for speech.
4. *Programme Item Number (PIN)*: This code can enable receivers and recorders designed to make use of this feature to respond to the particular programme item(s) that the user has pre-selected.
5. *Clock-Time and Date (CT)*: Clock-time and date can be transmitted for the information of the listener.

The standard RDS features to assist automatic receiver tuning have already been implemented in many countries in Europe. RDS car receivers are being marketed since 1987 and more than 50 models are commercially available. With the growth of FM transmitters in our country such features would also become available in due course of time.

Radiotext Information Service

In this information age, the importance of data is increasing in our daily life. We have to spend a lot of money and time to access several valuable and necessary data. Fortunately, some data can be transmitted from the radio transmitters, along with the audio programme without disturbing the audio programme. This data can either be related to the programme known as the Programme Associated Data (PAD), such as, the name of the producer, director, singer, lyricist, film, year of production, etc., of the song being broadcast. It can be totally unrelated to the audio programme also. The unrelated information may be of stock market quotations, traffic details, etc. Not only text data, but even limited graphics can also be transmitted along with the audio programme from the FM transmitter.

To receive this RDS data, a special receiver is required. It may have a built-in monitor to display data. Alternatively, RDS data received from a conventional FM receiver can-be fed to an RDS monitor. This additional Radiotext (data information) can be decoded at the receiver end and displayed on the monitor screen. The system is usefully configured to provide a maximum of 960 characters per page, bearing in mind that the display capability of a low-cost monitor is 24 lines of 40 characters each.

The text data may be received from various agencies such as universities, banks, transport sector, etc., as well as information originated at the broadcast centre itself. At the transmitter end, this text information is formatted into different pages and transmitted along with a page index number based on a service classification. This data is kept in a PC and the text data required for each transmission sequence is recovered from the PC memory and formatted. The process is continued for the entire page of a particular channel, and further extended to all the channels in a particular transmission sequence. The processed data sequence assembled in this manner is then transmitted to the coder at the VHF/FM transmitting station via data circuit. After sending the sequence, the computer accesses the next batch of text data and the process is repeated.

At the receiving end, the base-band signal from a conventional FM receiver is fed to a microprocessor-based decoder unit. The decoder carries out the recovery of the text data. The output can be displayed on a monitor and a hard copy can also be obtained using a conventional printer. The decoder also incorporates channel selection routines and has a display panel to indicate the selected channel number.

In India, field trials for the Radiotext transmission were successfully carried out by the Research Department of All India Radio in 1990. As a pilot project, the field trial was conducted for educational services in collaboration with Yashwant Rao Chavan Open University at Nashik. A set of lessons of socio-economic relevance were prepared and accompanying audio were transmitted. For information services, field trials were taken up for displaying general election results and other commercial services. The service was extended to transmission of news, current affairs and public utility information.

Radio Paging

You must have seen or used a pager. It is a small receiver or a gadget, which is carried by the user to receive the paging messages. Every pager, like a telephone, has a number and messages are delivered based on these numbers. Pagers generally gives a beep sound when a message is received. Some pagers also have the facility for vibration to indicate the message so that the user is not disturbed in meetings, etc. Pagers have provision for storage of messages and their deletion as well. Paging message is sent to 'alert' or to 'summon' a person. It is generally sent to a person who is on the move. It is a One-way transfer of pre-coded messages. The concerned person only receives these messages. In other words, when a person is called or paged, other subscribers do not know what message was sent to him. The paging messages may be in a direct or coded language.

When paging is done using radio mode, it is called 'Radio Paging'. The radio paging is a specialised value added broadcast service with built-in selective calling features. From the application point of view, two types of Paging exist, i.e., Spot Paging or Private Paging and Wide Area or Citywide Paging. Two technical standards, which are prevalent and popular, are POCSAG (Post Office Code Standardisation Advisory Group) and the FM RDS Paging (Broadcast Standard). FM RDS Radio Paging is a value added service from the FM transmitter whereas POCSAG is not a value added service as a transmitter is required to be installed exclusively for this service.

The RDS Paging network includes the following components:

i. Paging Exchange: The person who wants to send a paging message delivers it first to the operator in the paging exchange by calling on the telephone lines.

ii. From the 'paging exchange', these messages are routed to the coder at the FM transmitter. 'Paging exchange' generally has data links with the FM transmitter from where these messages are broadcast.

FM RDS Paging.s used in many countries. In India, it was introduced in 14 cities by All India Radio (AIR) but it has been discontinued due to some contractual problems. However, there are private operators who provide this service at various centres.

Paging is an inexpensive way to communicate with the people on the move. Being a one-way device of communication, the sender is not sure whether his/her message has actually been delivered/read by the receiving person. However it is a very powerful and cost-effective method of instant communication.

SCA Sound

Not only the RDS text data, but an additional audio programme can also be broadcast over a FM transmitter by utilising its spare capacity by using its sub-carrier. This sub-carrier can be used for the transmission of speech quality sound known as SCA (Subsidiary Channel Authorisation) sound. In the USA, the SCA sound transmission is being used for broadcasting background music in departmental stores.

The speech quality sound, such as educational lectures, slow speed news, sports commentary, etc., is generally broadcast on this SCA channel. These signals are frequency modulated on a sub-carrier in a SCA coder, which is an additional unit in the FM transmitter. In the FM receiver, a SCA decoder recovers back this additional sound for simultaneous listening along with the main programme. The decoder is a simple circuit which could be a built-in unit in the receiver or an external add-on unit.

The main programme and the SCA sound are of totally independent natures. It means that RDS data can also be of independent nature and can be associated with the main audio programme in the form of Programme Associated Data (PAD). For example, if the main programme is a song, the PAD may be the textual information about the name, director, year of release, etc., of the film. The RDS data may also be associated with the SCA sound signal.

The receiver may receive only main programme, SCA sound or text data. These signals can also be received on a multifunctional FM receiver in any combination. The radiotext receiver was developed by the Research Department of All India Radio for experimental purposes so that the technology could be transferred to the industry. This type of receiver is capable of reproducing simultaneously the normal stereo programme along with the SCA sound and display radiotext on a monitor. It is also possible to connect a printer directly to the receiver to get the text.

High-Speed Data Systems

In the RDS system, the rate of digital data injected at the sub-carrier is very low. Several proponents have developed prototypes for a new high-speed data service, known as FM High-Speed data Service (FM HSS) prototypes. This new high-speed data service is incorporated into the FM signal in the same way a conventional sub-carrier is added. The difference between conventional sub-carriers and the high-speed sub-carrier systems is the data rate of the service.

The current FM HSS systems are designed to provide data services to mobile users. The primary interest is in providing mapping services and traffic information to automobiles as part of Intelligent Transportation Systems. The FM HSS systems are not designed to provide this type of service exclusively. However, the system architecture allows any type of data service to be provided. The data can be addressed to a specific user or group of users with compatible receivers. FM HSS technology is more advanced and is currently available for broadcast. FM sub-carrier systems are typically installed and administered by a company that is separate from the broadcaster. Thus there are no equipment costs for the broadcast station to include this service. In fact, it generates revenues for the broadcaster in the form of fees paid by the sub-carrier service provider.

The high-speed data service is faster than RDS and more robust in terms of performance. In addition to text information, voice, picture and multi-media could also be transmitted over the high-speed data channel. The broadcaster can use the existing transmitter for these services without affecting the main sound programmes. S/he only needs to add the data encoder to transmit data. With a large coverage area available in commercial FM services, radio users can benefit from these data services which perform adequately even under mobile conditions.

Value Additions on AM Transmitters

High Frequency (HF) radio is one of the oldest forms of long distance broadcasting. Propagation of radio waves in the HF band of the spectrum occurs in two primary modes: the ground wave, in which radio wave energy remains near the surface of the Earth, and the sky wave, in which radio waves are reflected from ionised layers in the earth's upper atmosphere (ionosphere). The audio signal to be broadcast modulates the amplitude of the HF carrier and as such this type of transmitters are known as Amplitude Modulation (AM) transmitters.

At ranges of greater than 90 miles, HF communication depends upon sky wave propagation. Unlike the ground wave, the sky wave returns are highly variable and dependent upon frequency, time of day, season, solar activity, and geographic location. In addition to this variability, sky wave signals also suffer from a number of impairments, including the interruption of communications by ionospheric storms, a large number of possible propagation paths resulting in time dispersion of a signal, high levels of interference, large and rapid fades, and frequency dispersion of wide-band signals.

Despite these shortcomings, HF has remained the communication medium for many applications, because a low transmit power can often provide extremely long range communications (without the need for repeaters or the use of satellites) when the proper transmission frequency is used. Moreover, progress in HF technology since the 1970's, has reduced the need for skilled operators. Modern HF equipment incorporates a high degree of automation as a result of developments in automatic tuning and antenna matching systems, remotely controllable systems, and automatic link establishment systems. In addition, hardware developments such as solid-state circuits, highly stable oscillators, frequency-agile synthesisers, fast-tuning antenna couplers, and solid-state power amplifiers have considerably improved HF communications. The advent of very large scale integration has led to smaller, lighter, more power efficient and more reliable equipment AM transmitters can also be used for value additions.

AM Data System (AMDS)

Supplementary data transmission as value addition on AM sound broadcast transmitters, has always held great interest for the broadcasters. High power AM transmissions have large coverage area, and useful data such as tuning information, time/date, programme type, weather information, radio paging, telemetry and control, etc., could be provided over the service area The UK, France and Germany have actually developed systems for AM data transmission. The technical specifications for the system await the approval of the International Telecommunication Union.

Skywave 2000

Digital technology can be used in the HF broadcasting for value addition. A project named Skywave 2000 developed for the short-wave band can transmit audio, data and multimedia in digital mode using the existing HF transmission infrastructure. Present receivers could be used along with add on modules. Some demonstrations of the system have been given in Europe and elsewhere and promise a bright future for HF broadcasting. Further work is in progress.

Value Additions on DAB Transmitters

The Digital Audio Broadcasting (DAB), now called DSB (Digital Sound Broadcasting), technology was developed to provide very high quality audio reception under static and mobile conditions. This was aimed at overcoming many of the deficiencies encountered in conventional analog and digital transmission techniques. DAB carries six channels of CD quality audio stereo channels. The DAB system can also be used to carry a large variety of additional programme-associated as well as independent data services. The programme-associated category provides finer information on the audio programme received off-air. Independent data could be a whole lot of information from real-time paging data to on-demand file downloads, games, finance, weather, news and many more directed to a dedicated receiver incorporated in a desktop, laptop or even a palmtop computer. DAB system's immunity to multipath and other reception impairments guarantee error-free data reception

Examples of DAB data services currently being implemented are given below. These services may be presented either in the form of text information still pictures or even video images on more sophisticated displays. These are:

— Programme-associated services, such as current song title, interpreter and performer, lyrics, news headlines, CD covers, etc.;
— News, including events, traffic messages, weather, sport, stock market, travel and tourist information;
— Traffic navigation by means of transmitted digitised road maps;
— Advertisements and sales, including sales catalogues, purchase offers, etc;
— Entertainment, including games and non-commercial bulletin boards; and
— Closed user group services, such as banking information, electronic newspapers, fax printouts and remote teaching.

A key to the success of the DAB will be its ability to address each receiver individually. This will allow the service provider to customise the "bouquet" of services provided to each user, and to identify the user in an interactive transaction.

Ideally, the value added services should be interactive, to enable the consumer to communicate with the service provider's database. Since the broadcast services are one-way only, the return channel has to be provided. A semi-interactive mode is also possible.

Interactive FM Radio Programmes

A few decades ago, a well-known playwright, Bertolt Brecht observed that the one-way nature of a communication medium would condemn it to sterility. Over the years, every communication medium has introduced new features to take away the odium of being 'one- way' in nature and invest it with a two-way character to the extent possible. The newspapers regularly devote considerable space to letters to the editor from the readers to highlight peoples' reactions to events, happenings and the like. The periodicals have gone one step ahead by introducing schemes of prizes to encourage readers' feedback. In the case of the electronic media, the OB or outside broadcasting method helps the media persons to get out of their studio confines and interact with the audience. The radio medium offers large scope for interactivity with the common people.

To interact means, 'to facilitate a two-way flow of communication'. This could be between two persons in a face-to face situation or at a distance using tools of technology. Think of a situation in which you are listening to a talk by a specialist on a subject of your interest. At the end of the talk you may have some questions or thoughts in your mind that you would want to share with the talker. If you get an opportunity of asking or interacting, the subject or issue under discussion becomes more clear in your mind and you may like to apply that information or knowledge in your personal life. For example, you are listening to a programme on tree plantation and you are motivated by the programme to plant some tree saplings. If you get the opportunity to ask the questions and get an appropriate reply, you will possibly go ahead and plant the desired saplings. However, if there was no such opportunity for interaction then the motivation may probably die down. The programme thus would have failed to get the desired result to inspire tree plantation and the objective of the programme would have remained unfulfilled. Therefore, interactivity is essential in any form of communication, especially when communication, radio communication in this case, is being used as a development tool. Interactivity has many facets and its scope is large. In the radio medium, it is useful not only in 'live' or pre-recorded broadcasts but also to:

— Know the audience

— Plan and design the programme

— Content formulation

— Ensure that the programmes are comprehensible, interesting and that message is clear;

— Know whether the desired objective is achieved and also to measure the impact of communication.

One of the important elements of broadcasting is planning. If broadcasts are to be effective, interactivity must begin at the stage of planning itself.

Interactivity in Planning

Both, formative and summative researches involve close interaction with the present and potential audience. Surveys and Focus Group Discussion (FGDs) are such interactive exercises of a researcher. The producer plans his/her programmes with reference to the communication needs gleaned from audience survey findings. This is an on-going exercise. The producer has to keep in constant touch with people of different strata of society to ascertain their needs and expectations. S/he looks forward to receiving their views and reactions to his/her programmes. At the conclusion of the broadcast of a series of programmes on a chosen subject, the producer can invite listeners' views or suggestions on the broadcast they had heard through an announcement. Very often, the suggestions serve as the basis for further programming.

This can be illustrated with an example. When a series of programmes on adolescents was about to conclude, the producer wanted to introduce a new serial retaining the same audience which was deeply involved in the serial. The listeners were asked what they would like to listen in the next serial. Announcements were made inviting suggestions from listeners and the response was overwhelming. A majority of the listeners wanted a serial on marriage problems as many of them were at the threshold of married life. This response made the decision of the producer easy. When the serial on marriage problems was introduced, it not only addressed the felt needs of the listeners, it also gave the impression that the radio station was sensitive to their needs.

Interactions with the potential audience are of great help in planning the content of the programme. A study of the available research literature can throw insight on contemporary issues which deserve extensive treatment in radio programmes. Focus group discussions also provide free and frank articulation of views and opinions of a representative segment of people. Such feedback is of immense value in designing programmes. To illustrate, before preparing the conceptual design of the serial on adolescents (referred to earlier) critical issues confronting them were identified. A series of group discussions and in-depth individual interviews with the target audiences in schools, homes, counselling clinics, and in drug de-addiction centres were arranged to record their impressions, grievances and views. During these interactions, it was felt that parents' viewpoint was vital to present a balanced view since many among the youth blamed their parents for not understanding their feelings, pressures and stresses. Problems posed by the youth and their parents were analysed by subject specialists and suggestions were offered.

Types of Interactive Programmes

From the early days of radio broadcasting, producers have endeavoured to involve the listeners and associate them in programmes. The development of technology and availability of miniaturised equipment have expanded the scope for producing different types of interactive programmes involving the listeners. Some of these methods are:

Listeners' Letters

For a long time, interaction between the broadcasters and the audience was mainly through the medium of letters. There are two types of listeners' letters - solicited and unsolicited. When a radio station invites comments of listeners on specific programmes, and a response is received from them, these are known as solicited letters. In the case of unsolicited letters, listeners write on their own to the radio station to express their views and comments. Both types of letters are important for a radio station as they provide the station with valuable feedback of the listeners. Radio stations usually make a provision for broadcast of weekly/biweekly programmes of replies to listener's letters. The general pattern followed by radio stations is that one announcer reads excerpts from listener's letters and another announcer answers the points raised. However, some more innovative approaches are also been undertaken.

Generally, there is a considerable time-gap in listeners sending their letters and the radio station replying on the air. This gap is being bridged by e-mail facility which is being increasingly used by listeners to convey their requests, queries or feedback to the radio station. When the facility of voice mail was introduced, the listeners were asked to telephone their comments, suggestions or assessment of the programmes. The replies to listeners' programmes included comments of the listeners in their own voice.

The format of receiving communication from listeners was expanded to serve the interests of public service broadcasting. Listeners are now encouraged to send their queries on the day-to-day problems relating to family, health, law, inheritance and so on. The producer would approach experts in these areas to provide clarifications and advise the listeners. These are put together in an integrated broadcast programme.

One of the most popular formats of radio broadcasts is the 'listeners' choice'. Even at a time when the market is flooded with music cassettes and CDs, listeners write to radio stations on their choice of songs which they would like to listen. Of late, listeners at some centres have the facility to dial the radio stations, get connected to the producer or disc jockey and get the song of his/her choice broadcast immediately.

OB-based Programmes

Radio stations organise programmes outside the studios where the producers come into direct contact with their audience. These programmes are known as Outside Broadcasts or OB programmes. These are of different types: public functions, seminars or colloquia, etc. Some are in the form of features where a producer records views/opinions of the people connected with the topic of the feature. They are Vox pop type programmes. Vox pop is derived from Latin word Vox populi which means, 'voice of the people'. In such programmes the common people get access to the microphone to articulate their views and interact with the producers.

Some radio stations arrange programmes in interior villages for dissemination of information on a given issue. The producer accompanied by two or three experts goes to a village where an interactive session with the local people is organised. During the course of one such programme, a chief engineer of electricity board was participating and explaining to the villagers the use of electricity to energise their irrigation pump sets. While he was explaining to the villagers, there was a sudden drop in the voltage in power supply. The villagers pointed out that this was a regular feature which handicapped their drawing power for irrigation. The chief engineer did the investigation on the spot, located the fault and took prompt action to remedy the situation. It was the case of a radio programme solving a long-standing problem of the people.

"Students' forums" are OB programmes which are organised in colleges and universities. These bring subject experts face-to-face with students and their interactions on subjects of interest to students are recorded. The subject chosen varies from academic and subjects of vital interest to the youth. The recording of the interaction is suitably edited for broadcast.

Forum Programmes

Radio stations provide a forum for voicing the grievances of the people. "People's forum" is an OB-based grievance programme format. The producer identifies a subject agitating the minds of the people. S/he records the complaints/grievances of a cross-section of people in their own homes or workplaces. For example, if there is shortage of water supply in a particular town or city, the producer takes this up as a subject of grievances programmes. S/he contacts cross-section of the people and records their grievances. The recording is played back to the Mayor/the administrative head/concerned authority. Their reaction to the complaints and plan of the action is obtained. The people's complaint and the administrator's response is put out as a composite programme presenting both the sides of the issue.

Generally, morning information programmes broadcast from various radio stations in the country include a segment devoted to OB recordings of people's grievances and the authorities' response to these. 'Zoona Dub' was a popular programme of yesteryears broadcast from Radio Kashmir, Srinagar. The programme brought the people's grievances to the notice of the government agencies. The Chief Ministers of some states also use the radio for ascertaining the difficulties being faced by people and take prompt action in resolving them.

Phone-in Programmes

"Phone-in" is a technique adopted by radio stations abroad for receiving listener's requests for pop music items which are played immediately. In India the concept is catching up. 'Phonerins' have been popular in our country not only for listening music but also for counselling services. The 'phone-ins' on health related subjects are more popular due to the benefit the listeners derive from counselling services offered. These are designed to provide immediate advice and guidance to listeners in the areas of immediate concern to them. A large number of listeners interact with the experts and get the counselling directly. If the subject of a 'phone-in' programme is 'arthritis', specialists in orthopedics and physiotherapy are brought to the studios. The subject is announced beforehand and the listeners are asked to telephone at the time of live broadcast and pose their problems to the specialists. A large number of listeners interact with experts and get the needed counselling directly. Based on the success and popularity of this format, radio programmers have expanded the scope of the programme to cover various areas including law, education, employment opportunities, etc. If listeners ask questions about matrimonial disputes, the dowry act, the divorce laws, the provision for alimony, etc, the legal experts provide them the answers immediately. Supplementary questions can also be asked to get further clarifications.

The phone-in technique can be used for innovative programming. To take an example, a radio producer was keen that truck drivers must get the benefit of the public service messages a particular radio station was putting out. A reporter was sent to a roadside restaurant where the truck drivers halted at night during their driving assignments. The reporter engaged them in conversation and asked them to mention the song they would like to listen to on the radio. When they indicated their choice of songs, he got in touch with the radio station on his mobile phone and conveyed what the drivers wanted to listen. Within a few minutes, the announcer played the first song to the delight of the drivers. The next song of their choice followed and along with it a message on AIDS which they listened along with the songs. The subsequent discussions revealed that the drivers got information on ADDS for the first time and understood the content of the message.

Once the confidence of the drivers was gained, the reporter then started collecting details of their lifestyles, habits, including sexual behaviour. While this was an extremely sensitive matter a small percentage among them did part with the required information. The drivers also reported that they often suffered from fatigue, backache, stomach upsets, cough, allergy, etc. Appropriate counselling was provided to them with the help of medical experts.

The phone-in technique has been used with considerable success by IGNOU in its radio counselling programmes through AH India Radio. During the counselling, presentations are made by subject experts followed by a question-answer session. Students' queries regarding admissions, tests, assignments, results, fees, etc. are also taken up during the sessions. Those students who do not have a telephone connection are asked to send their questions by post to the respective Regional Centres. These are taken up in the subsequent programmes. However, it has been found that students often prefer to telephone from a public phone booth rather than write letters. This could be because they get instant replies and also hear their own voice over radio.

The phone-in sessions are monitored by a researcher who notes down the telephone numbers of the callers. They are subsequently contacted to find out whether the jailer was satisfied with the answer given or not. According to a feedback study, the phone-in counselling has been especially found useful by specific sections of the student's population, e.g., in-service personnel such as, nurses, primary school teachers, the visually challenged, women and poor students.

Voice Mail and E-mail based Programmes

While phone-ins can be used for interaction in 'live' programmes, voice mail and e-mail can be used for counselling. Voice Mail is akin to Post Box service available at post offices wherein a telephone number gets allotted as Voice Mail Box number. Listeners can dial the voice mail box number of the radio station and convey his/her message which is recorded. The radio producer retrieves the message and transfers it to an audio tape.

E-mail, as you may be aware is electronic mail sent through computers using the Internet. The radio stations have email address on which listeners can send emails. For this one need not own a computer. Email messages can be sent through the cyber cafes available in various towns and cities by paying nominal charges.

Voice mail or e-mail can be sent to the producer wherein the listener can state the questions for which s/he needs clarification from the experts. The listeners can e-mail his/her question to the producer even during the course of a 'live' programme and get the response from the expert in the same programme.

Every segment of listeners including women, industrial workers, farmers, youth and others for whom radio broadcast special programmes has the benefit of counselling through phone-in programmes. Apart from adults, children also seek radio counselling. In an interesting case, children participating in a radio programme asked the UNICEF expert how to behave when their parents quarreled in their presence. They also sought guidance how to manage their life when both the parents were employed and they were left alone at home.

Audio Conferencing and Radio Bridges

Audio conferencing is an extension of the phone-in facility. It involves the linkage of two or more radio stations through satellite or telephone lines. Experts in the studios of several cities are able to discuss a subject and the listener has the benefit of interactions with the experts from different places. The facility of audio-conferencing could be enlarged in the form of Radio Bridges in which apart from experts' participation, listeners could also telephone the radio station which is transmitting the programme from their residence and interact with the experts. To illustrate, a listener from Mumbai can telephone the radio producer at Delhi and seek clarifications from the experts in Kolkatta and all this happens in the same 'live' programme.

At the time of the presentation of the annual budget of the Union Government, radio stations arrange a Radio Bridge programme and announce the telephone numbers which the listeners can dial for participation. Any listener from any part of the country can participate in the interactive programme which usually includes the government functionaries connected with the central budget and economists at different centres. A large number of listeners including income tax practitioners, business men, exporters and students seek and secure additional information they want. Innovative radio producers have been trying to make use of technology for interactive programmes in different ways.

Interactivity in Programme Evaluation

We have stated that for effective broadcasting, interactivity must began at the planning stage itself. However, sometimes programmes designed after a lot of discussion and consultation with experts may not find acceptance with listeners. This could be due to a variety of reasons. A pre-test survey can reveal the reasons for this. This methodology of pre-testing the programmes in the field before they are actually broadcast has been applied to a number of science communication initiatives to assess the utility, acceptability and appeal to the target audience. In pre-testing, prototypes of the programmes are played to a group of potential listeners and their reactions are recorded.

Pre-testing in the field is one way of evaluating the programmes for their content, clarity of message, and production values, etc. Another way of evaluating the programmes is to judge them during broadcast. You can do this by inviting listeners' response to provide you with the information you are seeking about your programmes, and also to help the listener understand the concepts. For example, you can design a quiz at the end of each programme and tell them in the beginning of the programme that you will announce questions in the end of each episode. They have to send the answer and the best respondents will be rewarded. Thus you can motivate the listeners to listen to the entire episode. You may involve them further by asking them to send in the possible questions: "What are the possible questions you could frame on this episode?" You can announce rewards for those whose questions matched yours.

In this process, you can make them reflect on what they gained from the episode. After a fortnight, when the responses are received, you can announce the names of the best respondent/s. Through this process, your target audience has started thinking and talking about the issues you have dealt with. In other words, you have sensitised them to certain issues you have presented in the programmes. This approach can be especially useful in programmes on developmental issues and education.

References

Briggs Asa. *The BBC—the First Fifty Years*, Oxford University Press, 1984.

Crisell, Andrew *An Introductory History of British Broadcasting.* 2nd ed. London: Routledge. 2002.

Kahn Frank J., ed. *Documents of American Broadcasting,* fourth edition, Prentice-Hall, Inc., 1984.

Kapoor, D N., *Broadcast Journalism.* Mohit Pubications, 2006.

Kumar, K. *Mass Communications in India.* Mumbai: Jaico Publishing. 2007.

Singhal, A. and E.M. Rogers. *The Emerging Information Revolution In India.* New Delhi: Sage 1988.

4

Digital Audio Broadcasting

Digital Audio Broadcasting (DAB) is a digital radio technology for broadcasting radio stations, used in several countries, particularly in Europe. As of 2006, approximately 1,002 stations worldwide broadcast in the DAB format.

The DAB standard was initiated as a European research project in the 1980s. The Norwegian Broadcasting Corporation (NRK) launched the very first DAB channel in the world on June 1, 1995 (NRK Klassisk), and the BBC and SR launched their first DAB digital radio broadcasts in September 1995. DAB receivers have been available in many countries since the end of the 1990s. DAB may offer more radio programmes over a specific spectrum than analogue FM radio. DAB is more robust with regard to noise and multipath fading for mobile listening, since DAB reception quality first degrades rapidly when the signal strength falls below a critical threshold, whereas FM reception quality degrades slowly with the decreasing signal.

An unblinded "informal listening test" by Sverre Holm has shown that for stationary listening the audio quality on DAB is subjectively lower than FM stereo (but this may be due to observer bias). Most stations using a bit rate of 128 kbit/s or less, with the MP2 audio codec, which requires 160 kbit/s to achieve perceived FM quality. 128 kbit/s gives better dynamic range or signal-to-noise ratio than FM radio, but a more smeared stereo image, and an upper cutoff frequency of 14 kHz, corresponding to 15 kHz of FM radio. However, "CD sound quality" with MP2 is possible "with 256..192 kbps".

An upgraded version of the system was released in February 2007, which is called DAB+. DAB is not forward compatible with DAB+, which means that DAB-only receivers will not be able to receive DAB+ broadcasts. DAB+ is approximately twice as efficient as DAB due to the adoption of the AAC+ audio codec, and DAB+ can provide high quality audio with as low as 64 kbit/s. Reception quality will also be more robust on DAB+ than on DAB due to the addition of Reed-Solomon error correction coding.

In spectrum management, the bands that are allocated for public DAB services, are abbreviated with T-DAB, where the "T" stands for terrestrial.

More than 20 countries provide DAB transmissions, and several countries, such as Australia, Italy, Malta, Switzerland and Germany, have started transmitting DAB+ stations. See Countries using DAB/DMB. However, DAB radio has still not replaced the old FM system in popularity.

History of DAB

DAB has been under development since 1981 at the Institut für Rundfunktechnik (IRT). In 1985 the first DAB demonstrations were held at the WARC-ORB in Geneva and in 1988 the first DAB transmissions were made in Germany. Later DAB was developed as a research project for the European Union (EUREKA), which started in 1987 on initiative by a consortium formed in 1986. The MPEG-1 Audio Layer II ("MP2") codec was created as part of the EU147 project. DAB was the first standard based on orthogonal frequency division multiplexing (OFDM) modulation technique, which since then has become one of the most popular transmission schemes for modern wideband digital communication systems.

A choice of audio codec, modulation and error-correction coding schemes and first trial broadcasts were made in 1990. Public demonstrations were made in 1993 in the United Kingdom. The protocol specification was finalized in 1993 and adopted by the ITU-R standardization body in 1994, the European community in 1995 and by ETSI in 1997. Pilot broadcasts were launched in several countries in 1995.

The UK was the first country to receive a wide range of radio stations via DAB. Commercial DAB receivers began to be sold in 1999 and over 50 commercial and BBC services were available in London by 2001.

By 2006, 500 million people worldwide were in the coverage area of DAB broadcasts, although by this time sales had only taken off in the United

Kingdom and Denmark. In 2006 there were approximately 1,000 DAB stations in operation world wide.

The standard was coordinated by the European DAB forum, formed in 1995 and reconstituted to the World DAB Forum in 1997, which represents more than 30 countries. In 2006 the World DAB Forum became the World DMB Forum which now presides over both the DAB and DMB standard.

In October 2005, the World DMB Forum instructed its Technical Committee to carry out the work needed to adopt the AAC+ audio codec and stronger error correction coding. This work led to the launch of the new DAB+ system.

DAB vs. FM/AM

Traditionally radio programmes were broadcast on different frequencies via FM and AM, and the radio had to be tuned into each frequency, as needed. This used up a comparatively large amount of spectrum for a relatively small number of stations, limiting listening choice. DAB is a digital radio broadcasting system that through the application of multiplexing and compression combines multiple audio streams onto a relatively narrow band centred on a single broadcast frequency called a DAB ensemble.

Within an overall target bit rate for the DAB ensemble, individual stations can be allocated different bit rates. The number of channels within a DAB ensemble can be increased by lowering average bit rates, but at the expense of the quality of streams. Error correction under the DAB standard makes the signal more robust but reduces the total bit rate available for streams.

Some countries have implemented Eureka-147 Digital Audio Broadcasting (DAB). DAB broadcasts a single station that is approximately 1500 kilohertz wide (~1000 kilobits per second). That station is then subdivided into multiple digital streams of between 9 and 12 programs. In contrast FM HD Radio shares its digital broadcast with the traditional 200 kilohertz-wide channels, with capability of 300 kbit/s per station (pure digital mode). Thus HD Radio is approximately twice as data-efficient as DAB.

The first generation DAB uses the MPEG-1 Audio Layer II (MP2) audio codec which has less efficient compression than newer codecs. The typical bitrate for DAB programs is only 128 kbit/s and as a result most radio stations on DAB have a lower sound quality than FM, prompting a number of complaints. The newer FM HD Radio uses a codec based upon the MPEG-4 HE-AAC standard. Psychoacoustic studies/tests have shown HE-AAC codecs achieve the same perceived quality as MP2, but at one-quarter the bit rate (CD quality at 64 kbit/s rather than 256 kbit/s).

A directly related issue with DAB's original inefficient compression is "downgrading" stations from stereophonic to monaural, in order to include more channels into the limited 1000 kbit/s bandwidth, smaller coverage of markets as compared to analog FM, radios that are overly expensive, poor reception inside vehicles or buildings, and a general lack of interest in DAB in many countries.

DAB gives substantially higher spectral efficiency, measured in programmes per MHz and per transmitter site, than analogue communication. This has led to an increase in the number of stations available to listeners, especially outside of the major urban areas.

Numerical example: Analog FM requires 0.2 MHz per programme. The frequency reuse factor in most countries is approximately 15, meaning that only one out of 15 transmitter sites can use the same channel frequency without problems with co-channel interference, i.e. cross-talk. Assuming a total availability of 102 FM channels at a bandwidth of 0.2MHz over the Band II spectrum of 87.5 to 108.0 MHz, an average of 102/15 = 6.8 radio channels are possible on each transmitter site (plus lower-power local transmitters causing less interference). This results in a system spectral efficiency of 1 / 15 / (0.2 MHz) = 0.30 programmes/transmitter/MHz. DAB with 192 kbit/s codec requires 1.536 MHz * 192 kbit/s / 1136 kbit/s = 0.26 MHz per audio programme. The frequency reuse factor for local programmes and multi-frequency broadcasting networks (MFN) is typically 4 or 5, resulting in 1 / 4 / (0.26 MHz) = 0.96 programmes/transmitter/MHz. This is 3.2 times as efficient as analog FM for local stations. For single frequency network (SFN) transmission, for example of national programmes, the channel re-use factor is 1, resulting in 1/1/0.25 MHz = 3.85 programmes/ transmitter/MHz, which is 12.7 times as efficient as FM for national and regional networks.

Note the above capacity improvement may not always be achieved at the L-band frequencies, since these are more sensitive to obstacles than the FM band frequencies, and may cause shadow fading for hilly terrain and for indoor communication. The number of transmitter sites or the transmission power required for full coverage of a country may be rather high at these frequencies, to avoid that the system becomes noise limited rather than limited by co-channel interference. .

Sound Quality

The original objectives of converting to digital transmission were to enable higher fidelity, more stations and more resistance to noise, co-channel interference and multipath than in analogue FM radio. However, the leading countries in implementing DAB on stereo radio stations use compression to such a degree that it produces lower sound quality than that received from non-mobile FM broadcasts. This is because of the bit rate levels being too low for the MPEG Layer 2 audio codec to provide high fidelity audio quality.

The BBC Research & Development department states that at least 192 kbit/s is necessary for a high fidelity stereo broadcast:

> A value of 256 kbit/s has been judged to provide a high quality stereo broadcast signal. However, a small reduction, to 224 kbit/s is often adequate, and in some cases it may be possible to accept a further reduction to 192 kbit/s, especially if redundancy in the stereo signal is exploited by a process of 'joint stereo' encoding (i.e. some sounds appearing at the centre of the stereo image need not be sent twice). At 192 kbit/s, it is relatively easy to hear imperfections in critical audio material.

When BBC in July 2006 reduced the bit-rate of transmission of Radio 3 from 192 kbit/s to 160 kbit/s, the resulting degradation of audio quality prompted a number of complaints to the Corporation. BBC later announced that following this testing of new equipment, it would resume the previous practice of transmitting Radio 3 at 192 kbit/s whenever there were no other demands on bandwidth.

Despite the above a survey of DAB listeners (including mobile) has shown most find DAB to have equal or better sound quality than FM.

Notwithstanding the above, BBC Radio 4 has extended the periods it broadcasts programmes with a lower bit rate (80kbit/s) and in mono in 2012, rather than 128kbit/s and in stereo. Programmes which had traditionally been broadcast on BBC Radio 4 DAB in stereo (from 1999 to 2011), can now only be heard in the evenings in mono, even though the same programnmes still go out in stereo on Radio 4 FM, Digital TV and On-Line. The BBC have issued a statement stating that stereo is still their default for BBC Radio 4 DAB, however post the Olympics, this does not appear to be the case in the evenings, making FM broadcasts (in good reception areas) superior. As very few car radios are currently fitted with DAB if the BBC switch FM off as indicated later in the decade, some listeners may be forced to receive mono broadcasts in the future, a somewhat backward step.

DAB Technology

Bands and Modes

DAB uses a wide-bandwidth broadcast technology and typically spectra have been allocated for it in Band III (174–240 MHz) and L band (1452–1492 MHz), although the scheme allows for operation almost anywhere above 30 MHz. The US military has reserved L-Band in the USA only, blocking its use for other purposes in America, and the United States has reached an agreement with Canada that the latter will restrict L-Band DAB to terrestrial broadcast to avoid interference.

DAB has a number of country specific transmission modes (I, II, III and IV). For worldwide operation a receiver must support all 4 modes:

— Mode I for Band III, Earth

— Mode II for L-Band, Earth and satellite

— Mode III for frequencies below 3 GHz, Earth and satellite

— Mode IV for L-Band, Earth and satellite

Protocol Stack

From a OSI model protocol stack viewpoint, the technologies used on DAB inhabit the following layers: the audio codec inhabits the presentation layer. Below that is the data link layer, in charge of packet mode statistical multiplexing and frame synchronization. Finally, the physical layer contains the error-correction coding, OFDM modulation, and dealing with the over-the-air transmission and reception of data. Some aspects of these are described below.

Audio Codec

The older version of DAB that is being used in Denmark, Ireland, Norway, Switzerland and the UK, uses the MPEG-1 Audio Layer 2 audio codec, which is also known as MP2 due to computer files using those characters for their file extension. (Both Ireland and Switzerland also use DAB+).

The new DAB+ standard has adopted the HE-AAC version 2 audio codec, commonly known as AAC+ or aacPlus. AAC+ is approximately three-times more efficient than MP2, which means that broadcasters using DAB+ will be able to provide far higher audio quality or far more stations than they can on DAB, or, as is most likely, a combination of both higher audio quality and more stations will be provided.

One of the most important decisions regarding the design of a digital radio system is the choice of which audio codec to use, because the efficiency of the audio codec determines how many radio stations can be carried on a multiplex at a given level of audio quality. The capacity of a DAB multiplex is fixed, so the more efficient the audio codec is, the more stations can be carried, and vice versa. Similarly, for a fixed bit-rate level, the more efficient the audio codec is the higher the audio quality will be.

Error-correction Coding

Error-correction coding (ECC) is an important technology for a digital communication system because it determines how robust the reception will be for a given signal strength - stronger ECC will provide more robust reception than a weaker form.

The old version of DAB uses punctured convolutional coding for its ECC. The coding scheme uses unequal error protection (UEP), which means that parts of the audio bit-stream that are more susceptible to errors causing audible disturbances are provided with more protection (i.e. a lower code rate) and vice versa. However, the UEP scheme used on DAB results in there being a grey area in between the user experiencing good reception quality and no reception at all, as opposed to the situation with most other wireless digital communication systems that have a sharp "digital cliff", where the signal rapidly becomes unusable if the signal strength drops below a certain threshold. When DAB listeners receive a signal in this intermediate strength area they experience a "burbling" sound which interrupts the playback of the audio.

The new DAB+ standard has incorporated Reed-Solomon ECC as an "inner layer" of coding that is placed around the byte interleaved audio frame but inside the "outer layer" of convolutional coding used by the older DAB system, although on DAB+ the convolutional coding uses equal error protection (EEP) rather than UEP since each bit is equally important in DAB+. This combination of Reed-Solomon coding as the inner layer of coding, followed by an outer layer of convolutional coding - so-called "concatenated coding" - became a popular ECC scheme in the 1990s, and NASA adopted it for its deep-space missions. One slight difference between the concatenated coding used by the DAB+ system and that used on most other systems is that it uses a rectangular byte interleaver rather than Forney interleaving in order to provide a greater interleaver depth, which increases the distance over which error bursts will be spread out in the bit-stream, which in turn will allow the Reed-Solomon error decoder to correct a higher proportion of errors.

The ECC used on DAB+ is far stronger than is used on DAB, which, with all else being equal (i.e. if the transmission powers remained the same), would translate into people who currently experience reception difficulties on DAB receiving a much more robust signal with DAB+ transmissions. It also has a far steeper "digital cliff", and listening tests have shown that people prefer this when the signal strength is low compared to the shallower digital cliff on DAB.

Modulation

Immunity to fading and inter-symbol interference (caused by multipath propagation) is achieved without equalization by means of the OFDM and DQPSK modulation techniques. For details, see the OFDM system comparison table. Using values for the most commonly used transmission mode on DAB, Transmission Mode I (TM I), the OFDM modulation consists of 1,536 subcarriers that are transmitted in parallel. The useful part of the OFDM symbol period is 1 millisecond, which results in the OFDM subcarriers each having a bandwidth of 1 kHz due to the inverse relationship between these two parameters, and the overall OFDM channel bandwidth is 1,537 kHz. The OFDM guard interval for TM I is 246 microseconds, which means that the overall OFDM symbol duration is 1.246 milliseconds. The guard interval duration also determines the maximum separation between transmitters that are part of the same single-frequency network (SFN), which is approximately 74 km for TM I.

Single-frequency Networks

OFDM allows the use of single-frequency networks (SFN), which means that a network of transmitters can provide coverage to a large area - up to the size of a country - where all transmitters use the same transmission frequency. Transmitters that are part of an SFN need to be very accurately synchronised with other transmitters in the network, which requires the transmitters to use very accurate clocks.

When a receiver receives a signal that has been transmitted from the different transmitters that are part of an SFN, the signals from the different transmitters will typically have different delays, but to OFDM they will appear to simply be different multipaths of the same signal. Reception difficulties can arise, however, when the relative delay of multipaths exceeds the OFDM guard interval duration, and there are frequent reports of reception difficulties due to this issue when there is a lift, such as when there's high pressure, due to signals travelling farther than usual, and thus the signals are likely to arrive with a relative delay that is greater than the OFDM guard interval.

Low power gap-filler transmitters can be added to an SFN as and when desired in order to improve reception quality, although the way SFNs have been implemented in the UK up to now they have tended to consist of higher power transmitters being installed at main transmitter sites in order to keep costs down.

Bit Rates

An ensemble has a maximum bit rate that can be carried, but this depends on which error protection level is used. However, all DAB multiplexes can carry a total of 864 "capacity units". The number of capacity units, or CU, that a certain bit-rate level requires depends on the amount of error correction added to the transmission, as described above. In the UK, most services transmit using 'protection level three', which provides an average ECC code rate of approximately ½, equating to a maximum bit rate per multiplex of 1184 kbit/s.

Services and Ensembles

Various different services are embedded into one ensemble (which is also typically called a multiplex). These services can include:

— Primary services, like main radio stations

— Secondary services, like additional sports commentaries

— Data services

— Electronic Programme Guide (EPG)
— Collections of HTML pages and digital images (Known as 'Broadcast Web Sites')
— Slideshows, which may be synchronised with audio broadcasts. For example, a police appeal could be broadcast with the e-fit of a suspect or CCTV footage.
— Video
— Java Platform Applications
— IP tunneling
— Other raw data

DAB+ AND DMB

The term DAB most commonly refers both to a specific DAB-standard using the MP2 audio codec, but can sometimes refer to a whole family of DAB related standards, such as DAB+, DMB and DAB-IP.

DAB+

WorldDMB, the organisation in charge of the DAB standards, announced DAB+, a major upgrade to the DAB standard in 2006, when the HE-AAC v2 audio codec (also known as eAAC+) was adopted. The new standard, which is called DAB+, has also adopted the MPEG Surround audio format and stronger error correction coding in the form of Reed-Solomon coding. DAB+ has been standardised as ETSI TS 102 563.

As DAB is not forward compatible with DAB+, older DAB receivers can not receive DAB+ broadcasts. However, DAB receivers that will be able to receive the new DAB+ standard via a firmware upgrade went on sale in July 2007. If a receiver is DAB+ compatible, there will be a sign on the product packaging.

DAB+ broadcasts have launched in several countries like Switzerland, Malta, Ireland, Italy, Australia and Germany. Malta was the first country to launch DAB+ in Europe. Several other countries are also expected to launch DAB+ broadcasts over the next few years, such as Hungary and Asian countries, such as China, Vietnam and Japan, and the U.S. If DAB+ stations launch in established DAB countries, they can transmit alongside existing DAB stations that use the older MPEG-1 Audio Layer II audio format, and most existing DAB stations are expected to continue broadcasting until the vast majority of receivers support DAB+.

DMB

Digital Multimedia Broadcasting (DMB) and DAB-IP are suitable for mobile radio and TV both because they support MPEG 4 AVC and WMV9 respectively as video codecs. However, a DMB video subchannel can easily be added to any DAB transmission, as it was designed to be carried on a DAB subchannel. DMB broadcasts in Korea carry conventional MPEG 1 Layer II DAB audio services alongside their DMB video services.

Norway, South Korea and France are countries currently broadcasting DMB.

Benefits of DAB

Current AM and FM terrestrial broadcast technology is well established, compatible, and cheap to manufacture. Benefits of DAB over analogue systems are explained below.

Improved Features for Users

DAB radios automatically tune to all the available stations, offering a list for the user to select from.

DAB can carry "radiotext" (in DAB terminology, Dynamic Label Segment, or DLS) from the station giving real-time information such as song titles, music type and news or traffic updates. Advance programme guides can also be transmitted. A similar feature also exists on FM in the form of the RDS. (However, not all FM receivers allow radio stations to be stored by name.)

DAB receivers can display time of day as encoded into transmissions, so is automatically corrected when travelling between time zones and when changing to or from Daylight Saving. This is not implemented on all receivers, and some display time only when in "Standby" mode.

Some radios offer a pause facility on live broadcasts, caching the broadcast stream on local flash memory, although this function is limited.

More Stations

DAB is not more bandwidth efficient than analogue measured in programmes per MHz of a specific transmitter (the so called link spectral efficiency). However, it is less susceptible to co-channel interference (cross talk), which makes it possible to reduce the reuse distance, i.e. use the same radio frequency channel more densely. The system spectral efficiency (the average number of radio programmes per MHz and transmitter) is a factor three more efficient than analog FM for local radio stations, as can be seen in the above numerical example. For national and regional radio networks, the efficiency is improved by more than an order of magnitude due to the use of SFNs. In that case, adjacent transmitters use the same frequency.

In certain areas — particularly rural areas — the introduction of DAB gives radio listeners a greater choice of radio stations. For instance, in South Norway, radio listeners experienced an increase in available stations from 6 to 21 when DAB was introduced in November 2006.

Reception Quality

The DAB standard integrates features to reduce the negative consequences of multipath fading and signal noise, which afflict existing analogue systems.

Also, as DAB transmits digital audio, there is no hiss with a weak signal, which can happen on FM. However, radios in the fringe of a DAB signal, can experience a "bubbling mud" sound interrupting the audio and/ or the audio cutting out altogether.

Due to sensitivity to doppler shift in combination with multipath propagation, DAB reception range (but not audio quality) is reduced when traveling speeds of more than 120 to 200 km/h, depending on carrier frequency.

Less Pirate Interference

The specialised nature and cost of DAB broadcasting equipment provide barriers to pirate radio stations broadcasting on DAB. In cities such as London with large numbers of pirate radio stations broadcasting on FM, this means that some stations can be reliably received via DAB in areas where they are regularly difficult or impossible to receive on FM due to pirate radio interference.

Variable Bandwidth

Mono talk radio, news and weather channels and other non-music programs need significantly less bandwidth than a typical music radio station, which allows DAB to carry these programmes at lower bit rates, leaving more bandwidth to be used for other programs. However, this had led to the situation where some stations are being broadcast in mono, see music radio stations broadcasting in mono for more details.

Transmission Costs

It is common belief that DAB is more expensive to transmit than FM. It is true that DAB uses higher frequencies than FM and therefore there is a need to compensate with more transmitters, higher radiated powers, or a combination, to achieve the same coverage. A DAB network is also more expensive than an FM network. However, the last couple of years has seen significant improvement in power efficiency for DAB-transmitters.

This efficiency originates from the ability a DAB network has in broadcasting more channels per network. One network can broadcast 6-10 channels or 10-16 channels (with HE AAC codec). Hence, it is thought that the replacement of FM-radios and FM-transmitters with new DAB-radios and DAB-transmitters will not cost any more as opposed to newer FM facilities. Cheaper transmission costs is backed by independent network studies from Teracom (Sweden) and SSR/SRG (Switzerland). Among other things they show that DAB is up to 6 times less expensive than FM.

Disadvantages of DAB

Reception Quality

The reception quality on DAB can be poor even for people that live well within the coverage area. The reason for this is that the old version of DAB uses weak error correction coding, so that when there are a lot of errors with the received data not enough of the errors can be corrected and a "bubbling mud" sound occurs. In some cases a complete loss of signal can happen. This situation will be improved upon in the new DAB standard (DAB+, discussed below) that uses stronger error correction coding and as additional transmitters are built.

Audio Quality

Broadcasters have been criticized for 'squeezing in' more stations per ensemble than recommended, by:

— Minimizing the bit-rate, to the lowest level of sound-quality that listeners are willing to tolerate, such as 128 kbit/s for stereo and even 64 kbit/s for mono speech radio.

— Having few digital channels broadcasting in stereo.

Signal Delay

The nature of a SFN is such that the transmitters in a network must broadcast the same signal at the same time. To achieve synchronization, the broadcaster must counter any differences in propagation time incurred by the different methods and distances involved in carrying the signal from the multiplexer to the different transmitters. This is done by applying a delay to the incoming signal at the transmitter based on a timestamp generated at the multiplexer, created taking into account the maximum likely propagation time, with a generous added margin for safety. Delays in the receiver due to digital processing (e.g. deinterleaving) add to the overall delay perceived by the listener. The signal is delayed by 2–4 seconds depending on the decoding circuitry used. This has disadvantages:

— DAB radios are out of step with live events, so the experience of listening to live commentaries on events being watched is impaired;

— Listeners using a combination of analog (AM or FM) and DAB radios (e.g. in different rooms of a house) will hear a confusing mixture when both receivers are within earshot.

Time signals, on the contrary, are not a problem in a well-defined network with a fixed delay. The DAB multiplexer adds the proper offset to the distributed time information. The time information is also independent from the (possibly varying) audio decoding delay in receivers since the time is not embedded inside the audio frames. This means that built in clocks in receivers will be spot on.

Coverage

As DAB is at a relatively early stage of deployment, DAB coverage is poor in nearly all countries in comparison to the high population coverage provided by FM.

Compatibility

In 2006 tests began using the much improved HE-AAC codec for DAB+. Virtually none of the receivers made before 2008 support the new codec, however, thus making them partially obsolete once DAB+ broadcasts begin and completely obsolete once the old MPEG-1 Layer 2 stations are switched off. New receivers are both DAB and DAB+ compatible; however, the issue is exacerbated by some manufacturers disabling the DAB+ features on otherwise compatible radios to save on licensing fees when sold in countries without current DAB+ broadcasts.

Power Requirements

As DAB requires digital signal processing techniques to convert from the received digitally encoded signal to the analogue audio content, the complexity of the electronic circuitry required to do this is high. This translates into needing more power to effect this conversion than compared to an analogue FM to audio conversion, meaning that portable receiving equipment will tend to have a shorter battery life, or require higher power (and hence more bulk). This means that they use more energy than analogue Band II VHF receivers.

As an indicator of this increased power consumption, some radio manaufacturers quote the length of time their receivers can play on a single charge. For a commonly used FM/DAB-receiver from manufacturer PURE, this is stated as: DAB 10 hours, FM 22 hours.

Use of Licensed Codecs

The use of MPEG previously and later AAC has prompted criticism of the fact that a (large) public system is financially supporting a private company. In general, an open system will permit equipment to be bought from various sources in competition with each other but by selecting a single vendor of codec, with which all equipment must be compatible, this is not possible.

DAB Systems

The DAB standard was designed in the 1980s, and receivers have been available in many countries for several years. Proponents claim the standard offers several benefits over existing analogue FM radio, such as higher-fidelity audio, more stations in the same broadcast spectrum, and increased resistance to noise, multipath, fading, and co-channel interference. However, listening tests carried out by experts have shown that the audio quality on DAB is lower than on FM due to the fact that 98% of stereo stations in the UK, Denmark, Norway and Switzerland (which are the only countries where DAB sales have taken off) are using bit rates levels that are too low.

DAB system could play in the future information highway. The present situation is characterised by the convergence of computer, telecommunication and broadcasting technologies, and the divergence of different delivery and storage media which use advanced digital signalprocessing techniques. Consumers are overwhelmed by the new electronic gadgets which appear almost daily on the market, and they are astonished by the radically new technical innovations that are being designed to change their lifelong habits. Even the broadcasting sector itself is facing profound changes, particularly a growing competition between the public and the private broadcasters.

Radio is witnessing an increasingly strong competition from non-broadcast media which use digital techniques to produce the optimum performance, at a cost that is acceptable to large consumer markets. The compact disc was the first mass-storage digital medium to offer superior sound quality in the domestic marketplace. The CD has now been joined by various other tape and disk storage formats, such as R-DAT and S-DAT, digital compact cassette, MiniDisc and CD-I. In parallel with these mass-storage developments, digital sound-broadcasting systems - which use relatively simple source- and channel-coding techniques - have been developed. These systems have been designed for specific purposes where immunity to frequency-selective fading is not required and where reception is only via a static receiver. They do not provide reliable reception in a multipath propagation environment.

NICAM 728

NICAM 728 is a digital stereophonic sound system which was developed for use with PAL terrestrial television broadcasting. Directional receiving antennas are used to eliminate, or at least reduce, any multipath problems.

DSR

The Digital Satellite Radio (DSR) system is a highquality stereo satellite system which provides sixteen sound programmes in an FSS/BSS satellite channel.

ADR

The Astra Digital Radio system has been developed recently for the satellite distribution of digital sound signals to fixed individual receivers and to feed national FM networks. It is planned that ADR services will commence later this year. The ADR system makes use of unused capacity available on the existing analogue transponders of Astra satellites. Each transponder can accommodate twelve digitally-modulated subcarriers, each of which can carry a digital stereo sound programme at a data rate of 192 kbit/s.

DVB

Recently, the European Digital Video Broadcasting Project has developed and standardised a digital television broadcasting system for satellite and cable delivery. The DVB system makes use of ISO/IEC MPEG-2 video/ audio source coding and transport packet multiplexing, in conjunction with either QPSK modulation or multilevel QAM modulation. The DVB system allows potentially large numbers of audio programmes to be carried in a BSS/FSS satellite channel, but it is only suitable for stationary reception at home.

Eureka 147 DAB System

The Eureka 147 DAB system has been developed by a European consortium which was established in 1987 and now has over 40 members; it is composed of manufacturers, broadcasters, network providers and research institutes. The Project Office of the Eureka 147 Consortium is managed by the DLR, based in Cologne, Germany.

The Eureka 147 DAB system has been designed to provide highquality, multiprogramme digital sound and data broadcasting services - not only for reception by fixed receivers but particularly for in-car and portable reception using a simple whip antenna. The Eureka DAB system can operate in any dedicated broadcasting band at both VHF and UHF. Even when working in severe multipath conditions, such as in dense urban areas, the system provides an unimpaired sound quality in the DAB receiver. The system has also been designed as a flexible, general-purpose, integrated services digital broadcasting system which supports a wide range of source- and channel-coding options, as well as programme associated and independent data services.

Unlike conventional analogue broadcasting, the DAB system enables several sound programmes to be multiplexed together and broadcast on the same radiofrequency channel. The number of programmes in an "ensemble" depends on the trade-off implemented between:

- the encoded bit rate per audio programme;
- the channel protection that is provided against errors occurring on the propagation path;

— the data capacity required for the various programme associated and independent data services that are included in the ensemble.

In the Eureka 147 system, a transmission technique called coded orthogonal frequency division multiplex is employed. In this system, the complete ensemble is transmitted via several hundred closelyspaced RF carriers which occupy a total bandwidth of around 1.5 MHz, the so-called frequency block. Each individual RF carrier transmits - at a fairly low data rate - only a tiny fraction of the total data which makes up the ensemble, thus providing a form of diversity reception.

With COFDM, multipath reception is practically eliminated. Due to the low data rate of each RF carrier, any delayed reflections of the signal add in a constructive manner to the direct signal already received. The only situation where passive echoes do not contribute in a constructive manner is when the delays are much greater than the time guard interval of the DAB signal, i.e. greater than 300 s at VHF.

Recently, the Eureka 147 Consortium has resolved the issues concerning DAB and Intellectual Property Rights. The DAB system is now considered as fully open; it can be manufactured by any interested party following the fulfilment of the licence conditions. The Consortium is willing to negotiate licences with other parties on a nondiscriminatory basis and on reasonable terms and conditions. No broadcaster will be charged for implementing DAB networks based on the Eureka 147 system.

Advantages of Eureka 147 System

CD Quality

DAB has several advantages over conventional analogue AM/FM broadcasting. The main benefit is that the high sound quality, normally indistinguishable from that of the CD, is effectively free from interference. However, DAB also has a unique ability to serve the mobile audience, thus providing highquality coverage wherever and whenever required.

Spectrum Efficiency

A further advantage of DAB is that it is spectrumefficient. This means that it will be possible to increase the number of radio stations - initially by a factor of at least three when compared with FM without congesting the radio waves. As more efficient audio coding (compression) methods are introduced, it will be possible to carry even more radio programmes with no degradation to existing services, and without needing to modify existing receivers. A radio set of the future will thus make it possible to choose, for example, a favourite type of music station from among hundreds of music stations.

"Active Echoes"

The Eureka 147 DAB system is able to use "passive echoes" such that they add in a constructive manner to the direct signals already received. The Eureka system is also able to use "active echoes" constructively -i.e. delayed signals generated by other co-channel transmitters. This leads to two important concepts:

— single frequency networks (SFNs);

— co-channel gap-fillers.

The SFN concept enables all transmitters covering a particular area with the same set of sound programmes to operate on the same nominal radiofrequency channel, i.e. within the same frequency block. All SFN transmitters need to be synchronised, in terms of both frequency and time, and the transmitted bit stream must be identical. Although the signals emitted by the various transmitters are received with different time delays, the receiver recognises this as a direct signal coming from the nearest transmitter, followed by "active echoes" coming from other transmitters in the SFN.

Gap-filling represents the second type of application which makes full use of the "active echo" concept. A gap-filler acts rather like a mirror; it receives the signals from the main transmitter and retransmits them at low power on the same frequencies to provide coverage in an area where the main transmitter is not received satisfactorily. Although the listener receives signals from both the main transmitter and the gap-filler at slightly different times, the two sets of signals add together constructively to enhance the reception of the programme.

The gap-filling concept is useful both for terrestrial and satellite broadcasting systems. As a result of these two concepts, DAB eliminates the problem of having to retune car radios at frequent intervals. At present, long-distance drivers who are listening to an FM programme are forced to retune as they move away from the area covered by one transmitter to that of another. With DAB, however, a car radio does not need to be retuned because the wanted station will be in the same frequency block everywhere within a national or regional service area.

Flexible Bit Rates

The Eureka 147 DAB system is a highly flexible and dynamically reconfigurable system. It can accommodate a range of bit rates between 8 and 384 kbit/s, with a range of channel protection mechanisms.

Some broadcasters are interested in using low audio bit rates per audio channel, say between 16 and 64 kbit/s, in order to transmit more channels at slighly reduced quality. With a bit rate of 32 kbit/s per audio channel, the Eureka multiplex of 1.5 MHz can accommodate as many as thirty-six channels, with ½ channel protection level.

DAB Transmission Modes

Technically, the Euraka 147 DAB system can be used at any frequency between 30 MHz and 3 GHz. This wide range of frequencies includes VHF Bands I, II and III, UHF Bands IV and V, and L-Band. Since the propagation conditions vary with frequency, four DAB transmission modes are used.

These modes are detected automatically by the receiver and are transparent to the user. Mode I is suitable for SFNs operating at frequencies below 300 MHz. Mode II has been designed for local and regional services at frequencies below 1.5 GHz and Mode III is available for satellite broadcasting below 3 GHz. Mode IV has recently been introduced to enable existing transmitter sites to provide optimum and seamless coverage of large areas by means of SFNs operating in L-Band. The parameters of Mode IV lie between those of Mode I and Mode II.

Data Services

Although audio has been its primary raison d'être, the Eureka 147 transmission system can also be used to carry a large variety of programme associated and independent data services. Many data services of the programme associated category will probably be transmitted from the outset and will be received by the first generation of DAB consumer-type receivers. Later on, independent data services may also appear. These would be received by dedicated data receivers, including those incorporated in desktop and laptop computers. Two examples of this application are the electronic delivery of newspapers and the transmission of compressed video images such as weather maps.

The Eureka system's immunity to multipath and other reception impairments will guarantee errorfree data reception in the mobile environment. Hence, the Eureka 147 system is an ideal complement to the wired Information Highway distribution system now being established worldwide.

Future-proofing

The Eureka 147 DAB system is future-proof. Once the receiver has been purchased, it will not become obsolete as the digital technology develops, nor as new services and applications emerge. In Europe, for example, DAB delivery will commence via terrestrial networks. Nevertheless, the receivers designed for use with these terrestrial services should, in principle, also be able to receive future DAB services delivered via satellite and cable. In other words, the Eureka 147 system will become a universal means to deliver sound programmes and data, irrespective of the transmission medium used.

System Constraints

The design of a new system is inherently a tradeoff between different technical and operational choices. Thus, when introducing DAB services, one must be aware of the technical constraints of the Eureka 147 system, which may generally be overcome by the use of suitable operational practiccs.

System Processing Delay

The DAB system chain includes several blocks which introduce a significant processing delay. For example, the time interleaver introduces a delay of 384 ms, and the audio coder/decoder introduces a delay of several tens of milliseconds. The total delay in the system may vary from one implementation to the next.

The system delay should be taken into account when the receiver switches between DAB and FM "simulcast" programmes, so that a seamless transition is obtained. It will become necessary for simulcast FM transmissions to be delayed by nominally the same amount, say one second, regardless of the receiver design. This nominal delay should be taken into account when signalling the current time information.

Frequency Accuracy in SFNs

In order not to reduce the performance of the DAB system, the difference in frequency between geographically adjacent transmitters must be kept to an absolute minimum - of the order of a few hertz in 108. Consequently, the local oscillators of all transmitters must be locked to a rubidium oscillator, or to a common reference which is distributed to all the transmitters.

Time Accuracy in SFNs

The time difference between geographicallyadjacent transmitters will have an implication on the system's capability to cope with "active echoes". Therefore, all the transmitters operating in an SFN should be time-synchronised with an accuracy of better than 25s.

Bit-by-bit compliance in SFNs

In principle, the bit-streams emitted from all transmitters operating in an SFN should be identical. If this condition is not fulfilled, there will be a "mush area" between the transmitters where the DAB receiver may be confused. Tests are being undertaken to assess the size of the mush area in the case where a local transmitter "opts out" from an SFN, thus emitting a different bit stream to the other transmitters in the SFN.

Receiver Speed Limit

As the speed of a vehicle increases, the performance of an on-board DAB receiver progressively degrades, due to the Doppler effect. The "receiver speed limit" may be considered as the vehicular speed at which the RF signal-to-noise ratio degrades by 4 dB, due to the Doppler effect. While this does not affect the audio quality, it may reduce the DAB coverage area slightly - but only in a fast-moving vehicle. In the case of an SFN operating at VHF, the receiver speed limit is about 200 km/h. When the receiver operates at 1.5 GHz and Transmission Mode IV is used, the speed limit is about 120 km/h.

Transmission Standards for DAB

While international regulations in regard to a cut off date for analogue broadcasting and its replacement by DAB the world over may be impracticable, broad technical criteria have been laid down for a concerted growth of DAB. These criteria are to:

— provide stereo multi-channels with CD quality sound;

— perform better even in cases if there is obstruction in the path of transmission;

— be capable of utilizing common receiver for satellite and terrestrial DAB reception; and

— provide easier operation and transmitter power efficiency.

Digital broadcasting uses the compression technique by which the sound signals or programmes transmitted by conventional modes are compressed so that the same line or cable is able to accommodate and transmit more programmes at the same time. A system known as Digital System 'A' (based on Eureka 147 technology) has been recommended for DAB. MUSICAM (Masking-pattern-adapted Universal Sub-band Integrated Coding And Multiplexing) system is adapted for base band compression.

A common transmission standard for DAB, as opposed to a multitude of proprietory standards, has always been preferred by EBU Members. A single standard would readily lead to the mass production of DAB receivers, bringing their prices down to an affordable level. It would open the door to free market competition, resulting in a wide variety of receiver brands offering a range of qualities and features. A unique DAB standard would mean that the same core electronic circuitry in the receiver could be used in all parts of the world, as is the case today with AM and FM radio. It would also reduce the need to perform standards conversion with its inherent degradation of the signal. A single DAB standard would introduce stability in the market and the DAB technology would last for a long time.

In pursuing the above objectives, the EBU has been instrumental in establishing a unique DAB standard at both the European and the worldwide levels.

ETSI

In late 1994, the Eureka 147 DAB system was adopted by ETSI as a European Standard. ETSI then published the standard - ETS 300 401 in February 1995. The ETSI Standard describes the technical details of the broadcast on-air signal and is applicable to terrestrial, satellite and cable delivery, in all the frequency bands that are available for broadcasting above 30 MHz. The concept of the Standard is such that it includes both mandatory and optional features of the system, and it allows for future functional refinements and additions by the application of appropriate software tools. The Standard permits different levels of implementation to meet a variety of market requirements, production costs and receiver types.

ITU

The global DAB standardisation process is being conducted within the International Telecommunication Union which, among other things, considers new developments in broadcasting technology and agrees the technical standards of broadcasting systems - for both radio and television - on a worldwide basis. Over the years, EBU Members have contributed extensively to different ITU working parties on the results of R&D work carried out in their own laboratories.

Since 1985, the ITU-R has studied proposals for new digital sound broadcasting systems - for both satellite and terrestrial delivery to vehicular, portable and fixed receivers in the frequency range 30 - 3000 MHz. This information has been included in Report 955 for satellite sound broadcasting and Report 1203 for terrestrial sound broadcasting. Both reports still provide useful background information for analogue and digital system characteristics and frequency planning considerations, but they are now being superseded by a new ITU-R Special Publication on Digital Sound Broadcasting.

Since 1987, the ITU-R has been attempting to agree on the technical and operational requirements that any digital sound broadcasting system should fulfill. In November 1991, Working Parties 10B and 10-11S adopted two new draft Recommendations on the system and service requirements. Two important requirements should be highlighted here:

— the satellite and the terrestrial systems should both provide significantly-improved performance in a multipath and shadowing environment, when compared with existing analogue systems;

— the satellite and the terrestrial systems should both be capable of utilising common signalprocessing circuits in the receivers.

Digital Systems A and B

The most important ITU-R effort for some years has been focused on agreeing a Recommendation on the sound broadcasting system itself. The Eureka 147 system - known in ITU parlance as Digital System A - was first recommended by Working Party 10B (as a terrestrial system) and by Working Party 10-11S (as a satellite system) in October 1993, but only provisionally. A formal Recommendation was not possible at that time because some delegates wished to await the successful outcome of tests being conducted by the US Electronic Industry Association (EIA) on the so-called "IBOC" and "IBAC" approaches, and on the satellite system proposed jointly by the Voice of America and the Jet Propulsion Laboratory, known as ITU-R Digital System B. These tests were originally planned to finish by the end of 1994 but the estimated completion date has now slipped back until well into 1996.

Common Worldwide Standard for Digital Radio

At the late-1994 meetings of ITU-R Working Parties 10B and 10-11S, it was decided unanimously to adopt two Draft Recommendations, BS.1114 and BO.1130. The first of these drafts recommends to ITU members to use Digital System A for terrestrial delivery in the frequency range 30 - 3000 MHz. The second one recommends that administrations wishing, in the near future, to implement BSS which meets some or all of the requirements stated in ITU-R Recommendation BO. should consider the use of Digital System A.

Both these Draft Recommendations include a Note which, in principle, opens the door to other systems as well - when they are sufficiently developed and tested, and when they have shown that they would meet the agreed and approved ITU requirements given in Recommendations 774 or 789 (for terrestrial and satellite systems, respectively). It was only possible for the ITU to adopt the above two Draft Recommendations because the EBU was able to present important evidence to the late-1994 meetings of Working Parties 10B and 10-11S.

This evidence included a final Eureka 147 system specification (corresponding to the ETSI standard), as well as comprehensive EBU evaluations on the RF performance characteristics of DAB (including the subjective audio quality versus the RF signal-to-noise ratio) and the interference protection ratios required to protect other services in the same or the adjacent bands, or to protect DAB services themselves.

In addition, many administrations were able to present the results of their own field tests and experiments. The achievement of a common worldwide Standard is rare in the history of broadcasting. In the case of the Eureka 147 system, it was only possible due to the joint efforts of, and extensive cooperation between, European and Canadian broadcasters, research institutes and the radio manufacturing industry. The Eureka system also had the support of many administrations outside Europe, particularly from the developing countries.

It should be pointed out that, so far, no other digital radio system submitted to the ITU has been able to achieve the level of success of the Eureka 147 system. However, the situation may change when, or if, other systems reach a level of maturity that is comparable to the present Eureka 147 system; the proponents of these new systems could then knock at the door of the ITU and claim worldwide recognition as well!

Common Worldwide Standard for Audio Compression

Following extensive subjective tests, ITU-R Task Group 10/2 has adopted for emission the ISO/ MPEG Layer II format at 256 kbit/s. This audio bit-rate reduction system has been developed and implemented within the Eureka 147 Project and is known as Musicam. It uses a range of bit rates between 8 and 192 kbit/s per monophonic channel to allow some flexibility in optimising the trade-off between the intrinsic audio quality and the service ruggedness. A highquality stereo channel will generally use bit rates at the higher end of the range, e.g. 2 x 96 kbit/s.

Special Publication on Digital Sound Broadcasting

The ITU-R has prepared a Special Publication on Digital Sound Broadcasting. This comprehensive book is based on the studies performed since 1991 by ITU-R Working Parties 10B and 10-11S, and covers both terrestrial and satellite digital sound broadcasting. It contains a theoretical part on the different systems, a section on frequency planning approaches and experimental evidence derived from laboratory and field tests carried out on the different systems.

This ITU-R Special Publication is particularly useful to those who are planning DSB services in the near future, but it may also be interesting for those who have a medium- to long-term interest in DSB services, particularly in the developing countries.

CENELEC

CENELEC is planning to release a receiver standard for Eureka 147 DAB, by the end of 1995. Based on a draft technical report already prepared by EACEM, the CENELEC Standard will define only those mandatory parameters which are necessary for Eureka 147 DAB receivers to interpret correctly the received signals; non-mandatory parameters will not be specified and may be open to competition in the marketplace.

A specification of the receiver data interface (RDI) of the Eureka 147 system has been drawn up and will be converted into a CENELEC European Standard in due course. Via the RDI, it will be possible to connect computers, printers and dedicated decoders for data applications, as well as devices for audio post-processing and recording.

International DAB Services

Currently, many pilot service trials and field tests at VHF and in L-Band are being conducted all over Europe. Although the situation varies very much from country to country, it is clear that the critical mass has already been achieved and that the introduction of the Eureka 147 DAB system in Europe is assured.

Belgium

In Belgium, audiovisual and broadcasting matters (including those which relate to DAB) are considered at the level of the different cultural communities (Flemish, French and German). Nevertheless, an informal coordination group has been set up at the federal level to address the issues which relate to DAB and other radio matters. This group includes all the interested parties throughout the country (broadcasters, network providers, manufacturers, cable operators, administrators, etc.). Some key players such as the Flemishlanguage public broadcaster, BRTN, and the French-language public broadcaster, RTBF, have become direct members of the EuroDab Forum. The BRTN is planning to start pre-operational DAB services at the end of 1997.

Denmark

Denmark is in the process of setting up a national DAB platform. The National Telecom Agency has already decided to allocate one or two VHF frequency blocks (225 to 230 MHz) for national SFNs, and two or three blocks (235 to 240 MHz) for regional networks. The L-Band between 1452 and 1467.5 MHz has been allocated for local services and the number of frequency blocks here has yet to be decided. In the Faeroe Islands, the frequency ranges 223 - 230 MHz and 235 - 240 MHz will be used.

In September 1994, a DAB transmitter of 500 W e.r.p. began tests at 237 MHz in Copenhagen. In September 1995, the test frequency was changed to 227.360 MHz, following the CEPT Planning Meeting. However, the transmissions on this new frequency have caused problems to the local Channel 12 cable television services and so the tests have now reverted to 237 MHz. Further experiments are planned in Western Jutland during 1996, to test an SFN network consisting of four 1 kW e.r.p. transmitters.

Danish Radio is planning to distribute some 500 receivers for a controlled evaluation of DAB, as soon as the financial details have been agreed.

Finland

The Finnish national DAB platform has been working for some months. The YLE started experimental transmissions in February 1994 on 105 MHz in Helsinki. Two transmitters of 2.5 and 0.8 kW e.r.p. are used. Problems in urban areas have been encountered with horizontal polarization, due to high levels of man-made noise. Further tests in Band III are foreseen. The Finnish manufacturing industry is developing a combined terrestrial/satellite DAB receiver, in cooperation with the European Space Agency.

France

The French DAB Club was established in autumn 1991. It comprises the French regulator (CSA), public and private broadcasters, professional and consumer manufacturers, and others. The activities of the DAB Club are diverse and include the promotion of DAB, communication with other DAB groupings, coordination of trials and experiments, etc. The French DAB Club has conducted experiments in Paris, both in VHF Band I and in L-Band, and has chosen in favour of L-Band. Radio France has established a Working Party on radio programming issues, to study which specific programmes would be particularly suitable for DAB broadcasts. Radio France has also signed an agreement with TDF to provide DAB coverage of all major metropolitan areas and motorways as soon as consumer receivers are available.

TDF is fostering close partnerships with both current and potential customers in order to define innovative multimedia applications of the DAB system. TDF has created a new "Infodiffusion" department, which is responsible for on-line and multimedia applications, and which aims to support the development of new services delivered over the air. In order to move into the consumer segment, TDF will team up with leading service providers to launch pilot services. These will be designed to assess and define the demand in key target markets such as interactive television, new radio-related services, electronic newspaper publishing and services for mobile users in conjunction with the French transport ministry and the City of Paris.

Germany

The German national DAB platform was formed in 1991 and consists of public and private broadcasters, manufacturers, R&D institutions, PTT/ Telecom operators and others. Recently, it established a Memorandum of Understanding which concerns two principal points:

— the implementation of pilot projects in several Lander and the carrying out of experiments;

— the introduction of regular DAB services in time for the Berlin IFA fair in 1997 and the achievement of near-complete coverage of Germany by the year 2000.

Among the pilot projects currently undertaken or in preparation are those in Baden-Württemberg, Bavaria, Berlin, Hessen, Lower Saxony, Mecklenburg-Western Pomeriana, North-Rhein Westphalia, Rheinland-Palatine, Saxony, Saxony-Anhalt, Thuringia and the border of Germany with Switzerland in the Lörrach and Basel area. In total, some 20 000 to 25 000 receivers, produced mainly by German receiver manufacturers, will be used to test technical and programming features of the DAB system. The funding is provided in part by the States Governments. The main organisations involved in organising these tests are: the IRT, DBP-Telekom, media authorities, regional broadcasters and some manufacturers. Both Band III and L-Band are being considered. The German platform is cooperating with neighbouring countries and has invited them to test DAB equipment and gain experience.

Hungary

The Hungarian DAB Group started in 1992 and includes all important entities in the field of DAB. In autumn 1995, a DAB experiment using one transmitter will be installed in Budapest, carrying five different programmes and data. Regular DAB services will most probably start in 1997. However, the availability of DAB receivers in sufficient volumes, and at affordable prices, is a key issue.

Italy

In Italy, several experimental activities are ongoing. RAI is completing the development of a DAB test-bed in the Aosta Valley, which currently consists of three transmitters operating as an SFN in VHF Channel 12. An extension to four transmitters is foreseen. The band 223 - 230 MHz has been identified for DAB services but has not yet been fully approved. There is some chance that L-Band could also be used.

The Netherlands

The Dutch national DAB platform has already been established. A frequency range 216 - 230 MHz has been identified, but not yet selected, to accommodate one frequency block for national services and four blocks for regional DAB services. L-Band may be used for local services.

Tests with an SFN are being carried out by NOZEMA in Haarlem, Hilversum and Rotterdam. In total, four transmitters operating in VHF Band III provide 40 % coverage of the Dutch population. In order to increase the spectrum efficiency of DAB services, extremely low coding rates (64 kbit/s and less per stereophonic programme) are of great interest. The Dutch experiments, which involve seven companies, include the datacasting of an electronic newspaper, company information, railway and travel information, etc. Recently, DAB was the subject of governmental auditing.

Norway

The Norwegian DAB Group has been in existence since 1990. The first DAB transmitter was installed by Telenor and NRK in Oslo during April 1994. There are two transmitters at present, operating as an SFN, and a third transmitter will be added soon. A fourth transmitter will be installed in Trondheim, which lies in a very mountainous region. The tests include coverage evaluations in mountainous areas and the evaluation of programme-feed techniques.

Poland

There are plans to establish a national DAB grouping in Poland. In Warsaw, an experimental DAB service may commence at the end of 1995.

Sweden

As a result of the collaborative efforts of Teracom and Swedish Radio, the first DAB experiments started in March 1992, covering the Stockholm area. An SFN experiment in Uppsala/Enköping, comprising three stations, started in March 1994 and it now has four DAB transmitters in operation. An official

DAB service was introduced in the Stockholm area on 27 September 1995. This will be followed by the opening of three SFNs in Stockholm, Gothenburg and Malmö as soon as possible.

One additional SFN may be introduced in a rural region, thus extending DAB coverage to 35 % of the population in 1996. Limited governmental support might be provided. In addition to the Swedish radio channels, which include a new classical music programme, there will be a programme in Finnish and a channel for Lapps. New data services will be tested also.

Switzerland

The Swiss national DAB platform has existed for nearly two years. For future DAB services, four frequency blocks will be allocated in VHF Channel 12 and a further nine blocks will be made available in L-Band (1452 - 1467 MHz). Swiss Télécom PTT is currently operating two SFNs, one in VHF Channel 12 and the other in L-Band. The Channel 12 tests in the Reuss Valley started in June 1993 and initially comprised two transmitters. In the same region, a trial in L-Band started in May 1994.

Tests in the Bernese Oberland area started in April this year, using three transmitters in Channel 12. This trial is planned to become a pilot project in October 1995 which will continue for a period of two years. The official introduction of DAB services in Switzerland is planned for 1997.

United Kingdom

The UK national DAB Forum has been established since 1992. Last year, the UK government allocated 12.5 MHz of radio spectrum in VHF Band III. This provides space for seven DAB frequency blocks. Each of those can carry an ensemble of six highquality stereo channels plus some data, or different combinations of audio and data services depending on the bit rates used. Of the seven frequency blocks, one has been allocated to the BBC for a national network. A second will be used for national commercial radio services, yet to be decided by the UK regulatory body. The other five blocks will be used for local and regional BBC and independent radio services.

The BBC launched its official DAB service on 27 September 1995. Initially, an SFN of five transmitters serves a large area of southeast England (about 20 % of the UK population). Within two and-a-half years, 27 transmitters will cover about 60 % of the UK population and will include the main motorway and trunk road network. The BBC is "simulcasting" (i.e.

simultaneously broadcasting) its five current national channels on DAB and will also introduce a number of new services. It plans to use the multiplex dynamically, varying the bit rate according to the programme content and the number of services available at any given time. The normal data rate is expected to be between 96 and 128 kbit/s per monophonic channel, reducing to a minimum of 64 kbit/s for some spoken material.

A new monophonic announcement channel is being considered, to be transmitted at 64 kbit/s. It will provide short spoken messages, each of around two to three minutes duration, which will be transmitted cyclically every ten minutes or so. These will be supported by the Announcements feature, within a BBC cluster, whenever new messages are introduced. Messages which are not new, but which remain relevant, will be assigned programme type (PTY) codes so that specific types of message may be requested on demand. In August 1995, the UK Government issued a White Paper entitled Digital Terrestrial Broadcasting.

Australia

To further the awareness of the Australian broadcast industry concerning digital radio matters, the Australian administration has implemented an ongoing series of demonstrations and investigations in L-Band. These are based on the Eureka 147 DAB system. During 1994, terrestrial demonstrations of DAB were held in Canberra and Sydney and, in June 1995, the first L-Band satellite trial involving the Eureka 147 system was undertaken using the Australian Optus B3 satellite. The results of these tests have been presented to the September 1995 meeting of ITU-R Working Party 10-11S.

More recently, the Australian administration announced a major initiative to fund DAB transmitter facilities in three capital cities. This will allow the local broadcast industries to investigate operational and practical implementation issues associated with digital radio. In conjunction with a similar initiative by the national telecommunications carrier, it is likely that experimental DAB facilities will be provided in Sydney and Melbourne by the end of 1996.

Canada

The first public demonstrations in Canada using the Eureka DAB 147 system were conducted in 1990. Digital Radio Research Inc. (DRRI) was then set up in 1993 to coordinate Canadian tests on digital radio systems. In 1994, Canada hosted the Second International DAB symposium in Toronto.

There are four sites where DAB experiments are currently being conducted in L-Band - Toronto/ Barrie, Trois Rivières, Montreal and Toronto -which cover more than 25 % of the Canadian population. A datacasting demonstration has been given over this network, featuring a routeguidance system developed by the Ministry of Transport of Ontario. New transmitters covering Ottawa and Vancouver were due to open by summer 1995, thus extending DAB coverage to 35 % of the Canadian population. Commercial operation will begin in 1996.

China

In cooperation with the European Commission and the German national DAB platform, the Eureka 147 DAB system will be used in terrestrial experiments in China, starting in December 1995.

India

Terrestrial DAB transmissions in India will be in VHF Band II and the satellite emissions will be in L-Band. Attempts to bring together all the major parties involved in DAB are being pursued by All India Radio and membership of the EuroDab Forum is being sought.

DAB services in India will be implemented in three phases. In the first phase, due to commence in 1998, a limited terrestrial DAB service - based on current regional radio programmes - will be initiated in four metropolitan cities: Delhi, Bombay, Calcutta and Madras. The regional programmes will be collected at New Delhi, via satellite contribution links, and subsequently distributed from New Delhi via an S-band transponder of the INSAT satellite. The received DAB signals will be converted to VHF Band II frequencies and then simulcast using the existing FM transmitting antennas and towers.

In the second phase, independent local services - carrying a mix of local, regional, national and sponsored programmes - will be added gradually to a number of FM stations by the year 2003. Finally, DAB services via satellite could commence after 2003. So far, a number of preliminary propagation studies have been carried out in L-Band. Experiments using the Eureka 147 system will start shortly, covering both terrestrial and satellite delivery.

Mexico

A highly successful terrestrial test and demonstration of the Eureka 147 DAB system was conducted at L-Band in Mexico City during 1993. Then, in July 1995, an L-Band satellite trial was conducted using the Solidaridad 2 satellite. In the latter case, only low satellite power was available (about 43.5 dBW). Although this gave insufficient propagation margin for mobile reception at speeds of greater than 60 km/h, both fixed and mobile reception were demonstrated with an antenna of gain 7 dBi.

Fixed reception with a 15-dBi antenna enabled the characteristics of the satellite channel to be defined while successfully operating it in all the transmission modes of the Eureka 147 system. At high elevation angles, Doppler effects were less of a problem than for terrestrial transmissions, and thus Mode-II operation via the satellite was shown to be more than adequate.

The USA

A number of mobile tests and demonstrations of digital radio were given in the USA in 1991. Since 1992, the Eureka 147 system has undergone formal evaluation in a public test programme, along with several "in-band" digital proposals. The recently-published results of these tests are discussed in the next Section.

Independent laboratory tests on the Eureka 147 system have been conducted in the USA by the Electronics Industry Association (EIA), in association with the National Radio System Committee (NRSC). The results of these tests were presented during August 1995 in Monterey, California.

In addition to the Eureka 147 system, the EIA tests have included five proponents of the so-called "in-band" concept, whereby the digital radio signals are transmitted in the same band as the current analogue services; the digital signals are effectively overlaid on the existing analogue signals.

Two variants of the concept have been proposed: in-band on-channel (IBOC) and in-band adjacent-channel (IBAC). The in-band proposals outlined in the EIA tests are generally of a very complex design and use advanced digital technology which is used in modern military applications for the professional market. Therefore it is likely that "in-band" receivers will be quite expensive. From the spectrum management viewpoint, the in-band digital systems currently being proposed in the USA are designed to overlay analogue signals where the channel spacing is 200 kHz. These systems are not directly applicable to Europe where the channel spacing in VHF Band II is only 100 kHz. The following in-band systems were tested in the laboratory by the EIA:

— USADR-AM (0.54 - 1.7 MHz) IBOC
— AT&T (FM band) IBAC
— AT&T Amati (FM band) IBOC
— USADR FM1 (FM band) IBOC
— USADR FM2 (FM band) IBOC

The EIA tests were divided into three categories as follows:

— subjective quality tests on the source coding system, operating in a clear channel (i.e. with no transmission errors);
— objective digital tests on the overall system performance;
— objective and subjective compatibility tests carried out to determine the interaction between the digital audio broadcasting system and the analogue transmission system within the FM band.

The quality assessment results show that the Eureka 147 system - using ISO MPEG Layer-II Musicam at 224 kbit/s - had the highest overall rank and the most consistent ratings across the whole range of audio material which was used for the tests. Eureka 147 was the only system that never fell below the "perceptible but not annoying" range. Out of nine critical audio passages that were evaluated, four were judged to be transparent. The published test results show that, in general, the in-band digital systems may cause intolerably high interference to, and suffer interference from, the analogue services that are overlaid - particularly in a multipath environment.

Therefore, those broadcasters who wish to preserve the high broadcasting standards of their existing FM services should not opt for an in-band digital solution, given the present stage of its development. The published test results on the Eureka 147 DAB system are more favourable. They confirm the conclusions of extensive laboratory and field tests conducted in Europe, Canada, Australia and elsewhere - that the Eureka system eliminates problems such as FM multipath and signal failure (dropout). It also enables digital radio to coexist with AM and FM services with no interference.

Distribution System

The Eureka 147 system can also be used for the distribution of radio and data services in cable networks and SMATV installations. It may be particularly useful in cases where the quality of the cable network is poor, due to standing-wave reflections. A standard DAB receiver could be used; apart from frequency conversion, no transcoding or remodulation would be necessary in this application. However, when the primary objective is spectrum efficiency, the service provider will probably wish to use the DVB cable system which is based on 64-QAM. In an 8-MHz cable channel, DAB can accommodate 24 stereophonic channels with a data rate of 256 kbit/s, each using the lowest protection level (i.e. ¾). A 64-QAM system, on the other hand, would allow for some 150 channels of the same audio quality.

Broadcasters Expectations

The BBC has produced a document which contains its expectations of first-generation consumer DAB receivers. The document is intended to assist receiver manufacturers in the production of attractive consumer sets which will respond adequately to the BBC's DAB signals and which will satisfy the UK public following the launch of the first BBC DAB services in September 1995. The document is broadly in line with an earlier EBU document which published the more general requirements of first-generation DAB receivers. The first consumer receivers are expected to be for use in vehicles and in home hi-fi units. Portable, personal and other types of receiver are expected to appear on the market somewhat later. If DAB is to achieve rapid acceptance and success, the development of all receiver types must be promoted in the early years of DAB service.

The BBC plans to include Service Information (SI) from the start, as well as the Multiplex Configuration Information (MCI).

DAB as a Multimedia Carrier

Within the Eureka 147 Project, further developments are underway to study the use of the Eureka 147 System as a multimedia and data broadcasting system. The use of the Eureka 147 DAB system beyond the provision of excellent sound reception in adverse mobile and portable environments. In addition to the conventional audio services, the system is opening up many new opportunities to carry a number of non-audio services, such as text, still pictures, moving images, etc.

The multiplex of the Eureka 147 system has been designed to carry a large number of digital services with a total bit rate of up to 1.7 Mbit/s, organised in up to 64 stream- or packet-mode subchannels. Four different data transport mechanisms have been defined in the DAB standard:

— Programme Associated Data (PAD)

— Fast Information Channel (FIC)

— Stream Mode (SM)

— Packet Mode (PM)

The choice of transport mechanism depends on the kind of data that it is necessary to transport. For example, the Programme Associated Data is suitable for services which bear a strong relationship to the audio signal. Since this data is taken from the audio frame, there is a trade-off between the intrinsic audio quality and the PAD data capacity.

The FIC Channel was originally intended to carry information on the organisation of the DAB multiplex. Nevertheless, the FIC can carry a limited amount of additional information, such as paging and emergency warning messages. Dedicated (or special-purpose) receivers which only decode the FIC part of the multiplex may be significantly less complex than general-purpose DAB receivers. In Stream Mode, a subchannel is assigned to a single data service, providing a fixed data rate (in multiples of 8 kbit/s) with specific error correction.

In Packet Mode, a number of services may share the same subchannel. Packet headers contain a service address which allows the receiver to restore the original data. The PM is a convenient way to carry asynchronous services (which use variable data rates). Examples of DAB data services currently being implemented are given below. These services may be presented either in the form of textual information, still pictures or even video images.

— Programme associated services such as current song title, interpreter and performer, lyrics, news headlines, CD covers, etc.;

— News including events, traffic messages, weather, sport, stock market, travel and tourist information;

— Traffic navigation by means of transmitted digitised roadmaps, combined with positional information provided via the GPS system.

— Advertisements and sales including sales catalogues, purchase offers, etc.;

— Entertainment including games and noncommercial bulletin boards;

— Closed user group services such as banking information, electronic newspapers, fax printouts and remote teaching.

The DAB Standard offers two modes for text transmission: Dynamic Label and Interractive Text Transmission (ITTS). The former mode is similar to the Radio Text feature of the Radio Data System (RDS) on the FM band. ITTS is a more sophisticated text transmission system. It allows for menu-driven operation and can also be used to transmit text at the rate a broadcaster prescribes. It can process several streams of textual information simultaneously to convey, for example, the same information in several languages or to transmit a programme schedule at the same time as giving details of the programme currently on-air.

Ideally, multimedia services should be fully interactive, in which case the consumer can communicate with the service provider's database. Since broadcasting services are one-way only, the return channel could be provided by GSM telephone or via a telephone line. Nevertheless, a semi-interactive mode is also possible. In this instance, information is downloaded by the service provider to the user's data terminal and stored there as a database. All interactivity is then handled within the user's data terminal, but the database contents have to be updated regularly by the data service provider. The storage capacity of the user's terminal is a trade-off between the service transmission rate, the repetition rate and the cost of the memory.

A key factor for the success of DAB will be its ability to address each receiver individually. This will allow service providers to customise the "bouquet" of services provided to each user, and even to identify the user in an interactive transaction. This feature has some far-reaching implications, particularly for privately-funded radio.

Studies are continuing on the suitable presentation of DAB data services. Currently, data services specified in the ETSI Standard have a text-based presentation. In order to improve the manmachine interface, the Eureka 147 System will be enhanced to support a graphical user interface, such as Microsoft Windows. This will be of importance for screen-based services which seem to be more relevant for stationary and portable receivers. For mobile receivers, synthesized speech-based interfaces are a better alternative, as they would be less distracting to drivers. For the user's data terminal, a unified transmission protocol will be very helpful, as no distinction between different transport mechanisms would be necessary. A software-based language for objectoriented page description is being developed to define a communication and a presentation layer. Such a unified protocol for the multimedia transport mechanism could be used not only with DAB services, but also in other communications systems.

Currently, within the Eureka 147 Project, a standard receiver data interface is being specified to transfer the data carried within an ensemble, from the receiver to any external devices such as a PC, tape recorder or conditional access decoder. A demonstration of both the audio and the multimedia usage of the Eureka 147 system was given during August 1995, at the IFA fair in Berlin.

DAB Programming

The technology of DAB is a means of delivering audio programmes and data; it is not an objective in itself. Hence, the debate must eventually (if not soon) move away from the technical advantages of DAB to the programming issues which will actually drive this technology into the homes and cars of radio listeners.

People will buy receivers only if they can access interesting, entertaining and attractive programmes. Crisp digital sound is of course a good thing, but it is certainly not sufficient to persuade people to pay for it. Therefore, the content and the presentation of the audio, video, text and data information which is to be transmitted is of great importance. So far, insufficient new programming ideas have been put forward but it is hoped that the Eurodab Forum will help to generate some ideas on this matter.

In order to receive DAB services, consumers will need to buy a new kind of receiver. The consumer DAB receivers will also contain FM and AM circuits which, initially, will be analogue. However, it will not be long before the AM and FM circuits in a DAB receiver become digital. These alldigital AM/FM/DAB receivers will be based on advanced computer technology, which will allow the downloading of large quantities of information to programme the radio set and its associated equipment.

At the recent IFA fair in Berlin, six manufacturers displayed their current DAB receivers. In fact, they look more like semiprofessional equipment; the DAB part is in a separate box, mounted in the boot with a link to an FM/RDS receiver in the dashboard. These first-generation car receivers are not generally available yet; they can only be purchased on special order and in limited quantities for evaluation purposes.

The industry has been carrying out a lot of research and development on further applications of the DAB system, including:

— data-only receivers;
— picture radios and advanced teletext full bitstream video decoders;
— navigation systems;
— differential GPS;
— traffic information systems;
— Traffic Message Control (TMC);
— real time packet-mode multiplexers / demultiplexers;
— fax;
— videotext;
— audio in conjunction with radiotext (dynamic labels);
— electronic newspaper publishing, including text and pictures in packet mode;
— high-capacity storage using MiniDisc.

Internet Radio

Internet is the network of networks. A network is an interconnection of two or more computers to share data. Internet is a global network, which allows us to send and receive messages, and also to speak, on-line, and in real time to computers connected on the Internet Basically, the information whether data, voice or picture, is converted to digital data and sent on land lines/ satellites on the network. Any computer user with an Internet connection can download this information into the user's own computer. The Internet services are provided in our country by VSNL (Videsh Sanchar Nigam Limited) and a few other providers. Audio signals can also be converted into digital form and transmitted over the Internet. A user with a computer system can listen to this audio. Thus, the data transmission networks can be used for sending radio signals on the Internet. The Internet which is basically used for sending email file transfer or information exchange is being configured for telephony as well as transmission of radio and television signals.

Any broadcaster would like to broadcast his/her programmes world-wide for 24 hours a day. Listeners would also like to have access to high quality programmes from all over the world at the time of their choice. You have studied the principles of radio transmission and you know that any transmission has a limited range and the quality in many cases depends on the distance to the transmitter. Internet broadcasting will help get over some of these problems. The advantages of Internet broadcasting are:

1. *World-wide coverage.* The signals can be made available all over the world, wherever an Internet access is available. Generally, the quality is consistent throughout the world, but dependent on the quality of access technology, e.g. telephone based, dedicated leased, line, cable based technology.
2. *Programme availability.* In conventional broadcasting, once a programme is missed, it is missed for ever as far as the listener is concerned unless the programme is repeated. In Internet broadcasting, the programme is available on the Internet and a listener can access it anytime, anywhere.
3. *Large number of channels.* The listeners can access a large number of radio channels available on the Internet, unlike in the conventional broadcasting where number of channels available is limited.
4. *Less costly.* For a broadcaster, the expenditure to put radio programme on Internet is very low as compared to a conventional broadcast transmitter equipment. It takes less time to set up a transmission system and any Internet user can have access to the radio programme. The cost of transmission can be 10 times less than a FM transmitter.

Internet was established basically for transmitting text. It makes use of Hyper Text Mark-up Language (HTML) and it links one document to another and from one site to another. Information concerning any particular item can be downloaded into one's computer from any site.

The Internet provides, besides texts, graphics and scanned images at the web sites. But, the access time required for such file could be 10 to 15 times more than that required for data files. But Internet is not designed to deliver isochronoms, i.e., continuous time based information such as audio. Audio files have, therefore, to be downloaded, stored in computer's memory and then played back. Audio quality could be as good as that of a CD.

Rapid developments in the Internet technology have made it possible to have audio in real time over the ordinary telephone lines. Real time delivery means that the users do not have to wait for the whole file to be downloaded, the sound can be played back as it is delivered. Compression techniques are used to abridge the quantity of data to be transmitted. A number of proprietary systems have been developed. Some of these are real audio, true speech, winplay 3, etc. All of them utilise compression techniques to produce sound files, small enough to be transmitted in real time.

Several broadcasting organisations have set up their web sites on the Internet. All India Radio launched its on-line information service in text mode from May 2, 1996. It has also started its audio service.

One can listen to an audio broadcast on the Internet. For this, one has to use the web browser, a software package that displays web pages containing text graphics, audio and video files and a software player. After accessing the World Wide Web, (a system for accessing information on the internet) one can go through the various radio services available and select the desired one.

Internet uses a method known as the Hyper Text Transfer Protocol (HTTP) for transport of information through the web. To fulfill a request from a client, the web server triggers a request to the server called the Real Audio Server, which then sends the requested material to the listener.

Internet Radio Technology

Internet radio involves streaming media, presenting listeners with a continuous stream of audio that cannot be paused or replayed, much like traditional broadcast media; in this respect, it is distinct from on-demand file serving. Internet radio is also distinct from podcasting, which involves downloading rather than streaming. Many Internet radio services are associated with a corresponding traditional (terrestrial) radio station or radio network. Internet-only radio stations are independent of such associations.

Internet radio services are usually accessible from anywhere in the world—for example, one could listen to an Australian station from Europe or America. Some major networks like CBS Radio and Citadel Broadcasting (except for news/talk and sports stations) in the US, and Chrysalis in the UK restrict listening to in-country because of music licensing and advertising concerns. Internet radio remains popular among expatriates and listeners with interests that are often not adequately served by local radio stations (such as eurodance, progressive rock, ambient music, folk music, classical music, and stand-up comedy). Internet radio services offer news, sports, talk, and various genres of music—every format that is available on traditional radio stations.

Streaming

Streaming technology is used to distribute Internet radio, typically using a lossy audio codec. Streaming audio formats include "MP3, Ogg Vorbis, Windows Media Audio, RealAudio, and HE-AAC (or aacPlus)". Audio data is continuously transmitted serially ("streamed") over the local network or internet in TCP or UDP packets, then reassembled at the receiver and played a second or two later. The delay is called lag, and is introduced at several stages of digital audio broadcasting.

Simulation

A local tuner simulation program includes all the online radios that can also be heard in the air in the city.

Development

The first live internet only broadcast of a live band was Seattle based space rock group Sky Cries Mary on November 10th, 1994, by Paul Allen's digital media start-up Starwave, also based in Seattle.

A week later, during November 1994, Rolling Stones concert was the "first major cyberspace multicast concert." Mick Jagger opened the concert by saying, "I wanna say a special welcome to everyone that's, uh, climbed into the Internet tonight and, uh, has got into the M-bone. And I hope it doesn't all collapse."

On November 7, 1994, WXYC (89.3 FM Chapel Hill, NC USA) became the first traditional radio station to announce broadcasting on the Internet. WXYC used an FM radio connected to a system at SunSite, later known as Ibiblio, running Cornell's CU-SeeMe software. WXYC had begun test broadcasts and bandwidth testing as early as August 1994. WREK (91.1 FM, Atlanta, GA USA) started streaming on the same day using their own custom software called CyberRadio1. However, unlike WXYC, this was WREK's beta launch and the stream was not advertised until a later date.

In 1995, Progressive Networks released RealAudio as a free download. Time magazine said that RealAudio took "advantage of the latest advances in digital compression" and delivered "AM radio-quality sound in so-called real time." Eventually, companies such as Nullsoft and Microsoft released streaming audio players as free downloads. As the software audio players became available, "many Web-based radio stations began springing up."

In 1996, Edward Lyman created Sonicwave.com, the first American internet radio station, legally licensed by both ASCAP and BMI, to broadcast live, 24 hours a day on the internet.

In March 1996, Virgin Radio - London, became the first European radio station to broadcast its full program live on the internet. It broadcast its FM signal, live from the source, simultaneously on the Internet 24 hours a day.

Internet radio attracted significant media and investor attention in the late 1990s. In 1998, the initial public stock offering for Broadcast.com set a record at the time for the largest jump in price in stock offerings in the United States. The offering price was US$18 and the company's shares opened at US$68 on the first day of trading. The company was losing money at the time and indicated in a prospectus filed with the Securities Exchange Commission that they expected the losses to continue indefinitely. Yahoo! purchased Broadcast.com on July 20, 1999 for US$5.7 billion.

In 1998, The Raven started and ran Albuquerque's first Internet radio station Route 66 LIVE.

With the advent of streaming RealAudio over HTTP, streaming became more accessible to a number of radio shows. One such show, TechEdge Radio in 1997 was broadcast in 3 formats - live on the radio, live from a RealAudio server and streamed from the web over HTTP.

In 1998, the longest running internet radio show, "The Vinyl Lounge", commenced netcasting from Sydney, Australia, from Australia's first Internet Radio Station, NetFM (www.netfm.net). In 1999, Australian Telco "Telstra" launched The Basement Internet Radio Station but it was later shut down in 2003 as it was not a viable business for the Telco.

From 2000 onwards, most Internet Radio Stations increased their stream quality as bandwidth became more economical. Today, most stations stream between 64 kbit/s and 128 kbit/s providing near CD quality audio.

In October 1998, the US Congress passed the Digital Millennium Copyright Act (DMCA). One result of the DMCA is that performance royalties are to be paid for satellite radio and Internet radio broadcasts in addition to publishing royalties. In contrast, traditional radio broadcasters pay only publishing royalties and no performance royalties.

A rancorous dispute ensued over how performance royalties should be assessed for Internet broadcasters. Some observers said that royalty rates that were being proposed were overly burdensome and intended to disadvantage independent Internet-only stations—that "while Internet giants like AOL may be able to afford the new rates, many smaller Internet radio stations will have to shut down." The Digital Media Association (DiMA) said that even large companies, like Yahoo! Music, might fail due to the proposed rates. Some observers said that some U.S.-based Internet broadcasts might be moved to foreign jurisdictions where US royalties do not apply.

Many of these critics organized SaveNetRadio.org, "a coalition of listeners, artists, labels and webcasters" that opposed the proposed royalty rates. To focus attention on the consequences of the impending rate hike, many US Internet broadcasters participated in a "Day of Silence" on June 26, 2007. On that day, they shut off their audio streams or streamed ambient sound, sometimes interspersed with brief public service announcements voiced, written and produced by popular voiceover artist Dave Solomon. Official SaveNetRadio PSAs & Day Of Silence Network Audio.

Some broadcasters did not participate, such as Last.fm, that had just been purchased for US $280 million by CBS Music Group. According to a Last.fm employee, they were unable to participate because participation "may compromise ongoing license negotiations."

SoundExchange, representing supporters of the increase in royalty rates, pointed out the fact that the rates were flat from 1998 through 2005 (see above), without even being increased to reflect cost-of-living increases. They also declared that if internet radio is to build businesses from the product of recordings, the performers and owners of those recordings should receive fair compensation.

On May 1, 2007, SoundExchange came to an agreement with certain large webcasters regarding the minimum fees that were modified by the determination of the Copyright Royalty Board. While the CRB decision imposed a $500 per station or channel minimum fee for all webcasters, certain webcasters represented through DiMA negotiated a $50,000 "cap" on those fees with SoundExchange. However, DiMA and SoundExchange continue to negotiate over the per song, per listener fees.

SoundExchange has also offered alternative rates and terms to certain eligible small webcasters, that allows them to calculate their royalties as a percentage of their revenue or expenses, instead of at a per performance rate. To be eligible, a webcaster had to have revenues of less than US $1.25 million a year and stream less than 5 million "listener hours" a month (or an average of 6830 concurrent listeners). These restrictions would disqualify independent webcasters like AccuRadio, Digitally Imported, Club977 and others from participating in the offer, and therefore many small commercial webcasters continue to negotiate a settlement with SoundExchange.

An August 16, 2008 Washington Post article reported that although Pandora was "one of the nation's most popular Web radio services, with about 1 million listeners daily...the burgeoning company may be on the verge of collapse" due to the structuring of performance royalty payment for webcasters. "Traditional radio, by contrast, pays no such fee. Satellite radio pays a fee but at a less onerous rate, at least by some measures." The article indicated that "other Web radio outfits" may be "doom[ed]" for the same reasons.

On September 30, 2008, the United States Congress passed "a bill that would put into effect any changes to the royalty rate to which [record labels and web casters] agree while lawmakers are out of session." Although royalty rates are expected to decrease, many webcasters nevertheless predict difficulties generating sufficient revenue to cover their royalty payments.

In January 2009, the US Copyright Royalty Board announced that "it will apply royalties to streaming net services based on revenue." Since then, websites like Pandora Radio, Mog, 8tracks and even recently Google Music have changed the way people discover and listen to music.

In 2003, revenue from online streaming music radio was US$49 million. By 2006, that figure rose to US$500 million. A February 21, 2007 "survey of 3,000 Americans released by consultancy Bridge Ratings & Research" found that "[a]s much as 19% of U.S. consumers 12 and older listen to Web-based radio stations." In other words, there were "some 57 million weekly listeners of Internet radio programs. More people listen to online radio than to satellite radio, high-definition radio, podcasts, or cell-phone-based radio combined." An April 2008 Arbitron survey showed that, in the US, more than one in seven persons aged 25–54 years old listen to online radio each week. In 2008, 13 percent of the American population listened to the radio online, compared to 11 percent in 2007. Internet radio functionality is also built into many dedicated Internet radio devices, which give an FM like receiver user experience.

References

Hendy, David, *Radio in the Global Age*, Cambridge: Polity Press, 2000.

Hoeg, Wolfgang; Lauterbach, Thomas. *Digital audio broadcasting: principles and applications of DAB, DAB+ and DMB*. Wiley, 2009.

Michael Roberts. "Digital Dilemma: Will new royalty fees kill Web radio?". *Westword*. Retrieved 2010-03-14.

Priestman, Chris, *Web Radio: Radio Production for Internet Streaming*, Melbourne: Focal Press, 2002.

Reid, Alasdair, "Radio's Digital Challenge," *Campaign*, 14 November, 2003.

5

Community Radio

Community radio is a radio service offering a third model of radio broadcasting in addition to commercial and public broadcasting. Community stations serve geographic communities and communities of interest. They broadcast content that is popular and relevant to a local, specific audience but is often overlooked by commercial or mass-media broadcasters. Community radio stations are operated, owned, and influenced by the communities they serve. They are generally nonprofit and provide a mechanism for enabling individuals, groups, and communities to tell their own stories, to share experiences and, in a media-rich world, to become creators and contributors of media.

In many parts of the world, community radio acts as a vehicle for the community and voluntary sector, civil society, agencies, NGOs and citizens to work in partnership to further community development aims, in addition to broadcasting. There is legally defined community radio (as a distinct broadcasting sector) in many countries, such as France, Argentina, South Africa, Australia and Ireland. Much of the legislation has included phrases such as "social benefit", "social objectives" and "social gain" as part of the definition. Community radio has developed differently in different countries, and the term has somewhat different meanings in the United Kingdom, Ireland, the United States, Canada, and Australia.

Modern community radio stations serve their listeners by offering a variety of content that is not necessarily provided by the larger commercial radio stations. Community radio outlets may carry news and information programming geared toward the local area (particularly immigrant or minority groups who are poorly served by major media outlets). Specialized musical shows are also often a feature of many community radio stations. Community and pirate stations (in areas where they are tolerated) can be valuable assets for a region. Community radio stations typically avoid content found on commercial outlets such as Top 40 music, sports and "drive-time" personalities. A meme used by members of the movement is that community radio should be 10 percent radio and 90 percent community. This means that community radio stations should focus on getting the community talking and not solely on radio (which is a technological process); the social concerns of community radio are stressed over radio per se. There is also a distinction drawn in contrast to mainstream stations, which are viewed as pandering to commercial concerns or the personalities of presenters.

Communities are complex entities, and what constitutes the "community" in community radio is subject to debate which varies by country. "Community" may be replaced by terms such as "alternative", "radical" or "citizen" radio. In sociology, a "community" has been defined as a group of interacting people living in a common location. Community radio is built around the concepts of access and participation, and the term "community" encompasses geographical communities based around the reach of the radio's signal (the people who can receive the message) and their potential to participate in the creation of the message. This is complicated by the fact that many radio stations broadcast over the internet as well, thereby reaching a (potentially) global audience.

Two philosophical approaches to community radio exist, although the models are not mutually exclusive. One emphasizes service and community-mindedness, focusing on what the station can do for the community. The other stresses involvement and participation by the listener.

In the service model locality is valued; community radio, as a third tier, can provide content focused on a more local or particular community than a larger operation. Sometimes, though, providing syndicated content not already available within the station's service area is viewed as public service. Within the United States, for example, many stations syndicate content from groups such as Pacifica Radio (such as Democracy Now!) on the basis that it provides content not otherwise available (because of a program's lack of appeal to advertisers—in Pacifica's case, due to its politically controversial nature).

In the access (or participatory) model, the participation of community members in producing content is viewed as a good in itself. While this model does not necessarily exclude a service approach, there is some disagreement between the two.

History of Community Radio

The concept of community radio developed in the West as an alternative to or a critique of the mainstream broadcast media. Tracing its origins in Europe in the 1960s and 1970s, McCain and Lowe found "swashbuckling entrepreneurs boarded the airwaves illegally and seised as much of the audiences as they could carry away from the treasure chest monopolies controlled by the State with its public service model of broadcasting." Thus, pirate stations have been a major factor in motivating governments and national broadcasting systems to introduce legitimate local radio in Europe.

In Latin American countries, community radio came into being as a critique of, and alternative to, predominantly commercial oriented radio broadcasting networks. There, the thrust was to use radio as a medium to support education of the marginalised populations.

In Africa, establishment of community radio systems, in a broader sense, became a social movement after the demise of apartheid regime in South Africa, which was followed by democratisation, decentralisation, and structural adjustment elsewhere in the continent.

Systematic efforts to establish community radio in Asia were driven by initiatives taken by international agencies such as UNESCO, which was at the centre of the communication and development debate. These initiatives were mostly associated with externally funded development projects which were influenced by the discussions of participatory communication for sustainable development and new understanding of communication as a two-way process rather than just communicating 'to' the listener. Both participation and the two-way communication process are considered as mutually inclusive. The community was treated as the social space within which participation and two-way communication process would occur. This reinforced the need for planning communication strategies to catalyse development efforts in the immediate communities.

Communities are not monolithic units. They consist of people with different positions, individual/community priorities and varied approaches to their diverse questions and their solutions. There are also different levels of connectors and catalysts within communities. The community radio provides a platform for all segments of population to discuss common issues from different viewpoints in a positive atmosphere. What is sought out is a common good. All members of the community have to discipline themselves when participating in the programmes of community radio. They are expected to follow certain norms prescribed by the code of conduct of the radio station. In effect, community radio trains the community members in a very practical way for democratic behaviour. The community radio mode provides opportunities to project and discuss the community's common issues, helps promote a sense of belonging among community members and strengthens the community bond among individual members.

That is precisely why community radio, with the prime objective of promoting democratic discussions within the community and providing opportunities for divergent viewpoints is needed. The code of conduct established by many community radio stations emphasises that "programming should maintain a balance that properly reflects the differing interests of the various majority and minority sectors in the community."

Community radio can facilitate contextualising national development programmes within the immediate community and taking national development goals as close as possible to the intended beneficiaries. Through community radio, members are able to feed-forward on local development concerns, giving an opportunity for development agencies and authorities to get involved in a constructive dialogue on development priorities at local levels.

Similarly, the community radio provides opportunities to the community to make reiterative evaluation of programme implementation and eventually to make development inputs more relevant and efficient. This transparent process makes the community rely more on an integrated national system in which the degree of power sharing between the centre and the periphery is understood by each other. The ability of the communities to be involved in shaping programme implementation at the grassroots levels is well assured. A regular community dialogue and feedback facilitates continuous improvement in programme delivery and makes the radio centre more responsive. Therefore, the community members at large feel that their concerns are cared for and listened to.

At the same time, community radio helps facilitate self-reliance by mobilising resources readily available with the community. They can analyse their problems and propose their own solutions. This confidence makes them consider themselves as a part of the system they belong to. The very recognition that they have the possibility to influence national policy implementation at grassroots levels makes them feel a part of an inclusive nationhood.

Community radio is just one important element of the media channels. There are national and global level media reaching the communities though they do not provide access for and participation of the community. Nonetheless, the community media provide an opportunity to interpret the overall national media content with a local flavour.

In addition, community radio can present programmes based on what is disseminated by national media. This would enable those who cannot afford to purchase newspapers or access other national media channels, making the entire community aware of the national issues and programmes. Such a media environment not only makes them respond to the various national concerns, but also bonds them with the larger nationhood as they see the relevance of national issues and programmes within their immediate communities.

Community radio operations have distinct characteristics which differ from commercial and national Public Service Broadcasters (PSB) in regard to its mission and service. Community radio does not compete with commercial and PSB, rather plays a complementary role. But primarily, community radio is operated by and for the community and owned by the community itself. It is an empowering tool for the community. A nation consisting of empowered communities is more secure as they can make an equitable contribution to nation building.

Community radio ideally should have a broad-based ownership, which is accessible to any member of the community. If established with well-developed guidelines, there is no possibility for one particular group of the community to dominate community radio operations and programmes. In any case, such domination cannot sustain wider audiences in a community where most people know each other, and are easily able to discern group intentions, allegiances and partisan attitudes.

Models of Community Radio

Philosophically we can see two distinct approaches to community radio, though the models are not necessarily mutually exclusive. One stresses service or community model - focused on what the station can do for the community. The other stresses involvement and participation.

Within the service model localism is often prized, as community radio, as a third tier, can provide content focused on a more local or particular community than larger operations. Sometimes, though, the provision of syndicated content that is not already available within the station's service area, is seen as a desirable form of service. Within the United States, for example, many stations syndicate content from groups such as Radio, such as Democracy Now, on the basis that it provides a form of content not otherwise available.

Within the access or participatory model, the participation of community members in producing content is seen as a good in itself. While this model does not necessarily exclude a service approach, there is a tension between the two, as outlined, for example, in Jon Bekken's Community Radio at the Crossroads.

Characteristics of Community Radio

A community radio station is one that is operated in the community, for the community, about the community and by the community. The community can be territorial or geographical - a township, village, district or island. It can also be a group of people with common interests, who are not necessarily living in one defined territory. Consequently, community radio can be managed or controlled by one group, by combined groups, or of people such as women, children, farmers, fisher folk, ethnic groups, or senior citizens.

What distinguishes community radio from other media is the high level of people's participation, both in management and program production aspects. Furthermore, individual community members and local institutions are the principal sources of support for its operation.

Following are the characteristics of community radio:

— It serves a recognizable community.

— It encourages participatory democracy.

— It offers the opportunity to any member of the community to initiate communication and participate in program making, management and ownership of the station.

— It uses technology appropriate to the economic capability of the people, not that which leads to dependence on external sources.

— It is motivated by community well being, not commercial considerations.

— It promotes and improves problem solving.

Principles of Community Radio Operation

a) Access to the facility is the primary step towards the full democratization of the communication system. People have access not only to the media products but also to the media facilities. The feedback channel is always open and full interaction between the producers and receivers of messages is maintained.

b) Participation in the production and management of media is the logical step after access. Citizen's participation in radio is allowed at all levels - from planning to implementation and evaluation of the project. It involves the citizens in the decision-making process, including making decisions about the contents, duration and program schedule. The citizens, or their representatives, also have a voice in the management and financing of radio program projects.

c) Self-management of the communication facility follows participation. Once the community members gain necessary experience and assimilate the required skills there is no reason for preventing them from managing and owning the radio station.

d) Community mandate is the inevitable result of the process of democratizing the communication system. Community mandate encompasses not only management but also ownership of the radio.

e) Accountability is exercised. There is no sense in having the opportunity to operate, control and manage the station when accountability is not in the hands of the managers and broadcasters.

Community radio gives community members access to information because it gives them access to the means of communication. The most relevant information - educational and developmental - is disseminated and exchanged. Important local issues are aired. A free market place of ideas and opinions is opened up and people are given the opportunity to express themselves socially, politically and culturally. Community radio helps to put the community members in charge of their own affairs.

Distinct Features of Community Radio

Facilities

A community radio often uses the basic production and transmission equipment appropriate for the size, needs and capability of the community. Usual transmission equipment is comprised of a low-power FM transmitter of 20 to 100 watts. The production facility can range from a simple tape recorder or a karaoke playback machine to a simple studio that consists of an audio-mixer, tape decks, CD player and microphones.

In some facilities a simple loudspeaker or the community audio tower system (CATS) is used, either independently or coupled with a transmitter. Technically speaking, the community audio tower system is not radio. However, even with its apparent advantages and disadvantages the CATS serves a purpose similar to that of community radio. Regardless, the community prepares regular programs.

Sources of Support

Much, if not all, of the resources needed for operating the community radio come from individuals, institutions and organizations within the community. Private individuals are motivated to contribute to the station. Various fund raising schemes such as raffles draws, benefit dances, selling of FM receiver set are held. Institutional advertisements or sponsorships or outright donations are accepted. Host institutions such as schools, foundations, cooperatives, local government units and religious organizations may provide backstop support. Resource generation and appropriate fund raising schemes are planned and implemented by the station management.

Management

The management of a community radio station is entrusted to the Community Radio Council (CRC). The CRC is a multi-sectoral body, which obtains its mandate from the community to run the station. CRC is trained for the purpose for managing the station. It usually has seven to 25 members who are representatives from the most important sectors for the community such as farmers, fishermen, women, youth, laborers, ethnic communities, educators, and religious denominations. The members are initially selected from among wellrespected community leaders on the basis of their moral integrity, probity and community involvement. Eventually the council has a right to co-opt new members or replace those who retire. The functions of the council include, among other things, deliberating on the direction and polices of the station, and making major decisions for the situation.

Program Makers

A core of selected community members who have the time, ability and enthusiasm are chosen to prepare regular programs. Like the members of the management council, the program makers are from various sectors of the community. The program makers undergo training on preparing programs of various formats such as radio talk, interview, magazine, music, news, drama, documentary, or plugs.

The initial training normally lasts from two weeks to one month and is conducted by professionals and people from the academe. The production of community-oriented participatory programs is emphasized during the training.

The program makers are volunteers from the community. Although most of them do not receive honoraria, they undertake the day-to-day operation of the station. They serve as producers, announcers, hosts, scriptwriters, news gatherers, technicians and administrative personnel. Under the leadership of the designated senior manager, they prepare programs, operate the equipment, and handle the administrative responsibilities of the station.

Programs

Community radio's program format is similar to that of a mainstream radio including news, drama, talk shows, interviews and magazine. However, in community radio programs, there is a heavy emphasis on local contents. For instance a program will feature the availability of seedlings from local farmers and the price of vegetables in the market along with public service items. News content focuses on events coming from the municipality, villages and local organizations. Discussions centers on issues of local concern such as ordinances, bridges that have to be completed, or the setting up of a factory in the village. Broad participation by community members is encouraged. There is a dominance of local language, color and personality in the manner in which programs are presented.

Not only the regular production group produces programs. Cultural and neighborhood programs are prepared with a wider involvement from villagers who may not have formal training in production.

Broadcast Hours

The broadcasters and the management council determine the broadcast hours for a community radio on the basis of the following:

— capability and number of trained personnel;
— availability of electricity or power;
— technical feasibility;
— needs of the community/audience;
— availability of resources necessary for operation;
— competition with other radio stations.

With such considerations, community radio normally comes up with shorter broadcasting hours than commercial or government or public radio.

Stimulating Community Participation

Community residents can be motivated to participate in program making by inviting them to neighborhood and village level production workshops. Peasants, rural women and unschooled people can be trained in the rudiments of broadcasting.

By bringing production to the rural areas, radio is demystified for the people of the community. Many forms of cultural programs and village activities may be adopted and accommodated in radio programming. After all, radio is simply people talking with people.

Activities in Setting-up a Community Radio

Organizing. A core of responsible leaders, initiators and workers who are convinced of the benefits of community radio has to be organized. Research / Evaluation. Baseline research will determine the socioeconomic situation of the community at the start of the community radio project. During early operations a periodic assessment of progress and monitoring has to be done. Evaluative studies are also called for in the later stages of operation.

Training. Three groups of people need to acquire basic skills - the core of managers, program makers and technicians.

Documentation. With a new communication set up it will be in the interests of prospective evaluators, simulators, and adopters to record, on print, film, paper or video the progress of the community radio. Installation of equipment. There will be a need to purchase equipment, construct a studio and put-up a tower. Qualified electronic engineers and/or technicians are to perform these tasks.

Legitimizing Community Radio

Requirements for legalizing the operation of radio stations vary from country to country. Initiators must check with the communicationregulating agency of their respective state. The agency should provide a checklist of requirements for setting up low power radio. In the Philippines, there are two main instruments to be secured from government, which are (1) a congressional [parliament] franchise; and (2) a license from the National Telecommunication Commission (NTC). Low power stations [20 watts and below] that are set up for education and training are not required to get a franchise, only a license that will serve as a permit to buy, install and operate radio. In this case the license is renewed every year but ideally the community radio should have the license valid at least for three to four years without the fear of having to close after a short license period.

Sustainability of Community Radio

Contrary to popular assumption regarding the operation of a commercial station, community radio is not an expensive operation to maintain for the following reasons:

- The operating cost is very low, mostly related to electrical consumption, spare parts, maintenance and office supplies.
- Volunteers, who receive, if any, minimal honorarium, staff the station.
- Management is trained in how to raise money from local, national and international sources for example through donations other fundraising activities.
- Since a community radio serves the interests of the community, people easily assume responsibilities in the operation of the station.

Community Radio Movement

Community radio is fast becoming a sound system of communication all over the world. In most regions and continents, Europe, North America, South America, Africa and Australia there are hundreds, or thousands, of community radios. In Asia there are barely two dozen known community radios that are located in the Philippines, Nepal, Sri Lanka and East Timor. There are so few community radios in Asia because of the domination of governments in the use of radio. There is, however, a growing acceptance of the concept of community radio in many countries of the region.

Equipment

The simplest community radio set up can consist of a low-power transmitter harnessed with an antenna, a tape recorder and a microphone. A motorcycle battery provides the power source. Its total weight may be much less than 10 kilograms. When affordable and necessary, a more technical set up should consist of the transmission equipment, antenna, tower and a decent production studio. This will allow more possibilities for production and mixing of voice, music and sound effect. Listed below is a cost estimate of a basic equipment for community radio.

In addition to the above there may be a need to purchase small items, e.g. extension cords, electrical outlets, etc. A two-way communication system would be ideal for more dynamic newsgathering and reporting. Instead of the above-mentioned analog equipment it is possible to configure the entire production set-up using computers and USB supported recording equipment.

Transmitter

The transmitter is the core piece of equipment in a community radio. The transmitter makes it possible for programs to be sent to distant places. A low-power transmitter can be designed between 5 and 300 watts serving distances of up to an approximate 30 kilometers radius. The customary transmitter available, and often suitable for a town level community, is a 20-watt FM [frequency modulation] transmitter. It can be used as the sole transmission equipment and can also serve as an exciter. Another piece of technology called a linear amplifier, or a power booster, may be attached to the 20-watt transmitter. The power booster could be available, or fabricated, with multiples of 50, 100, 200, 250, 300, and 500 or even 1,000-watts. Electronics engineers claim that the booster is easier to build, hence cheaper, than a transmitter.

FM transmission is often preferred to AM (amplitude modulation) for its features. It is

— Less costly to acquire.

— More available in the market.

— Has better signal quality.

— Requires a less complicated antenna system.

— Consumes less electricity; and

— Has more available frequencies in the band.

The main disadvantage of the FM transmitter is that the signal travels in more or less line-of-sight fashion. FM is most suited to flat terrain where there are no mountain obstructions and tall buildings, or where an elevated site could be identified for putting up the antenna. Alternatively, an AM transmitter could be used with one distinct advantage. It works better where the terrain is hilly and mountainous. However, it needs a more sophisticated and costly antenna system and uses more electricity.

It must be pointed out that in most countries transmitters may be bought and possessed only upon securing a license from the telecommunicationregulating agency of the government. Depending on suppliers, the price of a 20-watt transmitter can be anywhere from US $400 to $2000. Unfortunately in most developing countries there are no local transmitter manufacturers. Most low-power transmitters are imported from Europe, China, Canada, Australia or the United States.

Signal Reach

The distance that the signal of a FM transmitter can reach is dependent on the following factors:

— Power of the transmitter

— Efficiency of the transmitter

— Height of the antenna

— Terrain of the community

— Atmospheric conditions.

A higher wattage transmitter will give a correspondingly wider coverage. However, the reach is not an exact numerical coefficient of the power. If the 20-watt transmitter hoisted on a 23-meter antenna could be heard with a Class A signal up to 10 kilometers on a flat terrain, the 100 watt transmitter could be expected to provide that same quality signal up to about 15 - 20 kilometers.

Understandably, the capacity of the receiver and its antenna could be factored in approximating strength and quality of reception. Where reception is rather weak, listeners could be advised to attach a metal wire to the antenna that extends to a pole above the roof possibly clear of structures and trees. A more sophisticated receiving antenna for FM radio may also be fabricated for better results. As much as 40% signal reception could be achieved with extended receiver antennas. 3. Mono or Stereo?

Most of the FM transmitter models available these days are stereo. If only for the advantage of more extended reach, a competent technician could disable the stereo function of a transmitter. By deleting the stereo chip, a signal could be strengthened by 20 to 35 percent. It is contended that rural people who crave for information do not mind if they get a mono signal. Stereo sound is more preferred in music broadcasting.

Transmission Antenna

Various antenna makes and designs could be fabricated, the most common of which is the folded single dipole. To increase signal propagation a two-bay or a four-bay antenna could be harnessed.

Antenna Tower

The height of the FM transmission antenna is an important factor that determines maximum signal reach. FM waves travel in nearly line-ofsight fashion. "If you can see it, you can hear it," says an experienced technician. Hills, ridges and building barriers can be overcome by raising the antenna up to approximately 20 to 30 meters. The higher the antenna the better and farther the signal can reach.

An antenna mast can be made of two-inch galvanized iron water pipe joined at the ends, erected and held firmly by guy wires. Triangular steps are also fitted on the side of the pipes to serve climbers. The base of the tower can be reinforced concrete, one square meter into the ground. The tower can also be erected above a strong roof where the mast needs to be fastened even more securely.

The water pipes, which are usually 20-foot sections in length, are arranged in descending diameters. The diameter of the lowest section can be three inches, followed by two inches and 1.5 inches. Bigger pipes are required for a more solid tower, appropriate for typhoon belt areas. Heavier pipes are more costly and will require some effort in erecting. Guy wires should be strong enough not only to hold the sway and weight of the antenna but also to withstand climbers. The guy wires must be secured strongly to the ground with iron pipes impaled about one and a half meters to the ground perpendicular to the direction of the guy wires. Guy wires are stretched in four isosceles directions. In some cases more sophisticated and expensive tower designs are used.

A lightning arrester is always recommended to avert any expensive tower damage on the transmitter during stormy weather situations. The major causes of breakdown for transmitters are unmatched antenna, faulty connections and lightning strikes, which ruin the expensive power module integrated circuit, called BGY 33, of the main transmitter output. The antenna mast should be grounded properly. If the mast is installed on top of a roof a half inch stranded copper wire can be welded to the mast and connected down to an iron bar that is driven into the earth. The iron bar should reach the wet part of the soil in order for the surge of high voltage electricity to be absorbed by the ground. The thick cable that runs from the transmitter to the antenna is usually a co-axial cable. An RG-ll or RG 58 cable is the most commonly used. Its cost is about US$2 per metre. Higher power transmitters of over 400 watts call for a heliax cable that offers the least power loss, but is more expensive than the co-axial cable. Heliax cable could cost about US$24 per metre.

The cable between the transmitter and the antenna must not be longer than 20 metres. With transmission lines longer than 60 feet, much of the transmitter power could be dissipated within the cable.

Location

The program production studio may be set-up in any existing house or room where there is enough space for the equipment and the operators to work. An optimum area for the announcer's booth is 30 square meters, technician's cubicle is 20 square meters, but smaller rooms are possible. In urgent need, the station could be provisionally operated in a cart, on a tricycle or even atop a walking horse.

In a more traditional set-up, a separate building that will house the station may be constructed. The station should preferably have an announcer's booth and a technician's cubicle as well as a receiving and working area.

The following criteria are recommended when choosing a studio site:

i. Closeness to center of population

ii. Accessibility to the participants

iii. Accessibility to the community members

iv. Low or no rental fee

v. Neutrality from vested interests

vi. Security from pilferers and vandals

vii. Availability of power source

viii. Freedom from uncontrollable noise [particularly when the studio is not enclosed tightly for air conditioning and noise proofing]

ix. Favorable technical conditions:

   a. There is an elevated location of transmitter.

   b. It is unobstructed by tall buildings.

   c. It is away from high voltage power lines.

The studio should be centrally located in the community where there is a tall building to hoist the antenna. A higher elevation for the studio location would be an advantage. Where it is necessary to hoist the antenna higher, the studio may be located up to several hundred meters away from the antenna. As mentioned earlier, the co-axial cable linking the transmitter to the antenna should not exceed 20 meters. A preferred set up would be for a program line [a pair of insulated wires connecting the studio to the transmitter] to be extended to the location of the transmitter and studio. Telephone drops wires, or even electric wires can be used as program line. The wire may be propped up on existing electric posts, or bamboo poles, throughout the length of the line. The length of the program line should preferably not be longer than one kilometer.

Building an Inexpensive Studio

The most important part of a studio is the announcer's booth, which houses the production equipment such as tape recorders, turntables, tape decks, audio mixer, amplifier, microphones, or speakers. This is where the announcer conducts his/her live broadcast. In some cases, the technician may control the equipment and the announcer has only the microphone to control. However, most announcers prefer to operate the turntables and tape recorders.

The announcer's booth should optimally have a minimum space of three metres by four metres and should be properly enclosed. The main features of a professional announcer's booth are that it is sound proof and it meets simple acoustical requirements.

It would also be a good idea to have a staff working area that can also serve as a receiving room.

Studio Acoustics

The acoustical balance of the studio room can be achieved by fitting some sections of the wall and ceiling with soft materials such as egg trays, styropor, drapes, coconut coir, curtains, cardboard or mats. The objective is to avoid too much bouncing of sound from the wall to the microphone. Sound reverberation makes for a "cathedral effect". Alternatively, too much of the soft materials can create an open field effect.

To limit noise from infiltrating the production room all passages should be sealed airtight with rubber lining if possible. Double walling is recommended, particularly if the partition is made of thin boards such as ¼ inch plywood. The usual passage of extraneous sound is through the gap between the panel and the doorframes, as well as the gap between the door panel and the floor. Some rubber fittings can be made to seal off these sound passages.

A small, silent-type air-conditioning unit may be installed inside the big studio. To avoid the hum from being picked up by the microphone the unit should preferably be installed in the technician's room or the working area. The cold air is then blown to the announcer's booth through an airduct with a silent exhaust fan.

If the studio is directly below galvanized iron roofing, there must be an intact ceiling to avoid too much heat during sunny days and to prevent the sound of raindrops being picked up by the microphone. Holes on a wooden floor should also be plugged.

The usual announcer's booth has a glass panel [possibly double] between it and the working area. This glass panel is necessary to facilitate communication between the announcer and the staff in the adjacent room. Hand signals, prompters, "idiot boards" and other means of non-oral communication are commonly passed between the announcer and the technician. The size of the glass panel can be one meter by 1.3 meters or larger. Again, this glass paneling must be tightly fitted to the frame to prevent external sound from being picked up by the sensitive microphone in the announcer's booth. It would be advisable for the assigned master carpenter or architect to visit local radio stations and to observe their respective acoustical treatment methods.

Production Equipment Layout

The pieces of equipment inside the studio are anchored on the audio console mixer, that processes, balances, amplifies and mixes any of the inputs and sends it to the transmitter, as well as to the monitoring speakers. The broadcast equipment such as turntables, tape player/recorders, cassette tape players, compact disc players and microphones should be laid out neatly where the announcer can easily reach the knobs, switches and faders.

Wiring and Installation of Equipment

Wires that connect the studio equipment to the audio console mixer should not be too long or short, and hence must be cut at proper lengths. Extraneous long wires are not only expensive but can also cause difficulties in a cramped studio space. Extra long wires can also cause humming sounds. Laid out wires must be laced or properly bundled together. Program lines that connect studio to transmitter, should not run close to electric power lines.

Dummy Load

It is a resistive element used as a substitute for the antenna element. The dummy load is useful in a situation where a proper antenna could not be connected, such as in a transmitter testing session. By connecting the transmitter output to a dummy load, any problems with antenna, transmission linc and output can be isolated and identified.

The transmitter should preferably be housed in one building with the studio. The technician and the announcer should occasionally check the transmitter to find out whether it is working. Its audio level and power meter indicate this. Should there be a need to locate the antenna in quite a distance from the studio, it is necessary that the transmitter be placed close to the antenna. This split operation would require a longer program line from the studio to the transmitter.

The telephone drop line/cable can be used to facilitate the conduct of studio sounds to the transmitter. It is durable, resistant to weather elements, and a good sound conductor. It is so designed for transmission of sound. If the telephone drop line is not available electrical wires may be used instead. However, these may have to be replaced more often as electrical wires easily develop cracks on the rubber insulators when exposed to heat and rain. Electrical wires with double insulation would be preferred for reason of durability. These electrical lines used as program lines should not exceed

500 meters. With longer distances noise or impedance of sound may manifest.

Microphone lines or standard studio audio lines are ideal sound conductors. However, they are more expensive and need to be laid out in a conduit to protect them from damage. They are not designed for outdoor installation.

Off-Studio Broadcast

In the absence of an outside broadcast van, program lines could be extended from the studio down to a coverage area such as the church, market place, gymnasium or the town plaza.

The program line will serve as link between the outside coverage points down to the studio. The telephone drop line is recommended for this purpose. Other electrical conductors such as flat cord or ordinary lamp cord could be used as cable. It should be noted that many of these types of cords are not designed for changing weather conditions, therefore expect to replace them when they show signs of brittleness such as cracking and when inner conductor is exposed. It is suggested that the program line must not exceed 1,000 meters.

While a microphone may be simply attached to the line at the coverage area, a remote microphone mixer is necessary, especially when several microphones and inputs are required. The remote mixer [sometimes called an auxiliary microphone mixer] can be bought for approximately US$150. The one that is powered by a battery instead of the alternating current is preferred so that it can still be used in case of blownout. Also look for mixers that are provided by individual output and input control knobs. Auxiliary mixers can be used to put on air recorded voice clips, interviews, music, sound tracks, and other material outside the live proceedings. During remote broadcasting, cables must be taped to the floor surface firmly to avoid accidental tripping and pulling that can cause disruption of on-air program or recording. Avoid running loose lines in passageways. Only the volume control knobs of switches to the microphones and inputs being used should be open. Turn off all others to minimize catching extraneous noise.

Remote broadcasts are usually exposed to various forms of audio interference such as mechanical, electrical or crowd noise. It is always wise to carry grounding materials. Copper wires may be used to ground the mixer to a water pipe or to any metal buried in the ground.

Community Radio Council

The community radio shall:

- serve as an avenue for the free flow of beneficial information aimed at uplifting the plight of the various sectors of the community. The station shall open up possibilities for everyone, especially regular citizens, to express themselves socially, culturally, politically and spiritually, thus preparing each and every member of the community to participate in decision-making;
- strive to help create a self-reliant interactive community and seek its own development, fully harnessing locally available resources;
- be the catalyst for social, political, moral and cultural development and promote harmony among all community members and sectors.

Objectives

a) It will be the general objectives of the community radio to:
   - give voice to the people who normally have no access to the mass media nor opportunity to express their views on community development;
   - seize every chance to use the radio station in a constructive way ensuring fullest respect for, and adherence to, basic democratic processes and journalistic ethics.

b) Through its regular operations the community radio shall seek to:
   - provide a development forum for the community;
   - encourage participatory community development;
   - promote active involvement of underprivileged groups such as women and young people;
   - intensify the sharing of information within the community;
   - encourage innovation in community development;
   - increase the free flow of accurate and balanced information to, and within, the community;
   - provide a forum for local cultural expression; and
   - improve people's access to information in local languages.

c) Furthermore, the station was established with the understanding that:
   - it shall in no way give advantage or disadvantage to a political party or candidate, political platform or purely partisan interest;

— its newscasts and information programs shall be edited for strictly factual and objective presentation; and that
— in the case of error or shortcoming the community radio shall rectify the said error, and issue corrective statements immediately.

Composition of the Community Radio Council (CRC)

The community radio council (CRC) is a group of leaders representing a cross-section of the community. Its task is to make decisions and formulate policies with respect to the operation of the community radio. The CRC composition is based on representation by the principal sectors in the community such as the following:

— business groups
— church sectors
— civic organizations, notably NGOs
— education sector
— ethnic groups, if any
— farmers
— fishermen
— labor groups, including professionals and employees
— local /national government
— senior citizens
— transportation groups
— volunteer staff member of the community radio
— women
— youth

A minimum number of political factions represented in the CRC should be three or four, if any need to be represented.

The council members should preferably be selected, or nominated, by the sectors concerned.

The members must have demonstrated a genuine concern in uplifting the plight of the sector and the community at large. Should a sector be so divided that no outstanding person appears to be a deserving representative, the other members of the community media council may determine the criteria and considerations necessary to decide who should be eligible to sit on the CRC. Selective representation by influential groups such as politicians or businessmen should be strictly ruled out. The station manager and volunteer staff are eligible to be members of the CRC. Should it happen that no member of the staff is a member of the CRC by virtue of their representation of a sector enumerated above, the staff may elect a representative to the CRC.

Observers

It is possible that a sector such as farmers, fishermen, youth and the ethnic communities would nominate more than one representative for the purpose of taking a more active part in the deliberations of the council. During the time of voting, however, it may be decided that each sector should have only one vote. Voting privileges should have been decided beforehand.

Annual Review

The CRC shall review its composition at every annual meeting, to ensure that it adequately reflects the principal sectors of the community, including newly emergent sectors.

Selection Criteria

A wide representation of key leaders in the community should make the decision as to which sectors should be represented in the CRC. The community representatives should be in a good position to determine who is best suited to represent the various sectors shown above. Certain criteria should be laid down in order to avoid confusion.

To be a member of the CRC, a person must:

- have proven integrity;
- be able to participate effectively and soundly in a democratic deliberation of community matters;
- have demonstrated a high level of interest in the wellbeing of the community;
- espouse the cause of his/her sector but be willing to subjugate sectoral interest in favor of the greater community;
- possess leadership qualities; and
- be willing to participate in workshops/seminars on the operation of the community radio and related issues.

Functions

The CRC, representing the whole community, shall collectively make decisions and formulate policies with respect to the community radio. The CRC shall decide and resolve the major issues regarding the community radio and serve as its steering committee. Among the specific acts that shall reserved to the CRC as a collegial body, are the following.

1. Initiate, develop and approve the radio station's code of conduct.
2. Approve the job descriptions of the station manager, deputy station manager, the cashier and any other volunteer staff member as may be deemed necessary.
3. Appoint the station manager, deputy station manager, and cashier.
4. Appoint an external auditor.
5. Exercise the authority to review the decisions of the station manager to ensure that they are consistent with the goals and objectives of the station.
6. Decide on possible honoraria, salaries/ fees and allowances for the members of staff or management of the community radio.
7. Decide on what kind of fund-raising schemes, announcements, sponsorships and other income generating revenue should be allowed.
8. Confirm and review the fees for announcements, sponsorship arrangements, public awareness spots by individuals, local businesses, development agencies, government/non-government organizations, etc.
9. Decide on following matters:
   - broadcast hours
   - types of programs to be aired
   - weather to air political programs or not and approve the related guidelines, based on objectives of the station
   - type of religious program to be aired
   - programs to be accommodated
   - programs to be cancelled
   - program airtime.
10. Deliberate and make a decision regarding any other major issue that is presented by community members, the staff, and the station management.

The CRC should ensure that the program schedule is in line with the mission statement and objectives of the station, taking into account the needs of audiences and ensuring that the community radio is responsive to the needs.

The CRC should further

1. Decide how often it will meet, and how and when the meeting invitations should be delivered. Meetings can be weekly, fortnightly, monthly, bi-monthly or quarterly. All decisions should be recorded in minutes for reference of the staff/community and for documentary purposes;
2. Siscuss its own term of office, systems of decorum, honoraria [if any], and other matters relating to the CRC that it may truly represent the community in its decision-making functions.

The CRC should adopt measures to avoid making its deliberations an arena for political bickering.

Right to Sign

In situations where the CRC is taken as a mere deliberative body, not an organization, it is recommended that the operation of the radio station be placed in the hands of a duly registered co-operative, foundation or association. Without an existing organization or agency that is officially responsible for the operation of the station the CRC shall act as an organization by itself. For practical and legal purposes it may consider acquiring a juridical personality.

Until the CRC has been duly registered it should nominate the chairperson and the station manager to make transactions, enter into contracts, engage in business and receive grants on behalf of the community radio. It should also decide on the mechanism of receiving local announcements and payments for them, as well as the related financial reports.

Terms and Conditions

The term of office of the individual members of the CRC is one year. However the term may be renewed/extended based on recommendation of the sector and the acceptance of the CRC.

The CRC shall have the option to replace those members with unsatisfactory performance, including the chairperson or vicechairperson.

The CRC should request for an alternative representative from the sector concerned.

A member shall be replaced if he/she is absent from more than half of the meetings organized in six months. Should the sector fail to send another acceptable representative, it forfeits its chance to participate in deliberations.

The CRC as a body may terminate, suspend or refuse to accept an individual member for any misconduct that it deems to be prejudicial to the deliberations of the council. Habitual tardiness, absenteeism, nonobservance of proper decorum, coming to the meeting under the influence of liquor and drugs, along with other recognized forms of misbehavior, shall be grounds for sanction by the council.

Official invitation letters indicating the period of time for which office is to be held should be sent to each member of the CRC.

Election of officials

The chairperson of the CRC shall be subject to yearly election, renewable for three years. Any member in good standing can be nominated and elected to the chair. While observers and resource persons can be invited to the meetings of the CRC, voting rights shall be limited to the membership of the council.

The council can decide whether election shall be by secret ballot or by viva voce.

The CRC shall also elect a vice-chairperson, cashier and secretary, subject to election every year.

Relations with Volunteer Staff

The station manager, and/or in his/her absence the deputy station manager, should attend the CRC meetings. The chairperson, station manager and/ or deputy station manager should hold regular [weekly or bi-weekly] meetings with the volunteer staff to discuss editorial policy on important community matters, new program schedules and formats and inform them of decisions of the CRC. Feedback should be collected from reporters to ensure their views, experience and contact with the community are adequately reflected in the policy decisions.

The preceding suggestions may be adopted, improved, modified or altered by the community leaders. They can also be taken as either the terms of reference or the constitution of the CRC. Each member of the CRC must sign the constitution to make it a binding document.

Community Radio around the World

Australia

In Australia, community radio is structured similarly to the United States, where stations operate as non-profit organisations, generally funded through sponsorship and listener subscriptions. One of the most successful Australian community radio stations is Melbourne's 3RRR. Like commercial radio stations, community stations need to apply to Australian Communications and Media Authority (ACMA) for a license to broadcast.

Contributing factors to the creation of community radio in Australia include the frustration felt by Vietnam War protestors at the mainstream media, classical music aficionados counteracting government inaction on the introduction of FM broadcasting and universities who wanted to explore the educational potential of radio.

Existing to support and represent community stations nationally is the Community Broadcasting Association of Australia (CBAA), which provides advice, assistance and also a satellite network so that stations can share content. A comprehensive list of Australian community broadcasters, and other information is available from CBOnline which also hosts a history of the Australian sector, "Diversity On The Airwaves".

Canada

Community radio stations in Canada are also similar in format to American community stations. Most commonly, Canadian community radio stations target commercially underserved minority language communities such as Franco-Ontarians, Acadians or the First Nations, although some small communities also have English language community stations. Community radio stations are most commonly operated by cooperatives.

In larger cities, community-oriented programming more commonly airs on campus radio stations. Some cities do, however, have community radio stations as well. Most community stations in Canada are members of the National Campus and Community Radio Association, or NCRA.

The province with the largest number of community radio stations in Canada is Saskatchewan. The majority of those stations are affiliated with Missinipi Broadcasting Corporation, an aboriginal public radio network.

India

In India, the campaign to legitimise community radio has been going on since almost the past decade. The Supreme Court of India ruled in judgement of 1995 that "airwaves are public property" came as an inspiration to groups across the country, but so far only educational (campus) radio stations have been allowed, under somewhat stringent conditions. First Indian Campus Community Radio. Anna FM is India's first campus community radio which is run by Education and MultiMedia Research Centre (EM²RC) and all programmes are produced by the students of Media Sciences Anna University.

A very strong movement to promote community radio in India began in 1996 when a group of communicators and academicians held a conference and pronounced the Bangalore Declaration Community Radio. The Deccan Development Society (DDS), an NGO was supported with funds and technical expertise to establish a community radio station in Pastapur, 100 kms south of Hyderabad in Andhra Pradesh under UNESCO's special project, entitled "Women Speaking to Women Community Radio." The DDS involved around 70 women's organisations, most of which have been set up by the dalit women for the managing and production of the programmes for this radio station. Currently, the studio facilities are being used to produce and distribute audio-cassettes on the issues related to women's empowerment. However, actual broadcasting at the station, in spite of its long-time readiness to go on air, has not begun because the Central Government has not approved the DDS's request for a community broadcasting licence.

The government does not want community radio to become, "a platform to air provocative, political content that does not serve any purpose except to divide people". There is provision for the communities to buy time from AIR service and run their programmes. In this scheme of things, the ownership of the radio stations vests with a public corporation.

Within this legal framework, there have been successful instances of community broadcasting in the country. Namma Dhwani is a partnership between the Boodikote community in Kolar district, MYRADA, an NGO committed to integrated development and VOICES, a development communications NGO, based in Bangalore with technical support from AIR, Bangalore. The programmes produced by this radio centre are broadcast from AIR.

A similar model exists in Jharkhand in which a partnership between three NGOs, the National Foundation of India (NFI), New Delhi, Alternative for India Development (AID) Lesliegunj Section, and Manthan Media Collective, Ranchi has led to setting up a community radio station in Palamau district. The focus is on empowerment of communities with special emphasis on women. The local AIR FM station at Daltongunj (the district headquarters) is used as a channel.

Another experiment is the Kunjal Pachaee Kutch project, which is a partnership between Kutch Mahila Vikas Sanghathan (KMVS) Bhuj, and the Dhrishti Media Collective, Ahmedabad. The place of operation of the project is Kutch district of Gujarat. AIR station at Bhuj is used for broadcast of the programmes. The target group is women in Kutch villages and the focal area is empowerment of women for Panchayat functions.

Ireland

Ireland has had self-described community radio stations since the late 1970s, though it was not until 1995 that the first 11 licensed stations came on air as part of a pilot project run by the Independent Radio and Television Commission. Early stations were represented by the National Association of Community-Radio Broadcasters, which in 1988 published a guide to setting up new stations. More recently licensed stations have formed CRAOL as a representative group.

United Kingdom

"Community radio" has recently been taken up by the radio industry regulator Ofcom as the name for the new 'third tier' of the UK radio industry. The idea for this new level of radio broadcasting was piloted by the Radio Authority (now Ofcom) in 2002 with the licensing of 15 "Access radio" stations. The one-year licenses were extended in 2003 for a further year, and in 2004 a consultation was issued by Ofcom on the creation of community radio. The first full licences for Community Radio stations in the UK were issued in 2005. Community radio stations are usually limited to broadcast areas smaller than commercial or BBC local stations, usually within 5 kilometres (km) of their transmitter. They focus on a specific community or on a range of listeners inside their small broadcast area. Their job is to benefit communities rather than make a profit.

In order to get a community radio licence, applicants must demonstrate that the proposed station will meet the needs of a specified target community, together with required "social gain" objectives set out in the application. A target community can be defined either by geography or by reference to a particular sub-community in an area, otherwise known as a "community of interest". A geographic community can be any defined local area, particularly those which would not sustain a fully commercial broadcaster. A community of interest can be any identifiable local community; existing Community stations are aimed at groups as diverse as the elderly, religious groups such as Christian and Muslim, lifestyle groups such as gay and transgender and cultural/recreational groups such as artists.

Community stations are not permitted to raise more than 50% of operating costs through on-air advertising and/or sponsorship; the remainder of operating income must be met through other sources. This can include public funding via grants, donor income, lottery funding or charities. Alternative methods of broadcasting include short-period licences, known as Restricted Service Licences, allowing community groups and special events to run local area low power stations for up to 28 days, and webcasting.

The Access Radio Pilot: The Access Radio Pilot, initiated by the UK Radio Authority, was designed to test the demand for community radio and to see whether such small-scale radio broadcasting projects were feasible. Some of the projects targeted a particular community of interest, ranging from religious and minority groups to children and older people, others such as Manchester's ALL FM and WythenshaweFM targeted geographical communities.

Access Stations included:

— Resonance FM - in London, run by the London Musicians Collective.
— Sound Radio - serving a range of groups in Hackney in London.
— BCB 96.7 - serving Bradford's diverse communities, with a mix of ethnic programming, specialist music and sport.
— Desi Radio - in London, serving the Punjabi community.
— ALL FM 96.9 - serving the communities of Ardwick, Longsight & Levenshulme in Manchester.
—]WythenshaweFM - serving the large housing estate of that name in Manchester.
— Cross Rhythms City Radio - Stoke-on-Trent

The Ofcom Community Radio Consultation: The Ofcom community radio consultation was issued on 17 February 2004. The consultation gave a brief outline of the Access radio projects, and made some proposals as to how the new sector would be managed. Included in the consultation were a series of questions which interested parties were invited to suggest comments on. These included whether community radio stations should have a cap of 50% of their income coming from advertising, and the order and method by which licenses should be applied for.

The closing date for contributions was 20 April 2004, and since this date all of the contributions have been published on the Ofcom website. Following the success of the pilot scheme, applications for full licences were invited in 2004 and the first full licences awarded in 2005.

United States

American community radio stations are often staffed by volunteers and air a wide variety of programming. They are generally smaller than public radio outlets. Community radio stations are distinct from public radio in that most of their programming is locally produced by non-professional DJs and producers, where public radio tends to rely on more syndicated programming. Community stations often try to reduce their dependence on financial contributions from corporations in comparison with other public broadcasters. Some examples of community stations are WAIF in Cincinnati, Ohio, KGNU in Boulder, Colorado, KSPC in Claremont, California, KDVS in Davis, California, KBOO in Portland, Oregon, WDBX in Carbondale, Illinois, WLUW and WZRD in Chicago, Illinois, WERU in Blue Hill, Maine, WMNF in Tampa, Florida, WORT in Madison, Wisconsin and Coast Community Radio (KMUN-Astoria and KTCB-Tillamook) in Oregon. These stations are licensed by the Federal Communications Commission. Many community stations are licensed as full-power FM stations, while others - especially newer community stations - are licensed under low-power broadcasting rules. The National Federation of Community Broadcasters formed in 1970 as an umbrella organization for community-oriented, non-commercial radio stations. The NFCB publishes handbooks for stations and lobbies on behalf of community radio at the federal level. The Grassroots Radio Coalition is a very loose coalition of stations that formed as a reaction against increasing commercialization of public radio and lack of support for volunteer-based stations. Some stations are part of both groups.

Community Radio Initiatives

The advent of low-cost low-power FM transmission and downsizing of production equipment and the experiences in different parts of the world provided impetus for community radio. Some initiatives were taken to make community radio as a potential participatory and two-way communication tool to support development in rural societies of developing countries. UNESCO supported community radio projects in Homa-bay in Kenya, and Mahaweli in Sri Lanka, in the early 1980s are among some of the earlier efforts in this direction. But, given the fact that the countries were not yet ready to relinquish their broadcasting monopolies, these early initiatives had to be carried out within the Government-owned broadcasting systems. The history of Asian community radio began within the parameters of government broadcasting systems.

Mahaweli Community Radio, Sri Lanka

The first Asian community radio was established at Girandurukotte in Sri Lanka in 1986 under the Mahaweli Community Radio project. In fact, the project was started in 1980 as a community programme service, serving the Mahaweli settlements under which nearly 60,000 families were resettled downstream the Mahaweli river. The purpose of this community radio project was to cater to the needs of the newly-settled families. It aimed to help them exchange their settlement experiences, learn new skills from each other, give timely information on day-to-day activities and help in catalysing development in the new communities. It was a new experience where both young and mature members of the settlers' families functioned as volunteer broadcasters. They identified various settlement issues, animated the community through their own programmes, much of which also related to cultural expressions which they brought from their place of origins.

Lively interaction between settlers and field officers responsible for various settlement administration matters were broadcast over the community radio. These broadcasts enabled policy makers and senior officials responsible for settlements to learn about problems and prospects of the settlements. It also helped to establish an all inclusive decisions-making process to solve many important issues such as water distribution, marketing avenues, health, education, etc.

However, around this time there was no possibility of thinking of independent radio stations anywhere in Asia. The radio broadcasting systems were largely government monopolies except in the Philippines where traditionally broadcasting was not a major government function. But martial law, imposed at that time by President Marco, did not permit independent community radio to flourish. The Mahaweli community radio project of Sri Lanka in fact was administratively under the national broadcaster, Sri Lanka Broadcasting Corporation.

The unique feature of the Girandurukotte community radio system was the airing of the volunteers' produced programmes. There were the three expert producers assigned to the station by the Sri Lanka Broadcasting Corporation. They were all fresh recruits, specifically trained for community broadcasting and were therefore not highly influenced with the ideas of the so-called professional broadcasting or commercial programming of the urban centres. They acted as technical consultants and trainers of the volunteer broadcasters.

In Sri Lanka's Mahaweli radio project, there are community radio stations. These have not greatly deviated from the original model, i.e., these still continue to function under the authority of the national public broadcasting service. However, increasingly it has been found that national broadcasters' obligations towards these stations are on the decrease because national broadcasting systems are now facing financial crisis. Public funds allotted to the national broadcaster have been cut down. And these have been advised to generate operational expenditure through advertising revenue by competing with private broadcasters. This has had the effect of undermining the public service orientation of the national broadcaster. It is not surprising that under these circumstances community radio services are being looked upon as a burden by the national broadcasting systems. Therefore, policy makers are now considering alternate ways of keeping community radio stations outside the authority of the national broadcasting organisation.

Thambuli Community Radio, Philippines

The first truly community-owned and operated Asian community radio stations were established in the Philippines with UNESCO-supported Thambuli Community radio project. The "Thambuli Community Radio Project" has set up a management and training team that co-operates with communities to organise independent community radio stations in less developed rural areas. So far, twenty two community radio stations have been established in different rural communities.

In the project, the thrust is on the local communities to build the radio station. Through focus group discussions, they set the guidelines for the broadcasters; they organise the radio team from all sectors of the village. All team members volunteer to share work. The project provides" equipment, training, facilitates research and helps in identifying community development schemes. Devoid of commercial or sectarian interests, these small radio stations help strengthen the democratic process by providing access to different viewpoints, build tolerance and help animate the local development efforts.

For the communities involved, there is a deep sense of pride of being the masters of their own communication facility that allows them to correlate their activities with the wider national development goals.

Radio Sagarmatha, Nepal

Another independent community radio movement in Asia began in Nepal. Radio Sagarmatha is Nepal's first independent community broadcasting station and represents South Asia's first effort at "independent community radio." The Sagarmatha radio station was established with financial and technical assistance provided under UNESCO's International Programme for the Development of Communication (IPDC).

Radio Sagarmatha has been on air daily on 102.4 FM with its innovative combination of educational, informative and entertaining programming. Radio Sagaramatha's programmes concern vital issues affecting the everyday lives of the citizens of Nepal's capital Kathmandu and its environments. Radio Sagaramatha's programmes have looked at Kathmandu's growing problems such as air pollution, urbanisation and its impact on heritage sites, tourism, threat of HIV/AIDS and garbage disposal. Radio Sagaramatha serves the ethnic, religious and linguistic diversity of over two million people around the Kathmandu valley.

Under Nepal's National Communication Policy Act (1993), a special task force, Radio Sagarmatha prepared the guidelines for the radio project. Private sector participation in FM broadcasting is one major provision of this act.

Community broadcasting is a relatively new concept in Nepal. Radio Sagaramatha's listeners are mostly urban citizens of Kathmandu which is the nation's social, economic and political centre. Thus, the radio is dealing with an intelligent, informed community. This listener profile is both a challenge as well as an opportunity. Getting attention of this audience demands programming that is competitive, comparable and superior to what already exists. It is an opportunity, because Sagaramatha is dealing with a public that has always influenced Nepal's political and economic decision-making. Thus, the community radio is also in a position to influence change. This environment shapes Radio Sagaramatha's mission.

Nepal now has a strong community radio movement with nearly six community radio stations in different parts of the country. Some of them have been established by people who have formed in to community co-operative societies, deemed to be a good model to ensure community ownership.

Another Development Paradigm

The theoretical underpinnings for these efforts were based on an emergence of "Another Development" perspective which emphasised alternative communication systems and media practices. The stress was on inclusive forms of participation of people in the economy, political system and media within particular locale.

'Another Development' perspective evolved as a critique of, and an alternative to, the modernisation and dependency theories, which influenced development communication paradigms until the late 1970s. Modernisation theorists advocated a universal model of development whereby development was a mirror of what happened in Western European countries and North America. Dependency theorists put forward the transitional and structural conditions needed to eliminate under-development. Both modernisation and dependency theorists were on two extremes of a psychological warfare that prevailed during the cold war period.

A significant feature of "Another Development" is its strong emphasis on the "community" as a level of analysis as against both modernisation and dependency paradigms which were based on tensions between developing and developed countries, and therefore focused more on nation state.

The "Another Development" paradigm argued that it is at the local community level that the problems of living conditions are discussed, and interactions with other communities and outside agents are elicited. Therefore, it highlighted the critical role of local participation in development and demanded that participatory decision-making strategies be encouraged in the design and implementation of development programmes. For this purpose, communication systems were seen as a means for those local groups to seriously consider development initiatives and desires, and elicit participation.

The "Another Development" was less theoretical, but more focused on the need of alternative communication systems and media practices that can be easily assimilated and used by the communities in developing countries. The stress was on inclusive forms of participation in the economy, political system and media within the communities. The nation state in this case is considered to be consisting of any number of individual communities. The mainstream media which are usually associated with the concept of nation state were generally left out in support of small and alternative media.

In out analysis so far, two key determinants of suggested alternative communication systems and media practices underscored in the "Another Development" are relevant. First, the "new understanding of communication as a two-way process" is underscored. Secondly, "participation" is recognised as a central concern of development communication. Here there was an absolute recognition of interactive nature of communication, as opposed to its linearity upon which the modernisation and dependency theorists relied.

To give sufficient emphasis on the two-way communication process, and to disassociate from the one-way communication approaches of preceding theories, some choose to use the term "participatory development communication" as a synonym to "Another Development". While what is meant by two-way communication as a process was rather clear, the defining of participation was engulfed in ideological debates, by those who felt that true participation puts people in charge of making all the decisions, and those who felt that participation at other levels was also valid.

Irrespective of the complex and varied nature of intended communication function in participatory approach, the widely held belief was that the new approach could help in the "development of a community's cultural identity, act as a vehicle for people's self-expression, or serve as a tool for diagnosis of a community's problems". While fewer efforts were made to define participation, the exact nature and role of communication in "Another Development" were believed to depend on normative goals and standards set by the host communities to ensure participation.

The participation, access and self-management define uses of communication media that include two-way communications as "community communication" or "community media". Taking into account the three normative elements, the definitions of community media tend to be based on the way in which the messages are planned and produced. Referring specifically to the term "community media", Berrigan says:

> "In the past, similar terms have been used to identify programming specially designed for particular community groups, such as ethnic or minority groups with special needs or interests. Other than this deliberate orientation, little in the production procedure was changed. Topics were chosen in the same way, by professional communicators, and targeted towards the apparent needs and interests of the audience. But.... community media are adaptation of media for use by the community, for what ever purpose the community decides. They are media to which the members of the community have access, for information, education, and entertainment when they want access. They are media to which community participates as planners, producers, and performers. They are the means of expression of the community rather than for the community. "

The discourse of "Another Development" supported the right to relevant local information, the right to answer back and the right to use the new means of communication for interaction and social action in small-scale settings of community, interest group or sub-culture.

In the place of uniform, centralised, high-cost, commercialised, professionalised or state-controlled media it encouraged multiple, small-scale, local, non-institutional, committed media which link senders to receivers and also favour horizontal patterns of interaction. Thus, the belief that the community should become the focus of development communication was strengthened.

Greater decentralisation and power-sharing plans have been recognised as essential reforms to support development efforts. But, decentralised administration alone would not bring the desired results unless there are possibilities for each and every community to influence and to take part in the decentralised decision-making process. This is where community radio has a great potential, particularly because it helps bottom-up decision-making from radio and every community in the decentralised administration. Therefore, community radio facilitates the process of true and democratic nation-building.

Community Radio Station

The community radio system has been opened up to educational institutions for establishing radio stations under a licence from the Government. NGOs, community groups and others in order to set up community broadcast stations may perhaps be taken up later after the various applications including security aspects are studied and cleared by the government.

The community radio station concept, as envisaged by the government usually extends the following benefits to the local community, particularly those in the rural areas:

— Enhancing participation of the people in the development process.

— Capacity building in the rural areas through education.

— Providing opportunities to people to upgrade their skills and enhance their creative talents.

— Preserve and promote the local language, arts, crafts, culture and traditions.

— Bring within easy reach of the rural population, topical information in areas of agriculture, social welfare, education, health and environment.

— Help create rural networks for the rural cottage and village industry.

Technical Aspects

Physical capital includes the main infrastructure for a radio station which consists of transmitting equipment, studio for production and transmission and a building to house all these. Working space will be required for the staff engaged to operate the radio station.

A radio station has to cover functions and festivals for which it needs special equipments often referred to as OB equipments. Let us examine each of these in detail.

Transmitting Equipments

The following are the main transmitting equipment required for a community radio station:

Transmitter

Licences are generally given for Low Power Transmitters of 50 Watts or less for FM radio stations. Several companies around the world now produce inexpensive FM transmitters for community radio using the frequencies mentioned above. They range In price from marginally over Rs 20,000 to Rs 2 lakh and are about the size of a thick paper back book. The technology of making and operating FM transmitters is now simple. Using locally available materials, the DANIDA/UNESCO Tambuli community radio project in the Philippines produced its first transmitter locally and successfully put it to work in 1998.

Low power transmitters may also have an amplifier or booster attached to them to increase their power output. Many of the UNESCO supported community radio stations have 20-Watt transmitters with a 100-Watt booster. This transmission equipment, especially the booster, generates considerable heat. Hence, it is important that it is accompanied by a cooling fan and installed in a well-ventilated place.

Most of the FM transmitters built for community radio require a 12-volt DC power supply. Thus, they can be run either off an electrical main source with a transformer that converts this into 12-volt DC output, or a vehicle battery or solar panels.

It is important to keep the audio signal from an FM Transmitter at the right level. If the signal is over modulated, it will result in distortion and possible interference from nearby stations. A device called limiter or compressor is therefore included in the audio chain to keep the signal at its pre-set level.

Antenna

The height, position and adjustment of the antenna play a crucial role in achieving high quality and the farthest possible reach of the FM broadcast signal. FM signals travel more or less in a straight line and follow the line of sight. The antenna that propagates the signal must therefore be as high as possible, and there should be no or few obstructions that can block the signal. Higher the Antenna, farther will be the signal reach. FM faces limitations in hilly areas because even if the antenna is placed on the top of a peak, there may be areas of signal shadow in the valleys. For using FM in hilly areas one or more relay transmitters need to be installed to cover the areas in shadow. The height of the antenna will depend on the terrain and on any obstacle that the signal may encounter. It is usually at least 20-30 metres above the ground. The Antenna may be placed on a building or hilltop to gain necessary height, or a mast must be constructed for it.

Antenna masts can be built locally using steel uprights and lathes to create a lattice construction. However, a simpler and cheaper version can be made by using galvanised steel water pipes. Stairs are welded on to them so that the broadcasting antenna itself, fitted high on the mast, can be reached for adjustments and repairs. The masts must be firmly anchored in a concrete block in the ground and they must be held vertical by guy wires, also anchored in concrete.

There are two broad categories of antenna: Omni-directional and Directional. As its name implies, Omni-directional radiates the signal in all directions, through 360 degrees around itself. Directional antenna radiates the signal towards one segment of the circle around it. In certain situations, directional antenna has been found better. One example is where an antenna is placed on the side of mountain overlooking the community to be reached. A directional antenna beaming the signal towards a particular area would be able to give additional power to that area. If the signal is beamed through omni-directional antenna, a part of the power would get dissipated or wasted resulting in weak signal reaching the listener.

FM antennas come in a variety of designs and sizes and can be bought ready made. But for most community radio stations they are fabricated on the spot by a metal worker, using materials that can usually be bought in a local hardware shop, such as copper piping and aluminum or PVC piping, all held together by hose-clamps and solder.

The tuning of antenna to get the best signal is the work of a specialist. Fine-tuning of the antenna to get the best signal is done with an instrument called SWR power metre which measures the Standing Wave Ratio (SWR). It costs less than Rs 5000. It is connected between the transmitter and the antenna to measure the ratio between the power coming from the transmitter and the power being reflected back from the antenna. If a lot of power is being reflected by the antenna, it implies that it is not properly tuned and broadcast power is being lost. The specialist adjusts the length and position of the movable radiating elements on the antenna until the SWR power meter shows that there is little, or almost no power being reflected back from the antenna. Many modern transmitters incorporate an SWR power meter. The setup mentioned above is suggestive in nature and can be suitably modified to suit individual requirements. It will provide an effective radiated power (ERP) of around 63 watts facilitating a stereophonic coverage of 8 kms with a 54 dbu or monophonic coverage of 10 kms with a 48 dbu. The concept of monophonic and stereophonic coverage is explained in detail in Course MJM-003. The coverage that a transmitter provides depends on the power radiated by it and the height of the antenna used. This is explained in Martin Allard "Broadcast Coverage Pattern". Some typical range figures, based on stereo transmission in a flat area with an antenna of 25 meter height would be:

20 watts ERP - 5 km

100 watts ERP - 12 km

1200 watts ERP - 30 km

However, each case is different. We have an example of a station running 1200 watts ERP with listeners living 80 kms away.

Frequency

The usual band for FM broadcasting ranges between 67.5 and 108 MHz. frequencies. The Government has framed guidelines for applying for licences for setting up community radio stations. The guidelines state, 'Licence will be issued in the shared frequency band from 87.5 to 100 MHz. However, in the event of frequency not being available in this band, the broadcast band of 104 to 108 MHz may also be considered. The frequency band from 100 to 104 MHz is earmarked exclusively for the use of All India Radio.

Equipment for OB Recording

OB constitutes an important segment of broadcasting. OB can be live or recorded. Live OBs are those which carry the proceedings of an event or happening with the commentary of a commentator. Recorded OBs refer to the field recording done at the scene of an event or happening. The recordings are taken back to the studio. They are edited to the extent required and used as a radio report or as an input in a feature or documentary. An interview with an expert can be recorded in the studio or at his/her residence or office. In the case of OBs, portable equipment are required which can be carried to the OB in a car or a van. The equipment can be handled by the person handling programmes if it is only recording. If it is a Live coverage, the recording of a technical person would be required.

The technical equipments required are given below:

— Portable recorders with microphones

— Dynamic microphones for portable recorders

— Portable mixing consoles
— Cassette recorders with mike outputs
— Microphone stand with audio cables.

Studio and Building

The radio station needs studios for production of programmes and their transmission. An available room in an existing building can be converted into a studio which must have the ideal acoustic conditions for recording and transmission. For this a special treatment of the walls and the roof of the room is done. After the treatment is completed the studio must be able to provide an optimum reverberation time (RT). The equipment to be provided in the studio must be able to meet the requirements of recording, editing and storage of programmes in analogue and digital mode. The technical details of analogue and digital are explained in detail in Course MJM-003. The recording and the playback facilities will centre around a hard disk based system assisted by CDs, cassette players etc! The production studio could also be used for transmission. This must be such as to accommodate three participants and the proceedings from there can either be recorded or broadcast live as "On Air Studio".

The basic module suggested is designed on the concept of a common 'On Air Studio' cum programme production studio, which will be acoustically treated to provide the optimum Reverberation Time. The equipment provided in the studio will meet the requirements of both production and transmission.

Financial Aspects

You have learnt that one of the key factors of sustainability is finance. The financial requirements of the community radio can be divided into two types of expenditure: Capital and Recurring.

Capital Expenditure

A community radio can be set up with a low power transmitter at a cost of about Rs 15 lakhs as on prevailing rates (2003 price level). This however, does not include the cost of the building.

Recurring Expenditure

If a community is to manage the entire show, it may not involve much recurring expenditure. However, this is easier said than done. A minimum core staff, such as a station manager, librarian and accountant need to be appointed. The role of the station manager is very important. S/he must imbibe the ethics of broadcasting and should have a thorough knowledge of the broadcasting code. S/he must have commitment to the concept of community broadcasting as well as to development communication. The station manager can also perform the duties of a producer. It would be helpful if the librarian can function as a technician as well as a storekeeper.

The recurring expenditure estimates should include some incentives to be given to the experts and participants of the radio programmes. It must also include the expenditure on equipment maintenance through annual maintenance contract.

The duration of broadcasts of different radio stations will vary widely. A standard model of a community radio station would have 8 hours of transmission. Usually, this comprises four hours of programmes broadcast in the morning which are repeated later, in the evening. In operating a radio station with 8 hours of transmission every day, the following recurring costs will be involved (the cost estimates are approximate):

Salary or remuneration or honorarium to the core staff	: Rs 3 lakhs/annum
Maintenance of equipment, studio, electricity, watercharges, stationery, telephone, fax, interest etc.	: Rs 3 lakhs/annum
Token remuneration to the artists, experts, participants, anchors, compere Rs 2000 (for a four hour broadcast)	: Rs 7 lakhs/annum
Miscellaneous expenditure	: Rs 2 lakhs/annum
Total cost	: Rs 15 lakhs approx.

There are, however, instances where a single person runs an entire radio station. In such cases, the cost will go down considerably.

Managerial Aspects

Management of a community radio has to be, handled with caution and tact. You will have to have a team comprising representatives of different groups among the community. Maintaining neutrality is of prime importance. With a skeleton team and scarce funds, the motivation and involvement of each and every member of the team is a sine quo non for the success of the station.

Local bodies such as municipality and panchayat must get involved in the generation of programmes. They must provide financial support. In Nepal, panchayats support community radio stations. An advisory committee, a management committee and marketing group will help the stations with efficiently managing these stations.

Managerial activities are wide and varied. When an infrastructure is created, then it has to be maintained. The listening audience would expect uninterrupted programme services for which stand by audio software has always to be kept. A radio station would incur both capital and recurring expenditure. Expenditure management would cover all the areas referred to under 'financial aspects'. The station has to constantly plan revenue generation to meet the expenditure involved. This in turn would involve marketing efforts and increase in the accountability of the station riot only to the listeners but also to those who contribute as donors, sponsors or advertisers. Accountability would also involve the managerial responsibility of ensuring fairness in broadcast as well as equitable participation by every section of the community. The responsibility would extend to strict adherence to the terms of licence and handling of any litigation arising from complaints of breach.

Public Relations (PR) is also an important managerial function of the radio station. It will cover relations with the opinion leaders, peoples' representatives and local authorities OB management would also require a lot of planning and liaison with the organisers. Apart from these, securing feedback from audience and reshaping programmes whenever required is also crucial. In a community radio station, these managerial activities may be on a lower scale but they cannot be overlooked.

Programming Aspects

Conventional radio programmes follow certain benchmarks based on the policies of an organisation. For example, in AIR music programmes are generally recorded in professional studios in which only approved and graded artistes perform. Even the tests for announcers are rigorous. However, in community radio the approach of conventional radio is difficult to follow. There is no need for 'fixed point programmes' which radio stations try to adhere to. The community radio can follow a 'flexible point programme' schedule. What is important is that programmes must be interesting. Conventional spoken-word programmes like formal talks, and interviews can be used in community radio. Efforts need to be made to use more interactive programmes.

Phone-in Programmes

The station can also go in for a toll free telephone facility wherein the station can pay for the calls received from its listeners. This will encourage more participation of the community. Experts sitting at the station or their homes can answer listener queries directly or the anchor connects the listeners to the expert.

Phone-out Programmes

The station may also organise 'brain teaser' type programmes by broadcasting suitable question-answer sessions in which the answer can be given by the listener using a telephone. The person who answers correctly can be called to the studio at a later date for a programme for which some honorarium can be paid.

Open House Programmes

In a small community, the listeners may not be able to send an email or make phone calls. They can come to the radio station in person in view of the proximity of the radio station. The station can earmark a particular time everyday for the people to walk into the station and express their feelings, talents, views, suggestions and get clarifications for the queries.

OB Programmes

A radio station gets requests for coverage of meetings, conferences, colloquia, poetic symposia and the like. Every community celebrates religious and cultural festivals by organising public functions. All these can be covered 'live' or they can be recorded and glimpses from them can be presented in the form of Radio Reports. Apart from these, regular radio formats can also be used for community radio.

Focus on Local Issues, Talent, Language a community radio station, local anchor-persons and local talents should be used. As far as possible, the programmes should be in the local language or dialect. The programmes should have to their knowledge and also aim to solve local problems. Commercial FM stations try to being friends together through their programmes. Community radio stations can imaginatively adapt these formats to convey developmental needs of the society. It can bring people together on the same platform. A sizable chunk must be allotted to local music and opportunities must be given to the budding artistes. It can also try to preserve the folk art of the region and go in for archiving such treasures. It can organise local competitions, debates, quiz programmes, music concerts, music competitions etc.

Radio stations produce at least half a dozen programmes in different formats. The station managers can make a selection of outstanding programmes among them which can be used by other public service broadcasters. They may charge a fee for the same. Broadcast of the station's programmes by other networks will be an incentive for the broadcasters. It will also give much needed publicity and also add to the credibility of the system. The programmes could be built as audio CDs and made available for sale. The dying folk arts can be canned and cut into CDs and sold. Radio tuition is another value added service which can be provided through community radio. Since the technical facilities are limited, the station could have more of live programmes eliminating the need for recording, editing etc.

Community radio may focus on the following areas for programming:

— Folk music
— Radio tuition for school children
— Agriculture, animal husbandry, community development
— Rural development
— Health and hygiene
— Adult education
— Communal harmony
— National integration
— Civic problems and solutions
— Women's empowerment
— Human Rights
— Resolution of community problems

Community broadcasters must ensure that the broadcasts are positive in nature leading to harmony and development and avoid anything that will lead to violence or communal tension.

Presentation

The presentation of community radio broadcasts needs to be taken care of seriously. Copying of the commercial FM or the conventional public broadcaster must be discouraged. While presenters or anchor-persons of these stations should have an exposure to various styles and techniques of presentation, they must develop their own style taking into account the local traditions and sensitivities. In this it is important that each community radio should first study the tastes and preferences of the audience. The day community radio deviates from these, their utility will be lost.

Value Added Services

The availability of experts in every field is limited in a community. The stations can subscribe to the Internet facility and can also answer the questions after surfing the net. Such experiments have become very useful in Kothamale community radio project in Sri Lanka. Information sought by a listener can be provided by the anchorperson by logging on to the Internet. Kothamale community radio has become popular due to its instant Internet connectivity. The listener who needs certain information, rings up or goes to the radio station and asks for the information. The anchorperson logs on to the Internet, accesses the information, translates it into the local language and offers it to the listener. In a country like ours where bandwidth problems are likely to exist for some time, this value added service provided by radio can prove very popular.

Programmes for Campus Radio

The campus radio may be managed by the academics and representatives of the student community. The duration of transmission and the programme content will depend upon the courses run by the educational institution concerned. Classroom lectures, extension lectures, interviews with visiting faculty, coverage of campus activities including sports and games will form the programme structure of the station. The stations will provide enough opportunities for the articulation of the artistic talents of the students and teachers. The programme can be produced and presented by students themselves after receiving some training. The teachers and technicians in the Physics and/or Telecommunication departments of the institutions could operate and maintain the equipments. The running expenditure of a campus radio could be easily absorbed by the management of the educational institutions. What would be required is one-time expenditure on purchase of hardware/transmitter and other equipments.

Ethical Aspects

The community radio ownership has legal parameters. There are rules and regulations governing the grant of a licence for operating a radio station. While applying for the licence, the specifications details regarding the infrastructure, hardware, programme production have to be studied. There must be clarity in regard to understanding of copyright laws, intellectual property rights, use of commercial film songs, or ready made material from tapes, cassettes, CDs etc and the formalities to be observed before using the copyright material.

Sustainable Models of Community Radio

Community radio exists in different parts of the world and there are various models of it. However, community radio, as popularly understood across the world, remains outside the legal periphery of the Indian landscape. The Government of India's recent decision to allow educational institutions recognised by the Centre and the State Governments the right to broadcast conforms more closely to the Campus Radio practices in other parts of the world. All India Radio started in the 80's a local radio with the lofty objective of its serving as community radio.

You may ask how community radio differs from local radio. While both outline the use of the medium by the community for its enrichment and development, local radio attempts to cover a large physical area which could be as large as a district itself. Whereas, the community radio concept envisages a very low power radio capable of information sharing within a village or two or a big campus or a cluster of housing colonies. In India, some community initiatives have been taken to use community participation in audio/radio as a central part of their work. One of the important aspects of community radio is sustainability. While the components of sustainability for community radio in general are distinct from other broadcast media, they are specific to the country scenario. In India, the airwaves are not accessible to communities unlike Community Radio in Nepal or Sri Lanka where a critical requisite for sustainability is legitimacy. The criterion for licence application and broadcasting articulates restrictions.

Factors Infulencing the Sustainability of Community Radio

In 2002, Community Radio practitioners and advocates met at Kathmandu to discuss ways on how to develop Community Radio in the region. The group determined that the sustainability of Community Radio was built on the following four capitals:

— Human Capital
— Social Capital
— Physical Capital
— Financial Capital

Human Capital

Human capital relates to the collective wisdom, knowledge and skills of a community. The human capital for community radio is different from private or Government radio, for e.g. Radio Sagarmatha in Nepal is different from Radio City or Radio Mirchi or Akashvani. The difference lies in that Community Radio is radio of, for and by the community. In simple terms, the community drives the radio in every sense, be it production, management or ownership. There are no divisions as in the case of a commercial enterprise between editorial and management. The producer of a community radio programme could well be a part of the management committee. This becomes evident on studying the models of community radio in the countries where it is practised.

Social Capital

Social capital pertains to the trust and commitment and one of the most important needs for community radio is to prove itself as a social entity. It has been found that most of the people involved in running a community radio station are volunteers. Attrition can become an issue of concern. How do community radio stations manage to sustain their personnel? The answer lies in motivation and ownership. A Community Radio station reflects the issues and concerns of the community and thereby it provides a great deal of local relevance and impact on the community. Local women provide the more reliable human resource as they do not usually look for jobs outside the community.

According to UNESCO's Community Radio Handbook, "sustainability should be seen as the ultimate responsibility of the community itself, and the challenge to the managers of the station and to his/her team of producers, reporters and technicians is to make the service so enjoyable, useful and valuable to its listeners that they will be willing to support it through subscription fees, voluntary donations in cash or kind, and the like."

Physical Capital

The physical capital comprises the medium or the channel. While the community drives the technology, the latter constitutes a critical component in the running of community radio. Technology assumes additional significance in the Indian context. The Cable Act, however, enables cable audio to be a viable model. This has been taken up by some NGOs, otherwise community interventions in audio are limited to narrow-casting or collaborations with All India Radio. In all the models of community radio stations, the technical infrastructure is characterised' by their ruggedness, adaptability and user friendliness. As far as possible, the accent is on durability and equipment that can be easily handled by the community.

Financial Capital

As its name suggests, this is all about the running costs. Many community radio stations are run by paid volunteers. Although their remuneration is not much, it needs to be built in to the day-to-day costs. The issues related to expenses for maintenance also need to be considered.

The Kathmandu Consultation for Community Radio was held recently which drew up various sources for revenue generation. These included:

1. *Diverse Funding:* Many community radio stations in Nepal receive funds from the Government as well as donors.
2. *Sponsorship:* Community programmes produced by groups for inclusion in the broadcasts of AIR like the Kutch Mahila Vikas Sanghathan have been sponsored by UNDP. Sponsorship can also come from the members of the community.
3. *Social Marketing*: community radio stations have marketed audio cassettes of programmes they have produced.
4. *Donations*: Radio Lumbini and Radio Madan Pokhara in Nepal accepted donations.
5. *Charge membership fees*: Radio Lumbini, Radio Madan Pokhara in Nepal charged membership fee from the members enrolled.
6. Listeners' contributions were also accepted by some community radio stations.

7. Volunteers' contribution by way of service was also one of the ways of revenue generation.

8. *Advertising*: Many community radio stations do not allow advertising. However, while community radio is symbiotic with community needs and community development, social /relevant advertising can play a useful role both in terms of revenue generation and awareness building. In order to prevent misuse or misrepresentation the decision to allow advertising rests with the management committee who in turn comprise members from the community. They determine whether advertising can play a legitimate role in community radio and the type of advertising that is compatible with the aims of the community radio station. Subsequently, regulatory mechanisms should be developed to ensure that appropriate advertising code of ethics is observed.

Apart from generation of revenues, there are also ways of minimising expenditure.

a) *Co-production*: Namma Dhwani, a community media partnership between NGOs VOICES, MYRADA and the community of Boodikote village, has jointly been involved in producing programmes with AIR Bangalore.

b) *Sharing programmes with other stations*: This is practised by community radio stations in Nepal..

c) *Linkages with educational institutions*: community radio practitioners can partner with other radio stations

Sustainable Models

Sustainable models of community radio exist in various parts of the developing and developed world. Nepal has a series of diverse and representative community radio models which have existed for the past decade. Based on these initiatives, an appropriate benchmark for analysis can be discussed. First, it has a vibrant tradition of community radio. Secondly, it is part of the South Asian canvas and shares similar socio-economic and political similarities with India. These factors could provide a framework for both discussion and analysis.

Co-operative Model

Radio Lumbini, which began in 1998, operates on a co-operative model. The co-operative system seemed the most suitable as it did not let the station be dependent either on donors or on business houses. The co-operative began with 69 members and has since expanded to 96 in mid 2002. The station charged a joining fee of Rs 20,000 from members to the station fund. Another source of revenue came from the Friends of Radio Lumbini group. The group which numbered about 600 people paid Rs 100 annually to the radio station. The station also received between Rs 4,000 and Rs 8,000 annually from 71 Village Development Committees (VDC) in the area.

There is an executive body which is elected for three years and meets monthly. There are also technical sub-committees. Day-to-day activities are carried out by the co-operative which |is also vested with the management and ownership components. In 2002, Radio Lumbini had a staff of 18 who were paid between Rs 2,000 and Rs 4,500 per month. Five people were paid @ Rs 200 each to produce a weekly programme. 10 weekly programmes were produced by the volunteers. Radio Lumbini broke even after its first year of operations. The schedule includes four local news bulletins a day and a range of programmes on health, agriculture, gender equality, children's education and good governance. Programmes about the VDCs and their activities are a part of the station's programming.

The Co-operative model enables easy and quick decision making as there is a strong sense of ownership and identity. The station is self-reliant as far as running costs are concerned, it accepts help from donors and sponsors for improving programmes and upgrading equipment. In the event of a crisis the co-operative could float shares.

Local Administration Model

The station Radio Madan Pokhara is owned by the Village Development Committee (VDC). It has set up a trust fund with 65 members who have paid Rs 1,000 each for membership. Running costs are met through the VDC and from the nearby District Development Council and through advertisements and sponsorships. The station also charges an entry fee at the rate of Rs 200 per group. Restricted and selective advertising is permitted. For example, there is no advertising of consumer products. Instead, advertising is more geared to announcements of births, deaths, marriages etc. There are 17 members on the managing board and 5 of these form a working committee for day to day management of the station. There is also an advisory board of 7 members headed by the local MP.

The studio is situated in a small ground floor room. The 100 watt transmitter can be heard in Palpa and 7 surrounding districts and the potential audience is some 400,000 people. Because of its growing popularity and wider than anticipated reach, the community planned to construct a purpose-built station in 2002, to erect a more powerful transmitter and to increase the daily broadcasts from the present 6 hours per day.

The station runs largely on volunteers from Madan pokhara and neighbourhood. Some are responsible for particular programmes; others work regularly as presenters. The station pays small amounts to its full-timers but much of the work is done voluntarily. The station is trying to build up a trust fund to cover capital expenses and to provide a regular income. It mostly relies on donations from local VDCs and the Palpa DDC, funding from donors, and charges for social messages and some local advertising. It also charges for visits to the station. The station is managing without a telephone. Installing one would be very costly because of the distance from the power-lines but they hope to get one installed soon. A VDC cannot float shares. Consequently, in the event of liquidation, the assets would go to the government. Decision making, in comparison to the Co-operative model was slow.

Trust Model

Radio Sagarmatha in Kathmandu, is the first Community Radio station in Nepal. The licence holder is the Nepal Forum of Environmental Journalists (NFEJ). It has a paid staff of 30 members and many volunteers. Sixty per cent of its funds came from donors, thirty percent from advertising and ten per cent from other sources. In a bid to strengthen ownership and its fund base, Radio Sagarmatha had formed a trust and encouraged the public to become members at Rs 1,000.

Indian Models of Community Radio

India does not have any of the models of community radio discussed above. However, some rural marginalised groups have developed viable models of community participation in audio/radio. Broadly, the examples throw up two distinct models, these are: Community participation and ownership model and use of existing channels of AIR.

Community Participation and Ownership Model

In this model, the communities work towards owning their media processes.

While both initiatives are supported by donor agencies, the concerned communities strive to work towards ownership by participation and subsidised funding.

Namma Dhwani (Our Voices)

Namma Dhwani is a partnership between the Boodikote community in Kolar district, MYRADA, an NGO committed to integrated development and VOICES, a development commu-nications NGO, based in Bangalore with technical support from AIR, Bangalore. The place of operation is Kolar District of Karnataka. The target group is communities living in and around Boodikote sector in Kolar. In the Boodikote-village which has a population of about 4,000, about 1930 families live below the poverty line. Their literacy levels are abysmally low, particularly among women.

Nairmia Dhwani has been operational for two years and has a community audio production centre which started in September 2001. Computers were introduced in April 2002 with a view to developing the project into a community information centre with web broadcasting playing a critical role. The objective of the radio centre was to develop community audio production and broadcasting skills using audio and the Internet with a view to ultimately developing Namma Dhwani into a full fledged community media information and broadcasting centre. The focus was on generating awareness about the concept of audio as a means of communication and empowerment. Cable audio, narrowcasting and loudspeakers were used as the modes of transmission.

Cable audio: Cable connectivity is currently being opera-tionalised across Boodikote village. This will enable cable audio programmes on health, education and income generation produced by the Namma Dhwani audio production centre to be cable cast to each and every house in Boodikote village. The first phase of cable audio to about 250 homes has already started. Cable audio educational programmes are cable-cast twice a week to the local school at Boodikote village.

Narrowcasting: In addition, narrow-casting using audio cassette technology is regularly carried out through self help groups across the Boodikote area which covers a cluster of 35 villages.

Loudspeaker narrowcast: Between January and December 2002, the Namma Dhwani audio production centre had weekly programmes which were narrowcast using loudspeakers. This was organised to coincide with the local mandi/market which meets every Tuesday.

Awareness and capacity building for making radio programmes marked the first stage of the project. This was done through a series of workshops. By the end of six months the community was producing programmes with support from AIR, many of which were broadcast over AIR FM. The Community Audio Production Centre, 'Namma Dhwani Samudayik Doorsampark Matu Mahiti Kendra' is managed and supported by community volunteers. A management committee comprising representatives from the Self Help Groups meets twice a month to take stock of the Production Centre's activities.

Pastapur Community Media Centre

This is a partnership between the Deccan Development Society (DDS) Pastapur, and "Women Speak to Women" project of UNESCO. The place of operation is Zaheerabad in Medak District of Andhra Pradesh. The owners as well as the audience groups are 100 Dalit women's groups (Sangams) consisting of nearly 4000 members in 75 villages of Medak district. The focus is on participatory development and empowerment of women. The media used is FM radio station designed to work on audio-cassette technology. It has a 100 watts transmitter, which can reach a radius of 30 kms.

DDS received part funding from UNESCO for the building, acoustics treatment, equipments including recorders, mixers, microphones, cables, installation etc. The building has three octagonal shaped blocks consisting of the studio, transmitting/control room, the dubbing section, the director's cabin and the reception area. The studio facilities are being used to produce audio cassettes. They already have over 200 hours of recorded programmes, some of which are being edited into one-hour magazine modules. In October 2001, a community media centre was inaugurated at Pastapur.

Using Existing Channels of AIR

In this model, community participation is facilitated through the production of its own audio programmes. Airtime is obtained from AIR for broadcasting programmes produced by the communities. By buying time from Akashvani, the programmes are broadcast on a regular basis. The programmes need to conform to AIR codes and packaging.

Chalo Ho Gaon Mein

A Partnership between three NGOs, the National Foundation of India (NFI),

New Delhi; Alternative for India Development (AID) Lesliegunj Section; and Manthan Media Collective, JL, Ranchi. The target group is 45 villages from Lesliegunj and Panki divisions. The focus is on empowerment of communities with special emphasis on women. The local AIR FM station at Daltongunj (the district headquarters) is used as channel. AID selected one project coordinator and each community volunteer was asked to identify three villages. The place, Palamau district of Jharkhand was selected keeping in mind geographic proximity to their native villages.

A series of workshops were organised to acquaint the volunteers with the techniques of audio production and presentation. A 30 minutes slot on Sundays at 7.20 pm on AIR Daltongunj was allotted on commercial terms for the community participatory programme 'Chalo Ho Gaon Mein'. The first community radio programme of Daltongunj went on air on 9 August 2001.

Kunjal Pachaee Kutch Ji

Kunjal Pachaee Kutch Ji is the project, which strengthens community participation through radio. It is a partnership between Kutch Mahila Vikas Sanghathan (KMVS) Bhuj, and Dhrishti Media Collective, Ahmedabad. The place of operation of the project is Kutch district of Gujarat. The target group is women in Kutch villages and the focal area is empowerment of women for Panchayat functions. AIR station at Bhuj was used for broadcast of the programmes. In the first year, a number of specific gender related issues including women's leadership and governance, girl child education, female foeticide, dowry/unnatural deaths/ suicides of women, pressure on women to produce boys, maternal mortality, reproductive health etc. were covered in the serial.

Strengths and Limitations of the Models

Both KMVS and AID provide facilitative mechanism which use existing channels, i.e., the local AIR radio to broadcast their programmes. Studies have revealed that audience reception and community participation is high. However, community ownership over the process is limited while it relieves the producers of the responsibilities of transmission and the problems associated with it. The models of community radio that we have talked about have been supported substantially by agencies like UNESCO, UNDP and National Foundation of India. However, underlying this support have been initiatives from the communities themselves as well as other partnership efforts which are easily replicable. The Namma Dhwani management committee has, for instance, a community base fund where the community contributes a small amount towards the programming costs. It is also in some ways similar to the efforts of community radio stations like Lumbini and Madan Pokhara in Nepal which have community contributions and friends of the community radio support. Funds are required constantly to sponsor the production of the programmes.

Impacts of Indian Models

The sustainability of community radio needs to be measured in terms of impact.

Gender Empowerment

All the four initiatives in community broadcasting in India have promoted the voices of women. The Namma Dhwani initiative's management committee which meets twice a month to take stock of the programming and management has representatives from eleven Self Help Groups in the area. Almost all of them, including the studio manager are women. Similarly, the Pastapur Media Centre is managed by a team of seven dalit non-literate women, and one man. In the case of KMVS, the women leaders of the sanghathans, who have been a part of the initiative; have asserted that they have acquired legitimacy among their counterparts working on other development issues, such as watershed sanitation.

In all the initiatives, the women involved in the projects have asserted that they would be ready to run a community radio station on their own. Many of the programmes have focused on women's participation in the political process, women's right to education, dowry deaths, violence against women, female foeticide, etc. Despite the fact that women play a strong role in these initiatives, a study however, has revealed that "socio-cultural barriers at the community and household levels affect women's listenership negatively."

Education

The school audio programme of the Namma Dhwani was born out of a concern regarding the Samudaya Dattashalay, a government initiative. The initiative aimed at providing a platform for parents to meet teachers and children to discuss the progress in education. Despite its laudable intentions and the presence of about 100 teachers and children, only a few parents used to attend. School Audio has brought about a significant change. Not only have parents begun to take a more active interest, but they want to know exactly what programmes are being made. School Audio has also triggered off the demand for cable audio across the village.

Poor children from the Government High School in Boodikote are a part of the School Audio programme which started in mid 2002 to make educational programmes on various subjects. Apart from expressing their own creativity and producing their own programmes, there is also an increased exposure to general knowledge and current affairs. Teachers have also begun to participate and make model lesson programmes which are then cable-cast by a cable which connects the audio production centre to the sch6ol. Today, the Namma Dhwani cable audio is cable-cast for two hours and reaches about 250 TV homes in the village.

Culture and Identity

The KMVS has a magazine format programme known as Musafari which resurrects Kutch history, art and culture and also attempts to reinterpret them in a contemporary context. KMVS believes that through these programmes, a bridge is built between tradition and modernity. During the programme, questions on traditional legends are constantly asked. KMVS's initiative was not only successful in using radio as a vehicle by which to reinforce ethnic identity but also to promote community cohesion and harmony. During the Gujarat riots, KMVS called upon the people of Kutch to practise the values of tolerance and plurality which are a part of their way of life and faith.

Namma Dhwani, is situated on the border of Karnataka and Andhra Pradesh. The people may be conversant with Kannada and Telugu, but they prefer to speak a mix of both. The nearest radio station is AIR Bangalore which broadcasts in Kannada. The Namma Dhwani audio production centre and cable initiative enabled them to overcome the language barriers.

Social Change

At DDS, programmes on a wide range of subjects from education and literacy, public health, environment to food security, gender justice and local /indigenous knowledge systems have been produced, narrow-cast and documented. Many community clubs have started functioning, such as Children's Club, Disabilities Club and Women's Groups. They meet about once a week, discuss relevant issues and examine how some of these can be developed into audio programmes. There have been interesting insights as a result of these programmes. For instance, a programme on disability helped the community to realise that bus passes were available free of cost for people with disabilities. Till then, middlemen were charging Rs 50 to fill up forms which should have been made available free of cost.

The station Madan Pokhra has been playing an active role in development, with programmes to improve farming and forestry and use of the environment, as well as working to eliminate social illusions, discriminations, injustice, superstitions and evil deeds. The station has added to the self-respect and identity of rural people and can be replicated in other parts of the country.

Community Radio: Security Threats

Some skeptics have expressed concerns about possible misuse of community radio when they are owned, managed and operated by distant communities. They fear that such community radio stations could contribute to disintegration of nationhood. However, the argument has no conceptual validity. There is no empirical evidence that armed groups have effectively used community radio to promote their own separatist agenda. No armed group will venture to acquire a community radio that belongs to the community as a whole and risk facing the community's wrath. This is more so because such an attempt will immediately expose the authoritarian nature of the armed group. The community will interpret it as an act of another dictatorial group which has no concern in community affairs other than dominating the community will. In any case, no listener can be forced to subscribe to unilateral viewpoints propagandised by such a radio. On the contrary, community radio has as much potential as an effective tool of integration.

Moreover a small community radio station covers only a limited geographic area with people known to each other. Any military takeover of community radio will make the armed group vulnerable to exposures. In the countries with conflicts such as Sri Lanka, South Africa, Nepal, community radio stations are operational without any threat of being acquired by armed groups. The radio stations with large geographic coverage, such as a national radio, are more vulnerable and have been targeted by armed groups because the ownership of national radio is normally associated with state power. But, a community radio station has not been recognised as a symbol of power as such does not attract the power-hungry armed groups. Decentralisation at the regional level can be effective only when there are democratic communication channels available for those who are living within the regional autonomy. Generally speaking, community radio makes it possible for individuals and communities governed by regional authorities to become more accountable to the people.

References

Dunaway, David *Community Media in the Information Age: Perspectives and Prospect,* Cresskill, NJ: Hampton Press. 2002.

Jankowski, Nicholas W.; Prehn, Ole. eds. *Community Media in the Information Age: Perspectives and Prospects*. Cresskill, NJ: Hampton Press.2001.

Jesse Walker, *Rebels on the Air: An Alternative History of Radio in America*. New York University Press, 2001.

Girard, Bruce (ed). ·*A Passion for Radio: Radio waves and community*. Black Rose Books. 1993.

UNESCO. *How to Do Community Radio: A Primer*. UNESCO. 2004.

Spurgeon, Christina L. and McCarthy, Joanna. "Mobilising the Community Radio Audience". *3CMedia: Journal of Community, Citizen's and Third Sector Media and Communication*, 1 (February), pp. 1-13. 2005.

Vinod Pavarala and Kanchan K. Malik. *Other Voices: The Struggle for Community Radio in India*. Sage Publications India Pvt. Ltd. , New Delhi, India , 2007.

6

Television Broadcasting

Television (TV) is a telecommunication medium for transmitting and receiving moving images that can be monochrome (black-and-white) or colored, with or without accompanying sound. "Television" may also refer specifically to a television set, television programming, or television transmission.

Commercially available since the late 1920s, the television set has become commonplace in homes, businesses and institutions, particularly as a vehicle for advertising, a source of entertainment, and news. Since the 1950s, television has been the main medium for molding public opinion. Since the 1970s the availability of video cassettes, laserdiscs, DVDs and now Blu-ray Discs, have resulted in the television set frequently being used for viewing recorded as well as broadcast material. In recent years Internet television has seen the rise of television available via the Internet, e.g. iPlayer and Hulu.

Although other forms such as closed-circuit television (CCTV) are in use, the most common usage of the medium is for broadcast television, which was modeled on the existing radio broadcasting systems developed in the 1920s, and uses high-powered radio-frequency transmitters to broadcast the television signal to individual TV receivers.

The broadcast television system is typically disseminated via radio transmissions on designated channels in the 54–890 MHz frequency band. Signals are now often transmitted with stereo or surround sound in many countries. Until the 2000s broadcast TV programs were generally transmitted as an analog television signal, but in 2008 the USA went almost exclusively digital.

A standard television set comprises multiple internal electronic circuits, including those for receiving and decoding broadcast signals. A visual display device which lacks a tuner is properly called a video monitor, rather than a television. A television system may use different technical standards such as digital television (DTV) and high-definition television (HDTV). Television systems are also used for surveillance, industrial process control, and guiding of weapons, in places where direct observation is difficult or dangerous. Some studies have found a link between infancy exposure to television and ADHD.

Television Technology

Elements of a Television System

The elements of a simple television system are:

— An image source - this may be a camera for live pick-up of images or a flying spot scanner for transmission of films

— A sound source.

— A transmitter, which modulates one or more television signals with both picture and sound information for transmission.

— A receiver (television) which recovers the picture and sound signals from the television broadcast.

— A display device, which turns the electrical signals into visible light and audible sound.

Practical television systems include equipment for selecting different image sources, mixing images from several sources at once, insertion of pre-recorded video signals, synchronizing signals from many sources, and direct image generation by computer for such purposes as station identification. Transmission may be over the air from land-based transmitters, over metallic or optical cables, or by radio from synchronous satellites. Digital systems may be inserted anywhere in the chain to provide better image transmission quality, reduction in transmission bandwidth, special effects, or security of transmission from theft by non-subscribers.

Display Technology

Thanks to advances in display technology, there are now several kinds of video displays used in modern TV sets:

CRT: The most common displays are the ubiquitous direct-view CRTs for up to 40in (100cm) (in 4:3) and 46in (115cm) (in 16:9) diagonally. These are still the least expensive, and are a refined technology that can still provide the best overall picture quality. As they do not have a fixed native resolution, in some cases they are also capable of displaying sources with a variety of different resolutions at the best possible image quality. The frame rate or refresh rate of a typical NTSC format CRT TV is 60 Hz, and for the PAL format, it's 50 Hz. A typical NTSC broadcast signal's visible portion has an equivalent resolution of about 640x480 pixels. It actually could be slightly higher than that, but the Vertical Blanking Interval, or VBI, allows other signals to be carried along with the broadcast.

Rear projection: Most big-screen TVs (up to over 100 inch (254 cm)) use projection technology. Three types of projection systems are used in projection TVs: CRT-based, LCD-based, and DLP(reflective micromirror chip) -based. Projection television has been commercially available since the 1970s, but could not match the image sharpness of the CRT; current models are vastly improved, and offer a cost-effective large-screen display. A variation is a vidco projcctor, using similar technology, which projects onto a screen.

F*lat panel LCD or plasma*: Modern advances have brought flat panels to TV that use active matrix LCD or plasma display technology. Flat panel LCDs and plasma displays are as little as 4in (10cm) thick and can be hung on a wall like a picture or put over a pedestal. Some models can also be used as computer monitors.

Signal Connections

The number of ways to connect a video device to a television has increased over the years:

— *HDMI* - a 19 or 29-pin industry-supported digital interface which supports standard, enhanced, or high-definition video, plus multi-channel digital audio on a single cable. The video signal is backward-compatible with DVI. Increasingly common on displays, DVD players, and high-end PC graphics cards. Copy protection is implemented using HDCP.

— *DVI* - a 17 to 29-pin connector that carries digital video signals, designed to carry HDTV but also used in current DVD players and latest digital displays. Copy protection is available using HDCP.

— *Component video* - three separate RCA jacks (colored red, green and blue) carry three analog video signals, one brightness (luminance) and two colors (chromas), and is usually referred to as "Y, B-Y, R-Y", "Y Cr Cb" (interlaced) or "Y Pr Pb" (progressive), or YUV. Audio is not carried on this cable. This connection provides for picture quality superior to S-Video and is typically used in home theater for DVDs, satellite and analogue HDTV; less common in Europe but is starting to become more widely available.

— *SCART* - a large 21 pin connector that may carry analog signals consisting of: one video signal composite video; or two video signals S-Video; or for picture quality similar to component video, three signals of separate red, green and blue or RGB; or for best picture quality, four video signals of separate red, green, blue and sync or RGBS; plus right and left line-level audio channels; along with a number of control signals including an aspect-ratio flag (e.g. widescreen). This system has been standard in Europe since mid-1980s for all consumer electronics, which meant that RGBS was available on even the earliest PAL DVD players and satellite receivers. Japan uses a 21 pin RGB connector which is visually similar to SCART but with different pin configurations. This connector is not used in the U.S.

— *S-Video* - small round connector with two separate analog video signals, one carrying brightness (luminance), the other carrying color (chroma). Also referred to as Y/C video. Provides most of the benefit of component video, with slightly less color fidelity. Use started in the 1980s for S-VHS, Hi-8, and early NTSC DVD players to relay high quality video before component was available. This will sometimes, completely incorrectly, be referred to as an S-VHS connector. Audio is not carried on this cable.

— *Composite video* - The most common form of connecting external devices, putting all the analog video information into one signal. Most televisions provide this option with a yellow RCA jack or occasionally a BNC connector. Audio is not carried on this cable, though two separate cables with similar red and white RCA jacks for right and left line-level audio are commonly bonded to composite video cables.

— *Coaxial RF* - All audio channels and picture components are transmitted through one coaxial cable and modulated on a radio frequency. Most TVs manufactured since the 1970s provide a coaxial connection, and this is the type of cable typically used for cable television.

Although still found on VHS tape-players, most modern DVD players and other video devices no longer supply an RF output, so very old TV sets made before composite video jacks became commonplace will need a modulator device. NTSC sets use a 75 ohm F-connector; most PAL sets use a 50 ohm Belling Lee. Most set-top TV antennas have a 300 ohm impedance, so to connect them to a coaxial input requires an inexpensive matching transformer to avoid signal degradation.

— *300 ohm twin-lead* - The predecessor to coaxial cable, generally a flat insulated cable with a pair of wires separated by 0.5 inch, found on NTSC television sets from 1940 to about 1985, and originally used to connect rabbit ears to a receiver. Connection to the set was by connecting the wire to a pair of screws on the back of the television set.

Nominal impedance was 300 ohms; connecting an older set to cable or VCRs requires an inexpensive matching transformer to avoid signal degradation due to impedance mismatch. Twin-lead wiring is sensitive to nearby metal objects. Long runs must be properly supported away from metal objects and should be mounted with a loose twist in the cable.

— *Fiber optic* - The latest in connections and only on extremly new and high quality TVs, fiber optics use a laser to transmit data along a glass fiber. Used for sound and/or video, can be found on newer TVs, high end video editing systems, as well as in high end computer systems. Can be referred to as S/PDIF digital-audio format.

Aspect Ratios

Aspect ratio refers to the ratio of the horizontal to vertical measurements of a television's picture. Mechanically scanned television as first demonstrated by John Logie Baird in 1926 used a 7:3 vertical aspect ratio, oriented for the head and shoulders of a single person in close-up. Most of the early electronic TV systems from the mid-1930s onward shared the same aspect ratio of 4:3 which was chosen to match the Academy Ratio used in cinema films at the time. This ratio was also square enough to be conveniently viewed on round cathode-ray tubes (CRTs), which were all that could be produced given the manufacturing technology of the time. The BBC's television service used a more squarish 5:4 ratio from 1936 to 3 April 1950, when it too switched to a 4:3 ratio.

In the 1950s, movie studios moved towards widescreen aspect ratios such as CinemaScope in an effort to distance their product from television. Although this was initially just a gimmick, widescreen is still the format of choice today and square aspect ratio movies are rare. Some people argue that widescreen is actually a disadvantage when showing objects that are tall instead of panoramic, others say that natural vision is more panoramic than tall, and therefore widescreen is easier on the eye.

The switch to digital television systems has been used as an opportunity to change the standard television picture format from the old ratio of 4:3 (approximately 1.33:1) to an aspect ratio of 16:9 (approximately 1.78:1). This enables TV to get closer to the aspect ratio of modern widescreen movies, which range from 1.78:1 through 1.85:1 to 2.35:1. There are two methods for transporting widescreen content, the better of which uses what is called anamorphic widescreen format. This format is very similar to the technique used to fit a widescreen movie frame inside a 1.33:1 35mm film frame. The image is compressed horizontally when recorded, then expanded again when played back. The anamorphic widescreen 16:9 format was first introduced via European PAL-Plus television broadcasts and then later on "widescreen" DVDs; the ATSC HDTV system uses straight widescreen format, no horizontal compression or expansion is used.

Recently "widescreen" has spread from television to computing where both desktop and laptop computers are commonly equipped with widescreen displays. There are some complaints about distortions of movie picture ratio due to some DVD playback software not taking account of aspect ratios; but this will subside as the DVD playback software matures.

Furthermore, computer and laptop widescreen displays are in the 16:10 aspect ratio both physically in size and in pixel counts, and not in 16:9 of consumer televisions, leading to further complexity. This was a result of widescreen computer display engineers' uninformed assumption that people viewing 16:9 content on their computer would prefer that an area of the screen be reserved for playback controls or subtitles, as opposed to viewing content full-screen.

The television industry's changing of aspect ratios is not without teething difficulties, and can present a considerable problem. Displaying a widescreen aspect (rectangular) image on a conventional aspect (square) display can be shown:

— in "letterbox" format, with black horizontal bars at the top and bottom
— with part of the image being cropped, usually the extreme left and right of the image being cut off (or in "pan and scan", parts selected by an operator)
— with the image horizontally compressed

A conventional aspect (square) image on a widescreen aspect (rectangular) display can be shown:

— in "pillar box" format, with black vertical bars to the left and right
— with upper and lower portions of the image cut off (or in "tilt and scan", parts selected by an operator)
— with the image horizontally distorted

A common compromise is to shoot or create material at an aspect ratio of 14:9, and to lose some image at each side for 4:3 presentation, and some image at top and bottom for 16:9 presentation. In recent years, the cinematographic process known as Super 35 (championed by James Cameron) has been used to film a number of major movies such as Titanic, Legally Blonde, Austin Powers, and Crouching Tiger, Hidden Dragon. This process results in a camera-negative which can then be used to create both wide-screen theatrical prints, and standard "full frame" releases for television/VHS/DVD which avoid the need for either "letterboxing" or the severe loss of information caused by conventional "pan-and-scan" cropping.

Technology Trends

In its infancy, television was an ephemeral medium. Fans of regular shows planned their schedules so that they could be available to watch their shows at their time of broadcast. The term appointment television was coined by marketers to describe this kind of attachment.

The viewership's dependence on schedule lessened with the invention of programmable video recorders, such as the Videocassette recorder and the Digital video recorder. Consumers could watch programs on their own schedule once they were broadcast and recorded. Television service providers also offer video on demand, a set of programs which could be watched at any time. Both mobile phone networks and the internet are capable of carrying video streams. There is already a fair amount of internet TV, while mobile phone TV is planned to become mainstream, if it can be effectively sold, early in 2006.

Digital television (DTV) is a telecommunication system for broadcasting and receiving moving pictures and sound by means of digital signals, in contrast to analog signals in analog (traditional) tv. It uses digital modulation and data digitally compressed which is decoded by specially designed television sets or special by special receivers. Digital television has several advantages over traditional TV, such as superior image and audio quality, smaller channel bandwidth, better reception, and special services such as multicasting (more than one program on the same channel), electronic program guides and interactivity.

All digital TV variants can carry both standard-definition television (SDTV) and high-definition television (HDTV). All early SDTV television standards were analog in nature, and SDTV digital television systems derive much of their structure from the need to be compatible with analog television. In particular, the interlaced scan is a legacy of analog television.

Attempts were made during the development of digital television to prevent a repeat of the fragmentation of the global market into different standards (that is, PAL, SECAM, NTSC). However, once again the world could not agree on a single standard, and hence there are three major standards in existence: the European DVB system and the U.S. ATSC system, plus the Japanese system ISDB. Note: For cable, in addition to ATSC standards, the SCTE standard is used to describe Cable out-of-band metadata.

Most countries in the world have adopted DVB, but several have followed the U.S. in adopting ATSC instead (Canada, Mexico, South Korea). Korea has adopted S-DMB for satellite mobile broadcasting. There could be other specialized high-resolution digital video formats in the future for markets other than home entertainment. Ultra High Definition Video (UHDV) is a format proposed by NHK of Japan that provides a resolution 16 times greater than HDTV.

Bandwidth

In current practice, HDTV uses 1280 × 720 pixels in progressive scan mode (abbreviated 720p) or 1920 × 1080 pixels in interlace mode (1080i). SDTV has less resolution (640 x 480 or 704 × 480 pixels with NTSC, 768 × 576 or 1024 × 576 with PAL in 4:3 and 16:9 aspect ratios respectively), but allows the bandwidth of a DTV channel (or "multiplex") to be subdivided into multiple sub-channels. The TV stations can use subchannels to carry multiple broadcasts of video, audio, or any other data, and can distribute their so-called "bit budget" as necessary, such as dropping one sub-channel down to a lower bitrate in order to make another one available to show higher quality video. Often, this is done automatically, using a statistical multiplexer (or "stat-mux").

In DVB-T, broadcasters can choose from several different modulation schemes, allowing them the option to reduce the transmission bitrate and make reception easier for more distant or mobile viewers.

Today most viewers receive digital television via a set-top box, which decodes the digital signals into signals that analog televisions can understand, but a slowly growing number of TV sets with integrated receivers are already available. Access to channels can be controlled by a removable smart card, for example via the Common Interface (DVB-CI) standard for Europe and via Point Of Deployment (POD) for IS or named differently CableCard. Some signals carry encryption and specify use conditions (such as "may not be recorded" or "may not be viewed on displays larger than 1m in diagonal measure") backed up with the force of law under the WIPO Copyright Treaty and national legislation implementing it, such as the U.S. Digital Millennium Copyright Act.

Characteristics of Television

While radio has sound, television content includes both sound and visuals. This audio visual character of television makes it a magic medium which allows us to watch the world from our drawing rooms.

You might remember how exactly Sachin hit a sixer in a crucial match. For most of us, "seeing is believing". This powerful visual nature helps television to create vivid impressions in our minds which in turn leads to emotional involvement. The audio visual quality also makes television images more memorable.

To watch television, you need not leave your drawing room. No need of going to the movie theatre or buying tickets. You can watch television in the comfort of your home with your family. This is why television is generally regarded as a domestic medium. It provides entertainment and information right inside our homes and has become an integral part of our everyday lives. It can actually pattern our daily activities. The domestic nature of television makes it an intimate medium. This makes the viewers experience a sense of closeness to the anchors of a show or with the characters in a serial.

What will you do if you hear that there is a bomb blast in a neighbouring city? You may switch on your television set for more information. This is because the live nature of television allows it to transmit visuals and information almost instantly. So, another important characteristic of television is that it is capable of being a live medium. The visuals of an earthquake in Indonesia can reach your television set in almost no time. This capacity of the medium makes it ideal for transmitting live visuals of news and sports events. If you are watching a football match in a television channel, you can almost instantly see the goal hit by your favourite team. On the other hand, you can read about the football match only in the next day's newspaper. Television allows you to witness events which happen thousands of miles away.

All of us know that there are a large number of people who cannot read or write. Such people may not be able to read a newspaper, but they can watch television. Any one with a television receiver can access the information shown on television. This makes it an ideal medium to transmit messages to a large audience.

We have gone through the unique characteristics of television. Now let us explore how different television is from other mediums of mass communication like radio, print and new media. Each of these mediums has their own strengths and imitations.

Print medium needs physical distribution of its limited products. If there is too much demand, the newspaper stand can run out of newspapers. Compare this with television. Any one with a television set can have access to it. Too many people tuning in to a particular programme does not affect its availability. On the other hand, we have already learnt that television is a transitory medium. Contrast it with the comparative "permanence" of print. You can easily make cuttings out of your favourite articles from your newspaper.

Television is a better medium for conveying documentary information. The visual content of television news makes it more appealing than radio news. This is because radio cannot outsmart television in providing the experience of physical reality. You can listen to radio while doing your household work. You can listen and drive or shave while hearing the news. However, watching television demands more undivided attention. You can play your radio in the living room and hear it from the kitchen. However, if you try to do the same with television, you are sure to miss most of the action. Many people keep their radios switched on in the background while they go about with their daily activities. This trait of radio has helped it to survive the onslaught of television. Radio stations have realised this advantage and have included more musical content in their programming.

Imagine hearing the commentary of the republic day parade on radio. How different will it be from watching it on television? You will notice that the radio commentary tries to paint the picture of the republic day parade through words. On the other hand, audio content in television is used to support the visuals. This is because television is an audio visual medium, while radio relies solely on audio content. This fundamental difference between the two influences the way in which news or other programmes are presented in the two media.

A television news show can bring the world to our homes. It can tell us about world leaders meeting in Washington, the effects of global warming in Antarctica and about an Indian athlete winning a gold medal in a world championship. We have learnt that television is generally regarded as a domestic medium. New media, on the other hand, is the medium of the individual. It allows you to connect with people around the world with just the click of a mouse. Television allows you to witness events happening around the world. New media empowers you further by allowing you to participate in these events by posting your comments on websites.

If you compare today's newspapers with those before the arrival of television, you will notice that the visual content of today's newspaper is much more. This is because the arrival of television has prompted the print industry to reinvent itself. People were impressed by the magic of the visual content offered by television. Not to be left behind, the print media started providing more photographs and other illustrations.

Every time a new medium emerges, the older media try to adapt to the new challenge. Before the advent of television, more than 60 percent of the print content was fiction based. However, soon television became the preferred source of entertainment for most people. This prompted print to shift more towards non fiction content. Pay attention to the way news is reported in both television and print. You will notice that while television delivers you the latest headlines in no time, the newspaper concentrates more on analysis and provides you with additional background information.

Do you watch audience backed shows? Here, the voters decide the outcome of the show. This is an attempt by television to include an element of interactivity into its content. The arrival of new media has prompted television to change itself to meet the new challenge.

Similarly, news shows and other programmes have started airing viewer's 'sms'. Some news channels allow you to send reports which might have been shot on your camera or mobile phone. This is termed as *'citizen journalism'*. This allows the viewer to participate in the content or programme production. Today, newspapers also try to be participatory in nature. Many major newspapers encourage viewers to send interesting photographs which are published.

When television first came into existence, it was predicted that it will wipe out newspapers. However, we have seen that it is not so. The newspaper reinvented itself to meet the new competitor. Similarly, many predict the death of television in the age of new media.

FUNCTIONS OF TELEVISION

Television can be used:

— to demonstrate processes or physical skills

— to show movement

— for those lacking reading skills

— to make distance learning more personalised

— to make teaching and learning more attractive,and dynamic

However, television has its limitations as an educator. In a class room you can always ask your teacher your doubts. Also, the teacher can repeat a difficult concept. Obviously, a television set cannot do this due to practical constraints. A few limitations of television in the educational field are due to the fact that:

— it is primarily a one-way communication medium

— both production and transmission of programmes are costly

— the production process is very lengthy

Many of us watch television to relax or to be entertained. Thus providing entertainment is one of the major functions of television. As a result serials, films or music based programmes are among the most popular television programmes. Television provides different kinds of programmes for different sections. Your brother might watch a football match while your sister may be more interested in a quiz contest.

Television Channels

Television keeps all types of audiences in mind whether they are children, women, youth, elderly, farmers, industrial workers, students or even illiterates and thus offers a number of channels for everyone.

Television telecasts many such programmes that are audience specific—these are known as special audience programmes like children's programmes, women's programmes, youth programmes and educational/ school telecasts.

Keeping the target audience in mind, these special programmes are planned, fulfilling the desires of specific groups. In case of children's programmes, stories, music, games and general knowledge are available. In women's programmes, tips on cooking, sewing, legal problems etc. are given. In the case of farmers programmes, subjects on agriculture, dairy farming, poultry, cooperative activities etc. are adequately covered.

The youth programme has a separate format which provides for discussion on the problems, desires and requirements of the youth, generally presented by young anchors and for the young audience. Now let us discuss the different categories of television channels available with us.

News Channels

Initially news on television meant a bulletin of half an hour or one hour usually telecast at the prime time comprising the top stories of the day. But today the meaning and definition of news has changed considerably. There are various programmes, various formats and a number of ways in which the news is being broadcast.

News may be defined as something that is new or information about recent events or latest happenings, especially as reported by newspapers, periodicals, radio, or television. But news has today come to mean much more. Just a little over a decade ago, only one television channel used to give us news and current affairs - that is, the sober old Doordarshan.

At present, we have more than half a dozen news channels in Hindi.Some of them are Aaj Tak, Star News, Zee News, NDTV India, Sahara Samay and ETV. There are English news channels which include NDTV 24x7, CNBC-TV18, Times Now and Headlines Today. In addition there are channels in all other major languages, including Tamil, Telugu, Malayalam, Kannada, Marathi, Gujarati, Bengali, Oriya and Urdu.

Sports Channels

Apart from news channels, another important category of television channels are sports channels. Sports channels are television specialty channels that broadcast sporting events like twenty-20 world cup- usually live, and when not broadcasting live events, they offer sports news and other related programmes. There are some channels that focus on only one sport, in particular or one specific region of a country, showing only their local team's games. These channels have greatly improved the availability of sports broadcasts, generating opportunities, such as the option to see every single sport our team plays in any part of the world. The concept of sports channels is also not that old. Earlier, you might even remember that in India many serials were not telecast at their routine timings because the cricket match was to be shown live. Today this is surely not the case. We now have exclusive sports channels which telecast live sports events thereby not hampering the schedule of other popular fiction and entertainment programmes available on other channels.

Cartoon Channels

The most popular category of television channels among kids are the cartoon channels. Cartoon Network India is the most popular cartoon-dedicated television channel in India. It airs English, Tamil and Hindi-dubbed versions of a variety of cartoons, including traditional Cartoon Network programmes featuring Tom and Jerry, Scooby-Doo and Popeye the Sailor. Programmes also include the superhero series including Superman: The Animated Series, Batman: The Animated Series and Justice League Unlimited, Pokémon, Beyblade, Xiaolin Showdown, Digimon, Duel Masters, Transformers: The Unicron Trilogy and the Teenage Mutant Ninja Turtles. Cartooon Network has also aired a few Indian-made cartoons, featuring *'Akbar and Birbal', 'Tenali Raman', 'Sindbad', 'Ramayan', 'Mahabharata' and 'Vikram and Betal'.*

Entertainment and Lifestyle Channels

There are channels dedicated to subjects such as home, garden, kitchen and family. These are called lifestyle channels and they offer a variety of programmes catering to various lifestyle conditions and patterns. Stylised anchors, well decorated and lit up sets, mesmerising locations and a cool attitude is how these channels can be best described. To know what your favourite celebrity likes or dislikes, you may watch the lifestyle channel. Zoom and Discovery's Travel and Living are some of the lifestyle channels.

Science and Discovery related channels

Just like sports channels offer a variety of programmes related to sports, science channels feature only science-related television shows. Each day has specialised blocks that cover certain topics such as weather, technology and space. If you want to lean about dinosaurs, snakes, tigers, waterfalls, nature, scientific inventions and discoveries, science channels like National Geographic and Discovery are a must for you.

Types of Television Programmes

Now we all know that there are different categories of television channels. Depending upon our mood, interests and other requirements, we select and watch the channels. Various programmes that are offered on these channels serve different purposes. Some programmes are used to inform the people, some to entertain the masses and others to educate the community. Time and again it has been proved that the television has provoked and persuaded the common people. Many of us have an emotional involvement with this medium.

Providing information, entertainment and education is the basic objective of television. Our priority changes from time to time and so does the channel that we select at a given moment. With time, new words like 'infotainment' and 'edutainment' have crept in, but in both the cases entertainment is common and that is what has become the main role of television.

Informative Programmes

Programmes whose main aim is to provide information to its viewers are termed as informative programmes. Different types of informative programmes are:

- *News and current affairs programmes:* For eg. News bulletins, news commentaries—direct coverage of proceedings of important events, news based interviews and panel discussions.
- *Sports programmes*: For eg. Cricket matches, sports diaries, sports commentary.
- *Cookery shows, food related programmes* eg. Cook it up with Tarla Dalal, Khana Khazana, Mirch Masala.
- *Programmes imparting information related to contemporary environmental issues*, scientific and technological inventions and discoveries and economic policies like *Surabhi, Bharat ek Khoj.*

Entertainment Programmes

Apart from programmes that provide us with information, there are a number of programmes on television that entertain us. These programmes are known as entertainment programmes. Examples of entertainment programmes are:

- Serials, soap operas, dramas and plays like: Junoon, Ghar ek Mandir, Kyunki saas bhi kabhi bahu thi, Banu mein teri dulhan.
- Comedy shows like laughter challenge, comedy circus.
- Musical programmes: Light music programmes, classical music programmes like Ghazal Goshthi
- Game shows like Master Card Family Fortune
- Chat shows like Koffee with Karan, Oye, its Friday!, Jeena isi ka naam hai.
- Cartoons like Tom and Jerry
- Fairy tales/ fantasy based programmes like Alladin ka Chirag
- Horror shows like Aahat
- Reality television shows like Indian Idol, Sa Re Ga Ma Pa and Voice of India.

Educational Programmes

Do you know that television can be an excellent teacher as well. It can act as an effective tool of distance education. *Gyandarshan* is the well-known educational channel of Doordarshan. Programmes telecast through this channel is a perfect example of educational programmes. Programmes that come under this category are:

— Open university and distance learning programmes (UGC and IGNOU)
— Social and development programmes: Health and science, fitness and hygiene, agriculture and rural development programmes, public service telecasts, literacy campaigns, family planning and welfare.
— Culture and gender studies programmes : Programmes related to literature, arts, theatre, cultural heritage and gender sensitisation.

Formats of Television Programmes

Man needs variety in his life, whether in taking food, getting dressed, making friends or even selecting entertainment. Here in television also we go by the saying 'variety is the spice of life'.

Many times while watching television you must have thought that some programmes are a work of the director's imagination while others appear to be real life experiences. This is very true because on one hand we have programmes which are based on imagination and on the other hand, we have programmes that are based on real incidents and events. Thus, we have two broad formats of television programmes which we shall discuss here.

— Fiction Programmes
— Non Fiction Programmes

Fiction Programmes

Almost all the fiction programmes that depend on imagination and dramatisation are meant for entertaining the audiences. Drama/ soap operas like *Humlog, Ghar ek Mandir, Kyunki saas bhi kbahi bahu thi* are ongoing, episodic works of fiction.

Interestingly, many film-based programmes with a mixture of fiction and song/ segments of film clippings etc are also available these days on television which blend various formats into one.

Non-fiction Programmes

Apart from different serials and other entertaining works of fiction, you must have watched programmes on television that provide a lot of information regarding various events that take place in our surroundings and also impart education on contemporary issues. Let us now discuss the various non-fiction programmes available on television.

News Bulletins: News bulletins essentially present a summary of news stories in their order of importance and interest. National and international happenings get the pride of place, while regional and local news are read out if time permits. Human interest stories and sports news generally round off the major bulletins. News bulletins in English, Hindi and various regional languages are presented on Doordarshan.

But with the advent of 24-hour news channels, half an hour bulletins are no longer popular. Rather the news has taken the 24X7 format where it is presented almost instantly as and when events occur.

Game/Quiz Show: You may have seen Derek O Brien presenting the most popular quiz programme, called Bournvita Quiz Contest (BQC) telecast every Sunday afternoon. Beginning with the Bournvita jingles, the programme gets off the ground quickly and moves at a hectic pace, taking the audience along with it.. It's the sense of participation and involvement in the quiz questions that makes the quiz programme an enjoyable family fare.

Talks and Discussion Programmes: There are many issues which are of importance and concern to us happening in our society. Reporting them through news alone is not enough. Several factors and viewpoints of experts help us to gain an insight into these issues. Talks and discussion programmes about topical issues are thus a very important format of television programming. Most of these shows feature a regular host, who interviews guest spakers. Typically, it includes an element of audience participation, usually by broadcasting conversations with listeners who have placed telephone calls to speak with the programme's host or guest. Generally, the shows are organised into segments which are separated by a break for advertisements.

Programme Production

While watching television, as viewers, we are largely unaware of the production complexities. But professional television production, regardless of whether it is done in a television studio or in the field is a complex creative process in which many people and machines interact to bring a variety of messages and information to a large audience.

Programme Production Stages

Let us consider a situation in which you are expecting some guests for dinner.

What preparations will you do? First of all, you need to decide the menu. Then you will arrange for all the vegetables and such other ingredients required for the preparation of food items. You may have to go to the market for buying the ingredients. Now after arranging for everything, you will start preparing the food. This again involves all the key ingredients to be mixed at the right time in the right quantity. Once the food is prepared, comes the presentation stage wherein you will put the various items prepared in different utensils and after garnishing, they will be ready to be served on the dining table.

So you have seen that there were three stages in the making of various food items. In stage one, you arranged for everything required for preparing the food items. In stage two, you actually prepared the food items and in the third stage, you presented them on the dining table.

Now imagine you have to produce a television programme. In a similar manner as above, you will first arrange everything required for the programme production. In the second stage you will actually carry on the production process, and thirdly you will polish the product for the final presentation on television. Thus, we can divide the entire production process into three major stages.

There are three stages of programme production

1. Pre production
2. Production
3. Post production

Pre-Production

This stage includes everything you do before entering the studio or reaching the shooting location. It involves idea generation, research, scripting, discussions with all the crew members and talents (actors), arranging equipment, video / audio tapes, properties, costumes, sets designing or location hunting and booking of editing shifts.

The first thing to know about any and every production is what you want the programme to look like, just like you need to know what you want to cook. This is the pre production stage. You need a clear idea of what you want to make. Only then will you be able to make a good programme, understandable by the audience. Once the idea is clear, the next stage is how to get from the idea to the television image. To translate an idea on screen effectively you need a good and detailed script.

In all it involves planning everything in advance. This is very essential to get desired results. If you have all the raw ingredients ready in your kitchen, you can easily cook the food. Similarly, if you have worked well in this stage of programme production, the other two stages become easy and workable.

Production

This is the stage when you are on the studio floor or on location and are ready to shoot or are actually shooting. It includes managing all the facilities, handling of talent and crew members, controlling the crowd, shooting without hurdles and solving any problem related on the spot at that time.

Post-Production

This is the third stage of programme production. It is the stage when you get the final shape of the programme, just like the way you garnished every food item to be presented on the dining table. It includes cutting the recorded visuals into appropriate length, arranging the visuals in a proper sequence, use of desired effects for the visuals or text/captions, commentary recording, music/song recording, and final assembly of the entire programme.

Television Production Process

We all know that in order to make a food item we need different materials like vegetables, utensils, knives, spoons, spices, water, oil etc. Similarly, in order to make a television programme we need various equipments and people required to operate them for the production of a specific kind of programme. Let us now discuss the equipments required for the production process.

Machinery and Equipment required for Production

Imagine you had to paint something on a canvas. Essentially, you will need a brush, colours and a palette. Similarly, if you want to make a good programme on television, you need some essential equipment like camera, lights, sound recorder etc. We can categorise the basic production elements as follows:

Camera

The most basic equipment in any and every production is the camera. In our lives also, many of us or our friends must have used the camera for capturing various events. If you carefully look at any camera, you will see a lens in it. This lens selects a part of the visible environment and produces a small optical image. The camera is principally designed to convert the optical image, as projected by the lens, into an electrical signal, often called the video signal.

Lights

Lighting any object or individual has three main purposes:

1. To provide the television camera with adequate illumination for technically acceptable pictures.
2. To show the viewers what the objects shown on screen actually look like, say, for instance, if there was no light in the room, we would not have been able to see how the chair, table or anything else for that matter would look like. Lights also help us know when the event is taking place, in terms of the season and the time of the day.
3. To establish the general mood of the event.

Microphone

Just as you have learnt that the camera converts what it sees into electrical signals, similarly the microphone converts sound waves into electrical energy or the audio signals. But the sounds that we produce are very feeble in nature and, therefore, cannot be sent to larger distances. Therefore it is amplified and sent to the loudspeaker which reconverts them into audible sound.

There are different types of microphones available for different purposes. Picking up a news anchor's voice, capturing the sounds of a tennis match, and recording a rock concert - all these require different types of microphones or a set of microphones.

Sound Recorder

Television sound/audio not only communicates infor-mation, but also contributes greatly to the mood and atmosphere of the visuals that come along with the audio on screen. The sound recorder essentially records the sound picked up by the microphone. With a sound recorder, you can:

1. select a specific microphone or other sound input
2. amplify a weak signal from a microphone or other audio source for further processing
3. Control the volume and ensure the quality of sound
4. mix or combine two or more incoming sound sources

Videotape Recorder

As we all know that television is an audio-visual medium, we need to record both audio and visual components. While the sound i.e. audio is recorded on sound recorders, visuals are recorded on video tape in a videotape recorder. Most of the television programmes that we see are recorded on videotape or computer disk before they are actually telecast.

Post-production editing Machine

Before we present any food item on the dining table, we need to garnish it. Likewise in television programmes also, before we actually telecast a programme on television, we need to do the post production. In the post production stage, you select from the recorded material, those visuals which seem to be most relevant and copy them onto another videotape in a specific order. This is called editing.

The post production editing equipment/machine helps to edit the programme after it is recorded. While many of the elaborate editing systems may help you to obtain the desired results, most of them cannot make the creative decisions for you. It is therefore important for you to know the desired result and shoot accordingly. Again, the better the pre production and production stages of the programme are, the more easier becomes the post production stage.

Professionals involved in Television Production

You know that your mother can cook tasty food and that too alone. Your sister can also do the same thing without any help. But in television programme production, this is not the case. Television production is a team effort. The team consists of creative talent as core members and there are other support staff also. The members may be required to perform more than one role and that depends on the type of organisation or a production house, and the type and scale of the production. Regardless of the specific job functions of the various members, they all have to interact as a team. Just like you know in every sport, say like cricket, each member of the team is very important; similarly in television production also, every member plays a crucial role. Television production is a team effort. Let us now discuss the key roles that the team members in a television production need to play.

Producer

In television programme production, the head of the production who is called a producer is in charge of the entire production. The producer manages the budget and coordinates with the advertising agencies, actors and writers. The producer is also responsible for all the people working on the production front and for coordinating technical and non technical production elements.

Director

In a television production, the Director is in-charge of directing the actors and technical operations. The Director is ultimately responsible for transforming a script into effective audio and video messages. Where the camera will be placed, what type of visuals need to be taken, where the actors will stand, all these are controlled by the director.

Production Assistant

The Production Assistant facilitates all that is required for the smooth execution of the television production. Both the producer and director are assisted by the production assistant.

Script Writer

One of the basic requirements of television production is the script. The script gives all the details of the programme such as the dialogues, the list of actors, details of the costumes, the mood required to be created for each scene and their respective locations. A script writer is the person who writes the script for the programme. In smaller productions, this task is generally done by the director and script writers are hired, if required.

Actors

Actors are the personnel who perform different roles according to the require-ment of the script.

Anchor

An anchor is a person who presents a programme formally on television. For example, news anchors present news on television while there are also anchors who present reality shows like Sa re Ga Ma Pa and Indian Idol.

Cameraperson

Camerapersons operate the cameras. They often do the lighting also for smaller productions. They are also called videographers.

Sound Recordist

A Sound recordist records the complete sound track of the programme. The sound recordist is also responsible for background music involved throughout the programme.

Art Director

The Art Director is the incharge of the creative design aspects, which includes set design, location and graphics of the show.

Property Manager

The property manager maintains and manages the use of various set and properties. It is found in large productions only, otherwise the props are managed by the floor manager only.

Floor Manager

A Floor Manager is in charge of all the activities on the studio floor. He coordi-nates talents, conveys the director's instructions and supervises floor personnel. He is also called floor director or stage manager.

Costume Designer

The costume designer designs and sometimes even constructs various costumes for dramas, dance numbers and children's shows.

Studio and Outdoor Recording

You may have noticed that the programmes which you see on television are either shot inside the rooms i.e. closed areas, or are shot in open spaces, or as we call outdoor areas. Thus, the recording of all the programmes that we see on television can be done in broadly two ways, either inside the studio or an outdoor location.

The recording done essentially within the four walls of the studio for the production of television programmes is known as *studio recording.* Whereas, any recording that involves shooting outside the studio is known as *outdoor recording.*

The success of a live programme entirely depends upon the performance of the talents and the crew members involved. Recorded programmes have a better chance for success as there is scope to go for retakes to get desired visuals with greater satisfaction. But on the other hand, live programmes can be made speedily. Live programmes generate a lot of excitement in the minds of viewers.

Recorded programmes have a better chance of marketing as such programmes can be polished and edited later, but they generally lack the excitement of live programmes. No matter what the programme format may be, live or recorded, the pre-production research and paper work is a must in television programme production.

Television: Impact on Society

We have seen that television is an immensely popular medium of mass communication. It is very much integrated into our daily lives and has the power to influence our outlooks. This influence can have both positive and negative results.. On the positive front, television can be an excellent teacher. Wouldn't your younger sister get thrilled if a cartoon show teaches her mathematics? Television can also be used as an excellent medium for mass education as in the SITE experiment. Identify one programme in your favorite channel which can have a positive impact on society.

Television can also open up new horizons for us. Sitting in your living room, you can access information about what is happening in a distant country like Iraq by just a click of the remote. Television can also be used to create awareness about various issues like environmental pollution and global warming. Can you recall any programme or public service advertisement which has increased your awareness about the need to conserve our environment? Television can also provide entertainment and can be used as a tool for relaxation.

Television viewing has also been linked with the creation of stereotypes. Watch some of the women based serials and observe where maximum time is spent by the heroine. You are most likely to find her spending most of the time inside a house. Here the stereotype that women are supposed to spend most of the time at home is subtly re-enforced. You would have come across the portrayal of a "madrasi" in Hindi comedy shows. This depiction may not have any real relation to a South Indian.

Television content can be delivered in a variety of ways. It can be distributed through terrestrial transmission. In this system, an antenna connected to the television viewer is used to receive the signals telecast by the broadcaster's transmitter. This is the traditional method of television broadcast. Other methods of delivery include distribution through cable networks and direct broadcast satellite.

The cable distribution in India can be seen as a chain which begins with the signal sent by the broadcaster to the cable operator. The cable operators then relay these signals to our homes. There are free to air channels and pay channels. For the free to air channels, the broadcaster does not charge the cable operator. Examples of free to air channels include Aaj Tak, Sahara and Times Now. Pay channels like Sony and Star Plus charge a certain amount of money per subscriber per month.

Television has invented its own ways to meet the challenges put forward by internet. Audience backed shows where the audience decides the winner is an example. Ask your mother if there were any such programmes on Indian television 15 years back. The answer will be 'no'. This is because new media is a recent addition to the media scene and television had no such challenges in the past. Reality television is another new trend. Thus, in this age of internet, television has been constantly reinventing itself as a medium. The new delivery platforms are steps in that direction. One of the disadvantages of television as a medium is delayed feed back. On the other hand, internet is all about interactivity. So to cope up with this, television has began to package its content as well as delivery in an interactive manner.

The social aspects of television are influences this medium has had on society since its inception. The belief that this impact has been dramatic has been largely unchallenged in media theory since its inception. However, there is much dispute as to what those effects are, how serious the ramifications are and if these effects are more or less evolutionary with human communication.

Positive Effects

Current research is discovering that individuals suffering from social isolation can employ television to create what is termed a parasocial or faux relationship with characters from their favorite television shows and movies as a way of deflecting feelings of loneliness and social deprivation. Just as an individual would spend time with a real person sharing opinions and thoughts, pseudo-relationships are formed with TV characters by becoming personally invested in their lives as if they were a close friend so that the individual can satiate the human desire to form meaningful relationships and establish themselves in society. Jaye Derrick and Shira Gabriel of the University of Buffalo, and Kurt Hugenberg of Miami University found that when an individual is not able to participate in interactions with real people, they are less likely to indicate feelings of loneliness when watching their favorite TV show.

They refer to this finding as the Social Surrogacy Hypothesis. Furthermore, when an event such as a fight or argument disrupts a personal relationship, watching a favorite TV show was able to create a cushion and prevent the individual from experiencing reduced self-esteem and feelings of inadequacy that can often accompany the perceived threat. By providing a temporary substitute for acceptance and belonging that is experienced through social relationships TV is helping to relieve feelings of depression and loneliness when those relationships are not available. This benefit is considered a positive consequence of watching television as it can counteract the psychological damage that is caused by isolation from social relationships.

Several studies have found that educational television has many advantages. The Media Awareness Network, explains in its article, The Good Things about Television, that television can be a very powerful and effective learning tool for children if used wisely. The article states that television can help young people discover where they fit into society, develop closer relationships with peers and family, and teach them to understand complex social aspects of communication. Dimitri Christakis cites studies in which those who watched "Sesame Street" and other educational programs as preschoolers had higher grades, were reading more books, placed more value on achievement and were more creative. Similarly, while those exposed to negative role models suffered, those exposed to positive models behaved better.

Negative Effects

There are many pejorative terms for television, including "boob tube" and "chewing gum for the mind", showing the disdain held by many people for this medium. Newton N. Minow spoke of the "vast wasteland" that was the television programming of the day in his 1961 speech.

Complaints about the social influence of television have been heard from the U.S. justice system as investigators and prosecutors decry what they refer to as "the CSI Syndrome." They complain that, because of the popularity and considerable viewership of CSI and its spin-offs, juries today expect to be "dazzled," and will acquit criminals of charges unless presented with impressive physical evidence, even when motive, testimony, and lack of alibi are presented by the prosecution.

Television has also been credited with changing the norms of social propriety, although the direction and value of this change are disputed. Milton Shulman, writing about television in the 1960s, wrote that "TV cartoons showed cows without udders and not even a pause was pregnant," and noted that on-air vulgarity was highly frowned upon. Shulman suggested that, even by the 1970s, television was shaping the ideas of propriety and appropriateness in the countries the medium blanketed. He asserted that, as a particularly "pervasive and ubiquitous" medium, television could create a comfortable familiarity with and acceptance of language and behavior once deemed socially unacceptable. Television, as well as influencing its viewers, evoked an imitative response from other competing media as they struggle to keep pace and retain viewer- or readership.

According to a study published in 2008, conducted by John Robinson and Steven Martin from the University of Maryland, people who are not satisfied with their lives spend 30% more time watching TV than satisfied people do. The research was conducted with 30,000 people during the period between 1975 and 2006. This contrasted with a previous study, which indicated that watching TV was the happiest time of the day for some people. Based on his study, Robinson commented that the pleasurable effects of television may be likened to an addictive activity, producing "momentary pleasure but long-term misery and regret."

Psychological Effects

There is a theory that when a person plays video games or watches TV, the basal ganglia portion of the brain becomes very active and dopamine is released. Some scientists believe that release of high amounts of dopamine reduces the amount of the neurotransmitter available for control of movement, perception of pain and pleasure and formation of feelings, although this remains a controversial conclusion. A study conducted by Herbert Krugman found that while viewers are watching television the right side of the brain is twice as active as the left which causes a state of hypnosis.

Physical Effects

Studies in both children and adults have found an association between the number of hours of television watched and obesity. A study found that watching television decreases the metabolic rate in children to below that found in children at rest. Author John Steinbeck describes television watchers:

> "I have observed the physical symptoms of television-looking on children as well as on adults. The mouth grows slack and the lips hang open; the eyes take on a hypnotized or doped look; the nose runs rather more than usual; the backbone turns to water and the fingers slowly and methodically pick the designs out of brocade furniture. Such is the appearance of semiconsciousness that one wonders how much of the 'message' of television is getting through to the brain."

The American Academy of Pediatrics (AAP) recommends that children under two years of age should not watch any television and children two and older should watch one to two hours at most. Children who watch more than four hours of television a day are more likely to become overweight.

TV watching and other sedentary activities are associated with greater risk of heart attack.

Alleged Dangers

Legislators, scientists and parents are debating the effects of television violence on viewers, particularly youth. Fifty years of research on the impact of television on children's emotional and social development have not ended this debate.

Some scholars have claimed that the evidence clearly supports a causal relationship between media violence and societal violence. However other authors note significant methodological problems with the literature and mismatch between increasing media violence and decreasing crime rates in the United States.

A 2002 article in Scientific American suggested that compulsive television watching, television addiction, was no different from any other addiction, a finding backed up by reports of withdrawal symptoms among families forced by circumstance to cease watching. However this view has not yet received widespread acceptance among all scholars, and "television addiction" is not a diagnoseable condition according to the Diagnostic and Statistical Manual -IV -TR.

A longitudinal study in New Zealand involving 1000 people (from childhood to 26 years of age) demonstrated that "television viewing in childhood and adolescence is associated with poor educational achievement by 12 years of age". The same paper noted that there was a significant negative association between time spent watching television per day as a child and educational attainment by age 26: the more time a child spent watching television at ages 5 to 15, the less likely they were to have a university degree by age 26. However recent research (Schmidt et al., 2009) has indicated that, once other factors are controlled for, television viewing appears to have little to no impact on cognitive performance, contrary to previous thought. However this study was limited to cognitive performance in childhood. Numerous studies have also examined the relationship between TV viewing and school grades.

A study published in the Journal of Sexuality Research and Social Policy concluded that parental television involvement was associated with greater body satisfaction among adolescent girls, less sexual experience amongst both male and female adolescents, and that parental television involvement may influence self-esteem and body image, in part by increasing parent-child closeness. However a more recent article by Christopher Ferguson, Benjamin Winegard, and Bo Winegard cautioned that the literature on media and body dissatisfaction is weaker and less consistent than often claimed and that media effects have been overemphasized. Similarly recent work by Laurence Steinbrerg and Kathryn Monahan has found that, using propensity score matching to control for other variables, television viewing of sexual media had no impact on teen sexual behavior in a longitudinal analysis.

Many studies have found little or no effect of television viewing on viewers (see Freedman, 2002). For example a recent long-term outcome study of youth found no long-term relationship between watching violent television and youth violence or bullying

On July 26, 2000 the American Academy of Pediatrics, the American Medical Association, the American Psychological Association, the American Academy of Family Physicians, and the American Academy of Child and Adolescent Psychiatry stated that "prolonged viewing of media violence can lead to emotional desensitization toward violence in real life." However, scholars have since analyzed several statements in this release, both about the number of studies conducted, and a comparison with medical effects, and found many errors.

Propaganda

Television is used to promote commercial, social and political agendas. Use of public service announcements (including those paid for by governing bodies or politicians), news and current affairs, television advertisement, advertorials and talk shows are used to influence public opinion. The Cultivation Hypothesis suggests that some viewers may begin to repeat questionable or even blatantly fictitious information gleaned from the media as if it were factual. Considerable debate remains, however, whether the Cultivation Hypothesis is well supported by scientific literature, however, the effectiveness of television for propaganda (including commercial advertising) is unsurpassed. The US military and State Department often turn to media to broadcast into hostile territory or nation.

Politics

While the effects of television programs depend on what is actually consumed, Neil Postman argues that the dominance of entertaining, but not informative programming, creates a politically ignorant society, undermining democracy: "Americans are the best entertained and quite likely the least-informed people in the Western world." However some broadcasters do offer Americans intelligent political narrative and argument. This offers otherwise ignorant viewers, who may not read about politics elsewhere, the opportunity to access current or historical political views, for example.

Gender and Television

While women, who were "traditionally more isolated than men" were given equal opportunity to consume shows about more "manly" endeavors, men's feminine sides are tapped by the emotional nature of many television programs.

Television played a significant role in the feminist movement. Although most of the women portrayed on television conformed to stereotypes, television also showed the lives of men as well as news and current affairs. These "other lives" portrayed on television left many women unsatisfied with their current socialization.

The representation of males and females on the television screen has been a subject of much discussion since the television became commercially available in the late 1930s. In 1964 Betty Friedan claimed that "television has represented the American Woman as a "stupid, unattractive, insecure little household drudge who spends her martyred mindless, boring days dreaming of love—and plotting nasty revenge against her husband." As women started to revolt and protest to become equals in society in the 1960s and 1970s, their portrayal on the television was an issue that they addressed.

Journalist Susan Faludi suggested, "The practices and programming of network television in the 1980s were an attempt to get back to those earlier stereotypes of women." Through television, even the most homebound women can experience parts of our culture once considered primarily male, such as sports, war, business, medicine, law, and politics. For the last since at least the 1990s there has been a trend of showing males as insufferable and possibly spineless fools (e.g. Homer Simpson, Ray Burone).

The inherent intimacy of television makes it one of the few public arenas in our society where men routinely wear makeup and are judged as much on their personal appearance and their "style" as on their "accomplishments."

References

Alan Taylor, *We, the Media: Pedagogic Intrusions into US Mainstream Film and Television News Broadcasting Rhetoric*, Peter Lang, 2005.

Albert Abramson, *The History of Television, 1942 to 2000*, Jefferson, NC, and London, McFarland, 2003.

Jacques Derrida and Bernard Stiegler, *Echographies of Television*, Polity Press, 2002.

David E. Fisher and Marshall J. Fisher, *Tube: the Invention of Television*, Counterpoint, Washington, DC, 1996.

Jerry Mander, *Four Arguments for the Elimination of Television*, Perennial, 1978.

Evan I. Schwartz, *The Last Lone Inventor: A Tale of Genius, Deceit, and the Birth of Television*, New York, Harper Paperbacks, 2003.

Beretta E. Smith-Shomade, *Shaded Lives: African-American Women and Television*, Rutgers University Press, 2002.

7

Digital Television Services

Digital television (DTV) is the transmission of audio and video by digitally processed and multiplexed signal, in contrast to the totally analog and channel separated signals used by analog TV. It is an innovative service that represents a significant evolution in television technology since color television in the 1950s. Many countries are replacing broadcast analog television with digital television to allow other uses of the television radio spectrum. Several regions of the world are in different stages of adaptation and are implementing different broadcasting standards. There are four different digital television terrestrial broadcasting standards (DTTB) and they are: Advanced Television System Committee (ATSC) uses eight-level vestigial sideband (8 VSB) for terrestrial broadcasting. This standard has been adopted in the United States and in other countries. Digital Video Broadcasting-Terrestrial (DVB-T) uses coded orthogonal frequency-division multiplexing (C-OFDM) modulation and supports hierarchical transmission. This standard has been adapted in Europe and Australia. Terrestrial Integrated Services Digital Broadcasting (ISDB-T) is a system designed to provide good reception to fix receivers and also portable or mobile receivers. It utilizes OFDM and two-dimensional interleaving. It supports hierarchical transmission of up to three layers and uses MPEG-2 video and advanced audio coding. This standard has been adopted in Japan and most of South America. Digital Terrestrial Multimedia Broadcasting (DTMB) adopts time-domain synchronous(TDS)- OFDM technology utilizing a pseudo random signal frame to serve as the guard interval (GI) of the OFDM block and the training symbol.

Technical Aspects of DTV

Formats and Bandwidth

Digital television supports many different picture formats defined by the broadcast television systems which are a combination of size, aspect ratio (width to height ratio).

With digital terrestrial television (DTV) broadcasting, the range of formats can be broadly divided into two categories: high definition television (HDTV) for the transmission of high-definition video and standard-definition television (SDTV). These terms by themselves are not very precise, and many subtle intermediate cases exist.

One of several different HDTV formats that can be transmitted over DTV is: 1280 × 720 pixels in progressive scan mode (abbreviated 720p) or 1920 × 1080 pixels in interlaced video mode (1080i). Each of these utilizes a 16:9 aspect ratio. (Some televisions are capable of receiving an HD resolution of 1920 × 1080 at a 60 Hz progressive scan frame rate — known as 1080p.) HDTV cannot be transmitted over current analog television channels because of channel capacity issues.

Standard definition TV (SDTV), by comparison, may use one of several different formats taking the form of various aspect ratios depending on the technology used in the country of broadcast. For 4:3 aspect-ratio broadcasts, the 640 × 480 format is used in NTSC countries, while 720 × 576 is used in PAL countries. For 16:9 broadcasts, the 720 × 480 format is used in NTSC countries, while 720 × 576 is used in PAL countries. However, broadcasters may choose to reduce these resolutions to save bandwidth (e.g., many DVB-T channels in the United Kingdom use a horizontal resolution of 544 or 704 pixels per line).

Each commercial broadcasting terrestrial television DTV channel in North America is permitted to be broadcast at a bit rate up to 19 megabits per second. However, the broadcaster does not need to use this entire bandwidth for just one broadcast channel. Instead the broadcast can use the channel to include PSIP and can also subdivide across several video subchannels (aka feeds) of varying quality and compression rates, including non-video datacasting services that allow one-way high-bandwidth streaming of data to computers like National Datacast.

A broadcaster may opt to use a standard-definition (SDTV) digital signal instead of an HDTV signal, because current convention allows the bandwidth of a DTV channel (or "multiplex") to be subdivided into multiple digital subchannels, (similar to what most FM radio stations offer with HD Radio), providing multiple feeds of entirely different television programming on the same channel. This ability to provide either a single HDTV feed or multiple lower-resolution feeds is often referred to as distributing one's "bit budget" or multicasting. This can sometimes be arranged automatically, using a statistical multiplexer (or "stat-mux"). With some implementations, image resolution may be less directly limited by bandwidth; for example in DVB-T, broadcasters can choose from several different modulation schemes, giving them the option to reduce the transmission bitrate and make reception easier for more distant or mobile viewers.

Reception

There are a number of different ways to receive digital television. One of the oldest means of receiving DTV (and TV in general) is using an antenna (known as an aerial in some countries). This way is known as Digital terrestrial television (DTT). With DTT, viewers are limited to whatever channels the antenna picks up. Signal quality will also vary.

Other ways have been devised to receive digital television. Among the most familiar to people are digital cable and digital satellite. In some countries where transmissions of TV signals are normally achieved by microwaves, digital MMDS is used. Other standards, such as Digital multimedia broadcasting (DMB) and DVB-H, have been devised to allow handheld devices such as mobile phones to receive TV signals. Another way is IPTV, that is receiving TV via Internet Protocol, relying on Digital Subscriber Line (DSL) or optical cable line. Finally, an alternative way is to receive digital TV signals via the open Internet. For example, there is P2P (peer-to-peer) Internet television software that can be used to watch TV on a computer.

Some signals carry encryption and specify use conditions (such as "may not be recorded" or "may not be viewed on displays larger than 1 m in diagonal measure") backed up with the force of law under the WIPO Copyright Treaty and national legislation implementing it, such as the U.S. Digital Millennium Copyright Act. Access to encrypted channels can be controlled by a removable smart card, for example via the Common Interface

(DVB-CI) standard for Europe and via Point Of Deployment (POD) for IS or named differently CableCard.

Protection Parameters for Terrestrial DTV Broadcasting

Digital television signals must not interfere with each other, and they must also coexist with analog television until it is phased out.

Digital TV is more tolerant of interference than analog TV, and this is the reason a smaller range of channels can carry an all-digital set of television stations.

Interaction

Interaction happens between the TV watcher and the DTV system. It can be understood in different ways, depending on which part of the DTV system is concerned. It can also be an interaction with the STB only (to tune to another TV channel or to browse the EPG).

Modern DTV systems are able to provide interaction between the end-user and the broadcaster through the use of a return path. With the exceptions of coaxial and fiber optic cable, which can be bidirectional, a dialup modem, Internet connection, or other method is typically used for the return path with unidirectional networks such as satellite or antenna broadcast.

In addition to not needing a separate return path, cable also has the advantage of a communication channel localized to a neighborhood rather than a city (terrestrial) or an even larger area (satellite). This provides enough customizable bandwidth to allow true video on demand.

1-segment broadcasting

1seg (1-segment) is a special form of ISDB. Each channel is further divided into 13 segments. The 12 segments of them are allocated for HDTV and remaining segment, the 13th, is used for narrowband receivers such as mobile television or cell phone.

Comparison Analog vs Digital

DTV has several advantages over analog TV, the most significant being that digital channels take up less bandwidth, and the bandwidth needs are continuously variable, at a corresponding reduction in image quality depending on the level of compression as well as the resolution of the transmitted image. This means that digital broadcasters can provide more digital channels in the same space, provide high-definition television service, or provide other non-television services such as multimedia or interactivity. DTV also permits special services such as multiplexing (more than one program on the same channel), electronic program guides and additional languages (spoken or subtitled). The sale of non-television services may provide an additional revenue source.

Digital and analog signals react differently to interference. For example, common problems with analog television include ghosting of images, noise from weak signals, and many other potential problems which degrade the quality of the image and sound, although the program material may still be watchable.

With digital television, the audio and video must be synchronized digitally, so reception of the digital signal must be very nearly complete; otherwise, neither audio nor video will be usable. Short of this complete failure, “blocky” video is seen when the digital signal experiences interference.

Effect on Existing Analog Technology

Television sets with only analog tuners cannot decode digital transmissions. When analog broadcasting over the air ceases, users of sets with analog-only tuners may use other sources of programming (e.g. cable, recorders) or may purchase set-top converter boxes to tune in the digital signals. In the United States, a government-sponsored coupon was available to offset the cost of an external converter box.

Analog switch-off (of full-power stations) took place on June 12, 2009 in the United States, July 24, 2011 in Japan, August 31, 2011 in Canada, February 13, 2012 in Pan-Arab States, and is scheduled for October 24, 2012 in the United Kingdom and Ireland,by October 31, 2012 in India (select cities only), by December 31, 2013 in Australia, by 2015 in the Philippines and Uruguay and by 2017 in Costa Rica.

Disappearance of TV-audio Receivers

Prior to the conversion to digital TV, analog television broadcast audio for TV channels on a separate FM carrier frequency from the video signal. This FM audio signal could be heard using standard radios equipped with the appropriate tuning circuits.

However, after the relatively recent transition of many countries to digital TV, no portable radio manufacturer has yet developed an alternative method for portable radios to play just the audio signal of digital TV channels. (DTV radio is not the same thing.)

Environmental issues

The adoption of a broadcast standard incompatible with existing analog receivers has created the problem of large numbers of analog receivers being discarded during digital television transition. An estimated 99 million unused analog TV receivers are currently in storage in the US alone and, while some obsolete receivers are being retrofitted with converters, many more are simply dumped in landfills where they represent a source of toxic metals such as lead as well as lesser amounts of materials such as barium, cadmium and chromium.

While the glass in cathode ray tubes contains an average of 3.62 kilograms (8.0 lb) of lead[unreliable source?] (amount varies from 1.08 lb to 11.28 lb, depending on screen size but the lead is "stable and immobile") which can have long-term negative effects on the environment if dumped as landfill, the glass envelope can be recycled at suitably equipped facilities. Other portions of the receiver may be subject to disposal as hazardous material.

Local restrictions on disposal of these materials vary widely; in some cases second-hand stores have refused to accept working color television receivers for resale due to the increasing costs of disposing of unsold TVs. Those thrift stores which are still accepting donated TVs have reported significant increases in good-condition working used television receivers abandoned by viewers who often expect them not to work after digital transition.In Michigan, one recycler has estimated that as many as one household in four will dispose of or recycle a TV set in the next year. The digital television transition, migration to high-definition television receivers and the replacement of CRTs with flatscreens are all factors in the increasing number of discarded analog CRT-based television receivers.

Technical Limitations

Compression artifacts and allocated bandwidth

DTV images have some picture defects that are not present on analog television or motion picture cinema, because of present-day limitations of bandwidth and compression algorithms such as MPEG-2. This defect is sometimes referred to as "mosquito noise".

Because of the way the human visual system works, defects in an image that are localized to particular features of the image or that come and go are more perceptible than defects that are uniform and constant. However, the DTV system is designed to take advantage of other limitations of the human visual system to help mask these flaws, e.g. by allowing more compression artifacts during fast motion where the eye cannot track and resolve them as easily and, conversely, minimizing artifacts in still backgrounds that may be closely examined in a scene (since time allows).

Effects of poor reception

Changes in signal reception from factors such as degrading antenna connections or changing weather conditions may gradually reduce the quality of analog TV. The nature of digital TV results in a perfectly decodable video initially, until the receiving equipment starts picking up interference that overpowers the desired signal or if the signal is too weak to decode. Some equipment will show a garbled picture with significant damage, while other devices may go directly from perfectly decodable video to no video at all or lock up. This phenomenon is known as the digital cliff effect.

For remote locations, distant channels that, as analog signals, were previously usable in a snowy and degraded state may, as digital signals, be perfectly decodable or may become completely unavailable. The use of higher frequencies will add to these problems, especially in cases where a clear line-of-sight from the receiving antenna to the transmitter is not available.

Direct-to-Home Television Service

Today, most satellite TV customers in developed television markets get their programming through a direct broadcast satellite (DBS) provider, such as DISH TV or DTH platform. The provider selects programs and broadcasts them to subscribers as a set package. Basically, the provider's goal is to bring dozens or even hundreds of channels to the customers television in a form that approximates the competition from Cable TV. Unlike earlier programming, the provider's broadcast is completely digital, which means it has high picture and stereo sound quality. Early satellite television was broadcast in C-band - radio in the 3.4-gigahertz (GHz) to 7-GHz frequency range. Digital broadcast satellite transmits programming in the Ku frequency range (10 GHz to 14 GHz). There are five major components involved in a direct to home (DTH) satellite system: the programming source, the broadcast center, the satellite, the satellite dish and the receiver.

Components of DTH

Programming sources are simply the channels that provide programming for broadcast. The provider (the DTH platform) doesn't create original programming itself; it pays other companies (HBO, for example, or ESPN or STAR TV or Sahara etc.) for the right to broadcast their content via satellite. In this way, the provider is kind of like a broker between the viewer and the actual programming sources. (Cable television networks also work on the same principle.) The broadcast center is the central hub of the system. At the broadcast center or the Playout & Uplink location, the television provider receives signals from various programming sources, compreses using digital compression, if necessary scrambles it and beams a broadcast signal to the satellite being used by it. The satellites receive the signals from the broadcast station and rebroadcast them to the ground. The viewer's dish picks up the signal from the satellite (or multiple satellites in the same part of the sky) and passes it on to the receiver in the viewer's house. The receiver processes the signal and passes it on to a standard television.

Programming

Satellite TV providers get programming from two major sources: International turnaround channels (such as HBO, ESPN and CNN, STAR TV, SET, B4U etc) and various local channels (SaBe TV, Sahara TV, Doordarshan, etc). Most of the turnaround channels also provide programming for cable television, so sometimes some of the DTH platforms will ad in some special channels exclusive to itself to attract more subscriptions. Turnaround channels usually have a distribution center that beams their programming to a geostationary satellite. The broadcast center uses large satellite dishes to pick up these analog and digital signals from several sources.

The Broadcast Center

The broadcast center converts all of this programming into a high-quality, uncompressed digital stream. At this point, the stream contains a vast quantity of data — about 270 megabits per second (Mbps) for each channel.

In order to transmit the signal from there, the broadcast center has to compress it. Otherwise, it would be too big for the satellite to handle. The providers use the MPEG-2 compressed video format — the same format used to store movies on DVDs. With MPEG-2 compression, the provider can reduce the 270-Mbps stream to about 3 or 10 Mbps (depending on the type of programming). This is the crucial step that has made DTH service a success. With digital compression, a typical satellite can transmit about 200 channels. Without digital compression, it can transmit about 30 channels. At the broadcast center, the high-quality digital stream of video goes through an MPEG-2 encoder, which converts the programming to MPEG-2 video of the correct size and format for the satellite receiver in your house.

Encryption & Transmision

After the video is compressed, the provider needs to encrypt it in order to keep people from accessing it for free. Encryption scrambles the digital data in such a way that it can only be decrypted (converted back into usable data) if the receiver has the correct decoding satellite receiver with decryption algorithm and security keys. Once the signal is compressed and encrypted, the broadcast center beams it directly to one of its satellites. The satellite picks up the signal, amplifies it and beams it back to Earth, where viewers can pick it up.

The Dish

A satellite dish is just a special kind of antenna designed to focus on a specific broadcast source. The standard dish consists of a parabolic (bowl-shaped) surface and a central feed horn. To transmit a signal, a controller sends it through the horn, and the dish focuses the signal into a relatively narrow beam. The dish on the receiving end can't transmit information; it can only receive it. The receiving dish works in the exact opposite way of the transmitter. When a beam hits the curved dish, the parabola shape reflects the radio signal inward onto a particular point, just like a concave mirror focuses light onto a particular point.

In this case, the point is the dish's feed horn, which passes the signal onto the receiving equipment. In an ideal setup, there aren't any major obstacles between the satellite and the dish, so the dish receives a clear signal. In some systems, the dish needs to pick up signals from two or more satellites at the same time. The satellites may be close enough together that a regular dish with a single horn can pick up signals from both. This compromises quality somewhat, because the dish isn't aimed directly at one or more of the satellites. A new dish design uses two or more horns to pick up different satellite signals. As the beams from different satellites hit the curved dish, they reflect at different angles so that one beam hits one of the horns and another beam hits a different horn.

The central element in the feed horn is the low noise blockdown converter, or LNB. The LNB amplifies the signal bouncing off the dish and filters out the noise (signals not carrying programming). The LNB passes the amplified, filtered signal to the satellite receiver inside the viewer's house.

The Receiver

The end component in the entire satellite TV system is the receiver. The receiver has four essential jobs: It de-scrambles the encrypted signal. In order to unlock the signal, the receiver needs the proper decoder chip for that programming package. The provider can communicate with the chip, via the satellite signal, to make necessary adjustments to its decoding programs. The provider may occasionally send signals that disrupt illegal de-scramblers, as an electronic counter measure (ECM) against illegal users.

It takes the digital MPEG-2 signal and converts it into an analog format that a standard television can recognize. Since the receiver spits out only one channel at a time, you can't tape one program and watch another. You also can't watch two different programs on two TVs hooked up to the same receiver. In order to do these things, which are standard on conventional cable, you need to buy an additional receiver. Some receivers have a number of other features as well. They pick up a programming schedule signal from the provider and present this information in an onscreen programming guide. Many receivers have parental lock-out options, and some have built-in Digital Video Recorders (DVRs), which let you pause live television or record it on a hard drive. While digital broadcast satellite service is still lacking some of the basic features of conventional cable (the ability to easily split signals between different TVs and VCRs, for example), its high-quality picture, varied programming selection and extended service areas make it a good alternative for some. With the rise of digital cable, which also has improved picture quality and extended channel selection, the TV war is really heating up. Just about anything could happen in the next 10 years as all of these television providers battle it out.

Digital Satellite Developments

All direct-to-home (DTH) system designs, whether analog or digital, have benefited from the fundamental advantages of satellite delivery—versus, for example, terrestrial broad-casting—that can be summarised as follows:

— line-of-sight transmission through the use of microwave frequencies, directive antennas, and high elevation angles;

— consistent picture quality across all channels received;

— broad, national coverage (and hence availability to reach customers in low density, rural areas).

Although satellite DTH television delivery was the dream of futurists for decades, little technological progress was made before 1980. DTH service in the United States began, serendipitously, in 1979, when the FCC declared that receive-only terminal licensing was no longer mandatory and individuals started installing dishes, initially with a diameter >4 m, to receive signals intended for distribution to cable head-ends. From roughly 1985 to 1995, millions of 2-3-m dishes were purchased by individuals to receive these analog cable feeds. Although the dish installations could cost several thousand dollars, the feeds were initially available without a monthly charge.

Reference discusses the various DTH business startup attempts in the 1980s that would have used smaller dishes, but planned to charge a monthly fee. None were financially successful. The major challenges of all system designs have been the need to generate, within project cost constraints, sufficient satellite power levels into a practical dish size, and the need for reception electronics requirements consistent with consumer electronics price expectations. The digital DTH satellite era began in 1994 and quickly captured the "big dish" market and other latent market demand.

Analog DTH

Reference provides a thorough review of analog satellite DTH issues and solutions as of 1990. The link geometry for homes in the contiguous 48 states typically affords an elevation angle—i.e., line-of-sight angle above the horizon—of at least 30°. This geometry means that potential obstacles such as trees or adjacent houses are rarely an actual impediment. The link geometry also means that multipath from hills and buildings is not an issue, especially for the microwave frequencies used by DTH systems. Except for the era of big dish DTH, which used a C-band downlink of 4 GHz, all DTH systems in the Americas have operated in the higher frequency Ku-band. For regulatory purposes, the DTH bands are divided into "fixed satellite service" and "broadcasting satellite service" bands. For systems licensed in the Americas for the Broadcasting Satellite Service (BSS) the uplink frequencies are in the band 17.3-17.8 GHz and the downlink frequencies are in the band 12.2-12.7 GHz. For Fixed Satellite Service (FSS) systems in the United States, the most common uplink and downlink bands are 14.0-14.5 GHz and 10.7-11.2 GHz, respectively. In either band the primary link environmental impediment is moisture along the line of sight—that is, rain—that causes signal fades. This degradation can be sufficiently estimated to establish margins for practical system designs. The DTH systems themselves cause intra-system interference, such as interference of cross-polarised signals at the same frequency, and inter-system interference, such as interference from satellites at neighbouring orbital locations received via consumer receive dish side-lobes.

Advent of Digital

Around 1990, a number of key technologies had made sufficient progress to make all-digital satellite DTH economically practical. These developments provided numerous benefits unavailable with analog solutions, as follows:

— Smaller consumer dish size

— Tuning to dozens of channels without the need to re-point the dish

— More standard-definition(SD) television channels per unit Radio Frequency (RF) bandwidth

— More consistent quality and the potential for improved quality, such as HDTV, and increased number of services without an increase in the dish size

— New innovative services using a high-quality, high-speed digital path into multiple homes

Although the DTH system designers recognised that they could utilize progress in key areas such as video/audio coding and cost reductions in Very Large Scale Integrated (VLSI) circuit technology, several areas were recognised as fundamental technical system interfaces and constraints, as follows:

— Home DTH receiver outputs compatible with home off-air television inputs

— Consumer dish and outdoor electronics power and control via established interfaces

— Set-top boxes consistent with consumer electronics industry practice, such as use of wireless remote controls and adherence to safety guidelines

— RF link design, such as RF channel bandwidth and polarisation reuse, should be consistent with existing FSS and BSS frequency plans

The first three constraints, along with a cost target, established many of the high-level requirements for the initial DTH home receivers. The last constraint set many fundamental requirements on the design of the RF portion of the uplink centers, the DTH satellites, and the tuner circuitry of the home receivers. For the BSS system designs, such as the DirecTV system that went online in 1994, the designers achieved compatibility with the ITU BSS Plan for the Americas,,, that based its intersystem interference planning on an analog FM implementation with 1 m receive dishes.

DTH Service Offerings

The "pay" business model of satellite DTH has created a technical role for the DTH service provider that has no counterpart in traditional advertising-supported terrestrial broadcasting.

Service and Technology Evolution

The DTH provider defines the services it believes to be compelling and then designs and deploys the infrastructure supporting that vision. For example, the DTH provider may set goals for the penetration of HDTV delivery. It then plans and implements the broadcast center and satellite resources and designs (or advocates the design) of the necessary customer receivers. Hence, each satellite DTH provider sets the direction and tempo of evolution of its delivery system. It may or may not tend to use open standards, but the service must be compelling, cost effective, and secure.

Customer Relationship

Each provider desires to create long-term customer relationships and the associated revenues associated with each successful relationship. The introduction of new services and receivers can attract new customers, but the needs of existing customers must also be accommodated. Hence, each new technology evolution can require a substantial investment in customer education, customer premises equipment provisioning and installation, and back-office systems, such as billing. For the U.S. providers, nurturing the customer relationship has been one of their great successes. A satellite DTH company has been selected as having the highest customer satisfaction rating among all multichannel programming providers for seven out of the last nine years.

DTH system service offerings include the following.

1) *Subscription TV*: The DTH providers offer channels on a tiered subscription basis—that is, most customers subscribe to a basic package of channels and one or more packages of premium channels, such as the HBO multiplex. Typically, the basic packages include access to an on-screen electronic programme guide and a number of audio-only music channels. Specialty television subscriptions such as international channels are available. Subscriptions are also offered for series of events, such as all available games from a professional sports league.
2) *Pay per view (PPV):* PPV services give customers the option to pick a specific programme or series of programmes and pay for the selected content as a one-time transaction. The DTH systems provide extensive PPV offerings including the atrical films, concerts, and sports events such as prize fights. In certain cases, the PPV concept has been extended to selling viewing rights for a movie for an entire day rather than for a single showing.
3) *Local channel rebroadcasts:* To provide a seamless, high-quality experience, the satellite DTH services offer subscription packages of the local NTSC "off-air" stations. In the United States, by law, these stations may only be rebroadcast into the same "local market" where they are broadcast terrestrially. By year-end 2004, Dish Network had announced that it was rebroadcasting local channels into 152 markets representing 93% of the U.S. population, while DirecTV's totals were 130 markets and 92%.
4) *High-Definition Television (HDTV)*: Since the enjoyment of HDTV necessitates purchase of a relatively expensive HD monitor, HDTV viewership has grown slowly in the United States since ATSC terrestrial broadcasts were initiated in 1998. This geographically dispersed market proved an excellent new application for satellite DTH. Satellite receivers for HD decoding have been available since 1999.

As they share many of the same processing functions, these receivers can typically decode an "off-air" ATSC signal as well. Most HDTV services are high-definition simulcasts of subscription, PPV, and local channel services already available in standard definition.

5) *Digital Video Recorders (DVRs):* DVRs have proven to be an excellent ancillary application for satellite services. The aggressive marketing of new receiver types to "early adopters" gave the U.S. satellite service providers a majority of all DVR households at year-end 2004. The DVR application benefits from two basic satellite DTH service attributes, the availability of electronic programme guide (EPG) information and of all-digital broadcasts. For a given programme, as indicated in the EPG, the digital content can be directly recorded to a hard disk drive without the need to perform A/D conversion.

6) *Interactive:* The simplest interactive television services are not associated with any particular video services: for example, an electronic programme guide, or screens displaying personalised and localised information, including weather, news, financial information, lottery results, and so on. More complex interactive services are integrated with programme video and as a result require more complex implementations. On-screen mosaics of multiple live channels and multicamera applications are examples of these applications.

   Special "middleware" receiver software is responsible for interpreting the received data and displaying the associated application. Due to the great complexity and the need for careful management of receiver resources, the technologies deployed to date by satellite DTH operators have used proprietary middleware implementations. Considerable work has been done to create standards for interactive services, and the ATSC "ACAP" standard and the Open Cable "OCAP" standard are noteworthy examples. As the services and technologies mature, these standards are likely to play a significant role in future digital DTH system implementations.

7) *Home Networking:* DTH providers' newest services feature satellite receivers with integrated home networking features, including support for connecting to a terrestrial broad-band path such as DSL. Networked receivers enable digital television to be recorded on one receiver and played on another. The linkage to the Internet permits remote DVR scheduling over the Internet and applications such as the transfer of

electronic photos from cell phones to the family's home network.

8) *Special markets:* Although satellite DTH may be symbolised by the small roof-mounted antenna on a single-family home, the services provide programming for various special markets including the following:

— multiple dwelling units—e.g., apartments and condos;

— hospitality market of hotels, bars, and restaurants;

— mobile vehicles ;

— commercial aircraft.

Broadcasting Facility

Most of the DTH subscription channels are delivered to the DTH broadcasting or uplink facility via existing "backhaul" satellites or fiber. These backhaul signals are often the same feeds used to deliver programming to other satellite and cable distributors. Some programming, such as theatrical films for PPV, arrives at the facility as prerecorded digital tapes.

The satellite delivery of local television channels has necessitated the use of in-market digital facilities to preprocess and backhaul, via leased terrestrial transmission facilities, the signals to a DTH broadcasting facility.

The broadcasting facility provides a number of functions common to any broadcasting facility, such as incoming signal monitoring, adjustment, and resynchronisation, signal routing within the facility, and for prerecorded content, quality control, cloning, and playback. The programme content for most channels is unchanged by the facility. Certain channels, by agreement with the originator, may have commercials or promotional spots inserted at points identified, by in-band tones for example, by the originator. Prerecorded material is copied from digital tape masters to video file servers. The video servers use redundant arrays of independent disk (RAID) technology and play back the content on a digital satellite channel at a time established by the daily broadcast schedule.

The "pay" business model of DTH systems also requires that the broadcast site provide conditional access equipment in addition to service information/electronic programme guide (SI/EPG) equipment, compression encoders, and multiplexing, error control, and modulation equipment. The conditional access system, which includes equipment within the home, permits customer access to programming services only when certain conditions are met—for example, the customer's account is in good standing and the customer is located in a geographic area where that particular programming is available per agreement with the content owner, e.g., is not subject to sports blackout. The SI/EPG equipment creates data streams that are used by the in-home electronics to display information about the programming channels and the individual programmes. The EPG data typically include programme title, start and end times, synopsis, programme rating for parental control, alternate languages, and so on.

The signal processing equipment performs redundancy reduction processing (compression) on both the television video and audio. Digital video/audio is typically routed within the broadcasting facility in the serial digital component format at 270 Mb/s, but is reduced to the range of 1–10 Mb/s prior to transmission via compression encoding. This signal processing dramatically reduces the transmission path investment—in satellites, for example—and, conversely, also increases the entertainment channels available for a given amount of transmission bandwidth and investment. Most operational digital DTH systems in the Americas use the Motion Picture Experts Group (MPEG)-2 encoding standard or a proprietary system with nearly identical signal processing characteristics. The compressed video/audio streams from multiple programming channels are typically multiplexed into a single high-speed stream. Each of the constituent streams may have a fixed data rate or the individual channel rates can vary dynamically depending on their instantaneous "image complexity." The latter approach is called statistical multiplexing. With either method, the resultant stream is processed by forward error control (FEC) logic.

Broadcasting Satellites

Each uplink signal from the broadcasting facility or facilities is received and rebroadcast by an RF "transponder" of a frequency-translating repeater on board a geosynchronous communications satellite. For BSS band operation, the satellite receives signals in the range 17.3–17.8 GHz, down converts each signal by 5.1 GHz, and retransmits each signal in the range 12.2–12.7 GHz. The satellites used in DTH systems are very similar in architecture to geosynchronous communications satellites that have been deployed for international and domestic telecommunications since the midsixties. For DTH systems, the satellites' greatly increased physical size and weight permit relatively high levels of received solar energy, and hence dc power, and relatively large on board antennas enabling downlink beam shaping. Each satellite's communications "payload" is a microwave frequency-translating repeater. A broad-band front-end receiver, one per polarisation, down-converts to the downlink frequency and drives multiple RF chains, one per carrier, with each RF chain or "transponder" having a high-power Traveling Wave Tube (TWT) transmitter. Typically, each TWT amplifier has a saturated-power rating of 240 W.

In the United States, to increase the total available capacity, a single system operator often uses multiple satellites at a given orbital location and, additionally, multiple satellites at adjacent orbital locations. Multiple satellites at a single orbital location—actually, separated in longitude by at least 0.1°—gives full use of the available spectrum by effectively pooling the capabilities of several satellites. This implements the futuristic visions from past decades for massive "earth-facing communications relay platforms" without the necessity for a single physical vehicle. Use of adjacent orbital locations permits spectrum reuse by a single system operator.

Customer Electronics

The DTH customer electronics consists of a small aperture antenna and low-noise block down-converter, an integrated receiver/decoder (IRD) unit (or simply "receiver") and a handheld remote control. The antenna is typically an off-set parabolic reflector in the range of 45–60 cm in diameter. The RF signal collected by the horn at the focus is coupled with a low-noise amplifier and then block down-converted to an L-band IF of 950–1450 MHz, or as wide as 250–2150 MHz for recent models. The "outdoor" electronics receives low-voltage dc power via the same coaxial cable used to deliver the down-converted signal into the customer's home and, specifically, to the receiver. The unit's circuitry includes an IF tuner, a QPSK demodulator, FEC decoder, stream demultiplexer (to capture a single programming channel), decryptor under conditional access control, an MPEG video/audio decoder, and TV signal regenerator.

In the Western Hemisphere, most DTH receivers also utilize a replaceable "smart card" with an embedded secure microprocessor used to generate cryptographic keys for decryption of the individual services. In the event that security is compromised, the system operator may only need to replace the smart card to allow economic upgrade of a portion of the conditional access logic instead of the far more costly replacement of entire receivers. The receiver outputs signals to various home entertainment devices such as standard definition and HD televisions and audio amplifier systems. The receiver may have front panel controls but it is routinely controlled via signals from a handheld remote control using IR, and in many cases RF, transmission.

ITU Recommendation ITU-R BO.1516, published in 2001, presents a generic reference model for a digital DTH receiver. This model presents the common functions required in a satellite IRD. The reference model is arranged in layers, with the physical layer located at the lowest level of abstraction, and the services layer located at the highest level.

Terrestrial DTV receivers share these reference model functional elements, with notable differences that reflect both business and technical differences in these services.

— The physical and link layers of the terrestrial receiver are designed to support the antennas and modulations required for off-air (terrestrial) signal reception.

— The conditional access layer of the terrestrial receiver is optional, whereas in satellite systems all services, even local channel rebroadcasts, tend to be encrypted. While there are "digital-cable-ready DTVs" having decrypt capabilities, there are no "satellite-ready DTVs."

— The EPG and interactive service capabilities tend to be highly customised in a satellite receiver, to meet the competitive needs of the service operator.

Functional Elements

Beginning in 1994 and driven by business imperatives, the first digital DTH satellite systems were launched prior to the creation of industry standards for either modulation and coding or transport and multiplexing or for video and audio source encoding. Nevertheless, standards for the digital DTH application did follow, and there are four of note for the Americas: ITU System A/DVB (used by Dish Network, Sky Brasil, Sky Mexico, and Bell ExpressVu), ITU System B (used by DirecTV and DirecTV Latin America), ITU System C (used by Star Choice), and the more recent ATSC A/81 standard (adopted in 2003, but not yet in use).

The ATSC A/81 specification defines extensions to audio, video, transport, and PSIP subsystems as defined in ATSC Standards A/53B and

A/65A. It also includes carriage of data broadcasting as defined in ATSC Standard A/90 without requiring extensions. Transmission and conditional access subsystems are not defined in A/81, allowing service providers to use existing subsystems.

High-Definition Television

High-definition television (HDTV) provides a resolution that is substantially higher than that of standard-definition television.

HDTV may be transmitted in various formats:

— 1080p - 1920×1080p: 2,073,600 pixels (approximately 2.1 megapixels) per frame

— 1080i - typically either:

   — 1920×1080i: 1,036,800 pixels (approximately 1 megapixel) per field or 2,073,600 pixels (approximately 2.1 megapixels) per frame

   — 1440×1080i: 777,600 pixels (approximately 0.8 megapixels) per field or 1,555,200 pixels (approximately 1.6 megapixels) per frame

— 720p - 1280×720p: 921,600 pixels (approximately 0.9 megapixels) per frame

The letter "p" here stands for progressive scan while "i" indicates interlaced.

The term high definition once described a series of television systems originating from the late 1930s; however, these systems were only high definition when compared to earlier systems that were based on mechanical systems with as few as 30 lines of resolution. The ongoing competition between companies and nations to create true "HDTV" spanned the entire 20th century, as each new system became more HD than the last.

The British high-definition TV service started trials in August 1936 and a regular service on 2 November 1936 using both the (mechanical) Baird 240 line and (electronic) Marconi-EMI 405 line (377i) systems. The Baird system was discontinued in February 1937. In 1938 France followed with their own 441-line system, variants of which were also used by a number of other countries. The US NTSC system joined in 1941. In 1949 France introduced an even higher-resolution standard at 819 lines (768i), a system that would be high definition even by today's standards, but was monochrome only. All of these systems used interlacing and a 4:3 aspect ratio except the 240-line system which was progressive (actually described at the time by the technically correct term “sequential”) and the 405-line system which started as 5:4 and later changed to 4:3. The 405-line system adopted the (at that time) revolutionary idea of interlaced scanning to overcome the flicker problem of the 240-line with its 25 Hz frame rate. The 240-line system could have doubled its frame rate but this would have meant that the transmitted signal would have doubled in bandwidth, an unacceptable option.

Color broadcasts started at similarly higher resolutions, first with the US NTSC color system in 1953, which was compatible with the earlier monochrome systems and therefore had the same 525 lines (480i) of resolution. European standards did not follow until the 1960s, when the PAL and SECAM color systems were added to the monochrome 625 line (576i) broadcasts.

The Nippon Hoso Kyokai (NHK, the Japan Broadcasting Corporation) began conducting research to “unlock the fundamental mechanism of video and sound interactions with the five human senses” in 1964, after the Tokyo Olympics. NHK set out to create an HDTV system that ended up scoring much higher in subjective tests than NTSC’s previously dubbed “HDTV”. This new system, NHK Color, created in 1972, included 1125 lines, a 5:3 aspect ratio and 60 Hz refresh rate. The Society of Motion Picture and Television Engineers (SMPTE), headed by Charles Ginsburg, became the testing and study authority for HDTV technology in the international theater. SMPTE would test HDTV systems from different companies from every conceivable perspective, but the problem of combining the different formats plagued the technology for many years.

There were 4 major HDTV systems tested by SMPTE in the late 1970s, and in 1979 an SMPTE study group released A Study of High Definition Television Systems:

— EIA monochrome: 4:3 aspect ratio, 1023 lines, 60 Hz

— NHK color: 5:3, 1125, 60 Hz

— NHK monochrome: 4:3, 2125, n/a Hz

— BBC color: 8:3, 1501, n/a Hz

Since the formal adoption of digital video broadcasting’s (DVB) widescreen HDTV transmission modes in the early 2000s the 525-line NTSC (and PAL-

M) systems as well as the European 625-line PAL and SECAM systems are now regarded as standard definition television systems. In Australia, the 625-line digital progressive system (with 576 active lines) is officially recognized as high-definition.

Early HDTV broadcasting used analog technology, but today it is transmitted digitally and uses video compression.

In 1949, France started its transmissions with an 819 lines system (737i). The system was monochrome only, and was used only on VHF for the first French TV channel. It was discontinued in 1983.

In 1979, the Japanese state broadcaster NHK first developed consumer high-definition television with a 5:3 display aspect ratio. The system, known as Hi-Vision or MUSE after its Multiple sub-Nyquist sampling encoding for encoding the signal, required about twice the bandwidth of the existing NTSC system but provided about four times the resolution (1080i/1125 lines). Satellite test broadcasts started in 1989, with regular testing starting in 1991 and regular broadcasting of BS-9ch commencing on November 25, 1994, which featured commercial and NHK programming.

In 1981, the MUSE system was demonstrated for the first time in the United States, using the same 5:3 aspect ratio as the Japanese system. Upon visiting a demonstration of MUSE in Washington, US President Ronald Reagan was most impressed and officially declared it "a matter of national interest" to introduce HDTV to the US.

Several systems were proposed as the new standard for the US, including the Japanese MUSE system, but all were rejected by the FCC because of their higher bandwidth requirements. At this time, the number of television channels was growing rapidly and bandwidth was already a problem. A new standard had to be more efficient, needing less bandwidth for HDTV than the existing NTSC.

The limited standardization of analog HDTV in the 1990s did not lead to global HDTV adoption as technical and economic constraints at the time did not permit HDTV to use bandwidths greater than normal television.

Early HDTV commercial experiments such as NHK's MUSE required over four times the bandwidth of a standard-definition broadcast, and HD-MAC was not much better. Despite efforts made to reduce analog HDTV to about 2× the bandwidth of SDTV these television formats were still distributable only by satellite.

In addition, recording and reproducing an HDTV signal was a significant technical challenge in the early years of HDTV (Sony HDVS). Japan remained the only country with successful public broadcasting of analog HDTV, with seven broadcasters sharing a single channel.

Rise of Digital Compression

Since 1972, International Telecommunication Union's radio telecommunications sector (ITU-R) had been working on creating a global recommendation for Analog HDTV. These recommendations however did not fit in the broadcasting bands which could reach home users. The standardization of MPEG-1 in 1993 also led to the acceptance of recommendations ITU-R BT.709. In anticipation of these standards the Digital Video Broadcasting (DVB) organisation was formed, an alliance of broadcasters, consumer electronics manufacturers and regulatory bodies. The DVB develops and agrees upon specifications which are formally standardised by ETSI.

DVB created first the standard for DVB-S digital satellite TV, DVB-C digital cable TV and DVB-T digital terrestrial TV. These broadcasting systems can be used for both SDTV and HDTV. In the US the Grand Alliance proposed ATSC as the new standard for SDTV and HDTV. Both ATSC and DVB were based on the MPEG-2 standard, although DVB systems may also be used to transmit video using the newer and more efficient H.264/MPEG-4 AVC compression standards. Common for all DVB standards is the use of highly efficient modulation techniques for further reducing bandwidth, and foremost for reducing receiver-hardware and antenna requirements.

In 1983, the International Telecommunication Union's radio telecommunications sector (ITU-R) set up a working party (IWP11/6) with the aim of setting a single international HDTV standard. One of the thornier issues concerned a suitable frame/field refresh rate, the world already having split into two camps, 25/50 Hz and 30/60 Hz, largely due to the differences in mains frequency. The IWP11/6 working party considered many views and throughout the 1980s served to encourage development in a number of video digital processing areas, not least conversion between the two main frame/ field rates using motion vectors, which led to further developments in other areas. While a comprehensive HDTV standard was not in the end established, agreement on the aspect ratio was achieved.

Initially the existing 5:3 aspect ratio had been the main candidate but, due to the influence of widescreen cinema, the aspect ratio 16:9 (1.78) eventually emerged as being a reasonable compromise between 5:3 (1.67) and the common 1.85 widescreen cinema format. (Bob Morris explained that the 16:9 ratio was chosen as being the geometric mean of 4:3, Academy ratio, and 2.4:1, the widest cinema format in common use, in order to minimize wasted screen space when displaying content with a variety of aspect ratios.)

An aspect ratio of 16:9 was duly agreed upon at the first meeting of the IWP11/6 working party at the BBC's Research and Development establishment in Kingswood Warren. The resulting ITU-R Recommendation ITU-R BT.709-2 ("Rec. 709") includes the 16:9 aspect ratio, a specified colorimetry, and the scan modes 1080i (1,080 actively interlaced lines of resolution) and 1080p (1,080 progressively scanned lines). The British Freeview HD trials used MBAFF, which contains both progressive and interlaced content in the same encoding.

It also includes the alternative 1440×1152 HDMAC scan format. (According to some reports, a mooted 750-line (720p) format (720 progressively scanned lines) was viewed by some at the ITU as an enhanced television format rather than a true HDTV format, and so was not included, although 1920×1080i and 1280×720p systems for a range of frame and field rates were defined by several US SMPTE standards.

HDTV Broadcast in the United States

HDTV technology was introduced in the United States in the 1990s by the Digital HDTV Grand Alliance, a group of television, electronic equipment, communications companies consisting of AT&T Bell Labs, General Instrument, MIT, Philips, Sarnoff, Thomson, Zenith and the Massachusetts Institute of Technology. Field testing of HDTV at 199 sites in the United States was completed August 14, 1994. The first public HDTV broadcast in the United States occurred on July 23, 1996 when the Raleigh, North Carolina television station WRAL-HD began broadcasting from the existing tower of WRAL-TV south-east of Raleigh, winning a race to be first with the HD Model Station in Washington, D.C., which began broadcasting July 31, 1996 with the callsign WHD-TV, based out of the facilities of NBC owned and operated station WRC-TV. The American Advanced Television Systems Committee (ATSC) HDTV system had its public launch on October

29, 1998, during the live coverage of astronaut John Glenn's return mission to space on board the Space Shuttle Discovery. The signal was transmitted coast-to-coast, and was seen by the public in science centers, and other public theaters specially equipped to receive and display the broadcast

European HDTV Broadcasts

The first HDTV transmissions in Europe, albeit not direct-to-home, began in 1990, when the Italian broadcaster RAI and Japanese broadcaster NHK used the HD-MAC and MUSE HDTV technologies to broadcast the 1990 FIFA World Cup. The matches were shown in 8 cinemas in Italy and 2 in Spain. The connection with Spain was made via the Olympus satellite link from Rome to Barcelona and then with a fiber optic connection from Barcelona to Madrid. After some HDTV transmissions in Europe the standard was abandoned in the mid-1990s.

The first regular broadcasts started on January 1, 2004 when the Belgian company Euro1080 launched the HD1 channel with the traditional Vienna New Year's Concert. Test transmissions had been active since the IBC exhibition in September 2003, but the New Year's Day broadcast marked the official launch of the HD1 channel, and the official start of direct-to-home HDTV in Europe.

Euro1080, a division of the Belgian TV services company Alfacam, broadcast HDTV channels to break the pan-European stalemate of "no HD broadcasts mean no HD TVs bought means no HD broadcasts ..." and kick-start HDTV interest in Europe. The HD1 channel was initially free-to-air and mainly comprised sporting, dramatic, musical and other cultural events broadcast with a multi-lingual soundtrack on a rolling schedule of 4 or 5 hours per day.

These first European HDTV broadcasts used the 1080i format with MPEG-2 compression on a DVB-S signal from SES's Astra 1H satellite. Euro1080 transmissions later changed to MPEG-4/AVC compression on a DVB-S2 signal in line with subsequent broadcast channels in Europe.

The number of European HD channels and viewers has risen steadily since the first HDTV broadcasts, with SES's annual Satellite Monitor market survey for 2010 reporting more than 200 commercial channels broadcasting in HD from Astra satellites, 185 million HD-Ready TVs sold in Europe (£60 million in 2010 alone), and 20 million households (27% of all European digital satellite TV homes) watching HD satellite broadcasts (16 million via Astra satellites).

In December 2009 the United Kingdom became the first European country to deploy high definition content using the new DVB-T2 transmission standard, as specified in the Digital TV Group (DTG) D-book, on digital terrestrial television. The Freeview HD service currently contains 4 HD channels and was rolled out region by region across the UK in accordance with the digital switchover process, finally being completed in October 2012. However, Freeview HD has not been the first HDTV service over digital terrestrial television in Europe; for example, in Italy the Rai HD channel started broadcasting in 1080i on April 24, 2008 using the older DVB-T transmission standard.

Notation

HDTV broadcast systems are identified with three major parameters:

— Frame size in pixels is defined as number of horizontal pixels × number of vertical pixels, for example 1280 × 720 or 1920 × 1080. Often the number of horizontal pixels is implied from context and is omitted, as in the case of 720p and 1080p.

— Scanning system is identified with the letter p for progressive scanning or i for interlaced scanning.

— Frame rate is identified as number of video frames per second. For interlaced systems an alternative form of specifying number of fields per second is often used.

If all three parameters are used, they are specified in the following form: [frame size][scanning system][frame or field rate] or [frame size]/[frame or field rate][scanning system]. Often, frame size or frame rate can be dropped if its value is implied from context. In this case the remaining numeric parameter is specified first, followed by the scanning system.

For example, 1920×1080p25 identifies progressive scanning format with 25 frames per second, each frame being 1,920 pixels wide and 1,080 pixels high. The 1080i25 or 1080i50 notation identifies interlaced scanning format with 25 frames (50 fields) per second, each frame being 1,920 pixels wide and 1,080 pixels high. The 1080i30 or 1080i60 notation identifies interlaced scanning format with 30 frames (60 fields) per second, each frame being 1,920 pixels wide and 1,080 pixels high.The 720p60 notation identifies progressive scanning format with 60 frames per second, each frame being 720 pixels high; 1,280 pixels horizontally are implied.

50 Hz systems support three scanning rates: 50i, 25p and 50p. 60 Hz systems support a much wider set of frame rates: 59.94i, 60i, 23.976p, 24p, 29.97p, 30p, 59.94p and 60p. In the days of standard definition television, the fractional rates were often rounded up to whole numbers, e.g. 23.976p was often called 24p, or 59.94i was often called 60i. 60 Hz high definition television supports both fractional and slightly different integer rates, therefore strict usage of notation is required to avoid ambiguity. Nevertheless, 29.97i/59.94i is almost universally called 60i, likewise 23.976p is called 24p.

For commercial naming of a product, the frame rate is often dropped and is implied from context (e.g., a 1080i television set). A frame rate can also be specified without a resolution. For example, 24p means 24 progressive scan frames per second, and 50i means 25 interlaced frames per second.

There is no standard for HDTV color support. Until recently the color of each pixel was regulated by three 8-bit color values, each representing the level of red, blue, and green which defined a pixel color. Together the 24 total bits defining color yielded just under 17 million possible pixel colors. Recently some manufacturers have produced systems that can employ 10 bits for each color (30 bits total) which provides for a palette of 1 billion colors, saying that this provides a much richer picture, but there is no agreed way to specify that a piece of equipment supports this feature. Human vision can only discern approximately 1 million colors so an expanded color palette is of questionable benefit to consumers.

At a minimum, HDTV has twice the linear resolution of standard-definition television (SDTV), thus showing greater detail than either analog television or regular DVD. The technical standards for broadcasting HDTV also handle the 16:9 aspect ratio images without using letterboxing or anamorphic stretching, thus increasing the effective image resolution.

A very high resolution source may require more bandwidth than available in order to be transmitted without loss of fidelity. The lossy compression that is used in all digital HDTV storage and transmission systems will distort the received picture, when compared to the uncompressed source.

Standard Frame or Field Rates

ATSC defines the following frame rates for digital high-definition television.

- 23.976 Hz (film-looking frame rate compatible with NTSC clock speed standards)
- 24 Hz (international film and ATSC high-definition material)
- 25 Hz (PAL, SECAM film, standard-definition, and high-definition material)
- 29.97 Hz (NTSC standard-definition material)
- 59.94 Hz (ATSC high-definition material)
- 60 Hz (ATSC high-definition material)

The optimum format for a broadcast depends upon the type of videographic recording medium used and the image's characteristics. For best fidelity to the source the transmitted field ratio, lines, and frame rate should match those of the source.

Although PAL, SECAM and NTSC frame rates technically apply only to standard definition television, not HD, with the roll out of HD, countries maintained the heritage of their former systems. HDTV in former PAL countries operates at a frame rate of 50 Hz and HDTV in former NTSC countries operates at 60 Hz.

Types of Media

Standard 35mm photographic film used for cinema projection has a much higher image resolution than HDTV systems, and is exposed and projected at a rate of 24 frames per second (frame/s). To be shown on standard television, in PAL-system countries, cinema film is scanned at the TV rate of 25 frame/s, causing a speedup of 4.1 percent, which is generally considered acceptable.

In NTSC-system countries, the TV scan rate of 30 frame/s would cause a perceptible speedup if the same were attempted, and the necessary correction is performed by a technique called 3:2 Pulldown: Over each successive pair of film frames, one is held for three video fields (1/20 of a second) and the next is held for two video fields (1/30 of a second), giving a total time for the two frames of 1/12 of a second and thus achieving the correct average film frame rate.

Non-cinematic HDTV video recordings intended for broadcast are typically recorded either in 720p or 1080i format as determined by the broadcaster. 720p is commonly used for Internet distribution of high-definition video, because most computer monitors operate in progressive-scan mode. 720p also imposes less strenuous storage and decoding requirements compared to both 1080i and 1080p. 1080p-24 frame/s and 1080i-30 frame/s is most often used on Blu-ray Disc; as of 2011, there is still no disc that can support full 1080p-60 frame/s.

Contemporary Systems

Besides an HD-ready television set, other equipment may be needed to view HD television. In the US, cable-ready TV sets can display HD content without using an external box. They have a QAM tuner built-in and/or a card slot for inserting a CableCARD.

High-definition image sources include terrestrial broadcast, direct broadcast satellite, digital cable, IPTV, Blu-ray video disc (BD), and internet downloads. Sony's PlayStation 3 has extensive HD compatibility because of the Blu-ray platform, so does Microsoft's Xbox 360 with the addition of Netflix streaming capabilities, and the Zune marketplace where users can rent or purchase digital HD content. The HD capabilities of the consoles has influenced some developers to port games from past consoles onto the PS3 and 360, often with remastered graphics.

Recording and Compression

HDTV can be recorded to D-VHS (Digital-VHS or Data-VHS), W-VHS (analog only), to an HDTV-capable digital video recorder (for example DirecTV's high-definition Digital video recorder, Sky HD's set-top box, Dish Network's VIP 622 or VIP 722 high-definition Digital video recorder receivers, or TiVo's Series 3 or HD recorders), or an HDTV-ready HTPC. Some cable boxes are capable of receiving or recording two or more broadcasts at a time in HDTV format, and HDTV programming, some included in the monthly cable service subscription price, some for an additional fee, can be played back with the cable company's on-demand feature.

The massive amount of data storage required to archive uncompressed streams meant that inexpensive uncompressed storage options were not available in the consumer market until recently. In 2008 the Hauppauge 1212

Personal Video Recorder was introduced. This device accepts HD content through component video inputs and stores the content in an uncompressed MPEG transport stream (.ts) file or Blu-ray format .m2ts file on the hard drive or DVD burner of a computer connected to the PVR through a USB 2.0 interface.

Realtime MPEG-2 compression of an uncompressed digital HDTV signal is prohibitively expensive for the consumer market at this time, but should become inexpensive within several years (although this is more relevant for consumer HD camcorders than recording HDTV). Analog tape recorders with bandwidth capable of recording analog HD signals such as W-VHS recorders are no longer produced for the consumer market and are both expensive and scarce in the secondary market.

In the United States, as part of the FCC's plug and play agreement, cable companies are required to provide customers who rent HD set-top boxes with a set-top box with "functional" FireWire (IEEE 1394) upon request. None of the direct broadcast satellite providers have offered this feature on any of their supported boxes, but some cable TV companies have. As of July 2004, boxes are not included in the FCC mandate. This content is protected by encryption known as 5C. This encryption can prevent duplication of content or simply limit the number of copies permitted, thus effectively denying most if not all fair use of the content.

Digital Video Broadcasting-Handheld (DVB-H)

The Digital Video Broadcast (DVB) Project started research work related to mobile reception of DVB-Terrestrial (DVB-T) signals as early as 1998, accompanying the introduction of commercial terrestrial digital TV services in Europe. In 2000, the EU-sponsored Motivate (Mobile Television and Innovative Receivers) project concluded that mobile reception of DVB-T is possible but it implies dedicated broadcast networks, as such mobile services are more demanding in robustness (i.e., constellation and coding rate) than broadcast networks planned for fixed DVB-T reception. Later in 2002, the EU-sponsored Multimedia Car Platform (MCP) project explored the excellent behavior of antenna diversity reception which, introducing spatial diversity in addition to the frequency and time diversities provided by the DVB-T transmission layer, improved sufficiently reception performance to allow a mobile receiver to access DVB-T signals broadcast for fixed receivers.

Five years after its inception, DVB-T shows sufficient flexibility to permit mobile broadcast services deployment in cities like Singapore or in Germany. But, during these five years, consumer habits have evolved, and in early 2002, the DVB community was asked to provide technical specifications to allow delivery of rich multimedia contents to handheld terminals, a property that has been missing in the original DVB-T. This would make it possible to receive TV-type services in a small, handheld device like a mobile phone.

This approach requires specific features from the transmission system serving such devices. First, as these devices are battery powered, the transmission system shall offer them the possibility to repeatedly power off some part of the reception chain to increase the battery usage duration. Second, as the technology is targeting mobile users, the transmission system shall ease access to the services when receivers leave a given transmission cell and enter a new one. Third, as services are expected to be delivered in an environment suffering severe mobile multipath channels and high levels of man-made noise, the transmission system shall offer additional means to mitigate these effects on the receiving capabilities.

Additionally, the system should be capable to handle a number of reception scenarios; indoor, outdoor, pedestrian and inside amoving vehicle; and, consequently, the transmission system shall offer sufficient flexibility and scalability to allow the reception of the services at various speeds, while optimising transmitter coverage. Also, the system should be usable in various parts of the world and should offer the flexibility to be used in various transmission bands and channel bandwidths. All this should be achieved with a system based on DVB-T in order to have maximal compatibility with the existing DVB-T networks and implementations. The work to define such a system within the DVB Project started in the beginning of year 2002 first by defining a set of commercial requirements for a system supporting handheld devices. The technical work then led to a system calledDigital Video Broadcasting-Handheld (DVB-H): , which was published as European Telecommunications Standards Institute (ETSI) Standard EN 302 304 in November 2004 . This standard is an umbrella standard defining in which way to combine the earlier existing-now updated-ETSI standards to form the DVB-H system.

The DVB-H system is defined based on the existing DVB-T standard for fixed and in-car reception of digital TV. The main additional elements in the link layer (i.e., the layer above the physical layer) are time slicing and additional forward error correction (FEC) coding. Time slicing reduces the average power in the receiver front-end significantly-up to about 90%-95%-and also enables smooth and seamless frequency handover when the user leaves one service area in order to enter a new cell. Use of time slicing is mandatory in DVB-H.

FEC for multiprotocol encapsulated data (MPE-FEC) gives an improvement in carrier-to-noise (C/N) performance and Doppler performance in mobile channels and, moreover, also improves tolerance to impulse interference. Use of MPE-FEC is optional for DVB-H. It should be emphasised that neither time slicing nor MPE-FEC technology elements, as they are implemented on the link layer, touch the DVB-T physical layer in any way. This means that the existing receivers for DVB-T are not disturbed by DVB-H signals-DVB-H is totally backward compatible to DVB-T.

It is also important to notice that the payload of DVB-H is IP-datagrams or other network layer datagrams encapsulated into MPE-sections. In view of the restricted data rates suggested for individual DVB-H services and the small displays of typical handheld terminals, the classical audio and video coding schemes used in digital broadcasting do not suit DVB-H well. It is therefore suggested to exchange MPEG-2 video by H.264/AVC or other high-efficiency video coding standards.

The physical layer has four extensions to the existing DVB-T physical layer. First, the bits in transmitter parameter signaling (TPS) have been upgraded to include two additional bits to indicate presence of DVB-H services and possible use of MPE-FEC to enhance and speed up the service discovery. Second, a new 4K mode orthogonal frequency division multiplexing (OFDM) mode is adopted for trading off mobility and single-frequency network (SFN) cell size, allowing single-antenna reception in medium SFNs at very high speeds. This gives additional flexibility for the network design. 4K mode is an option for DVB-H complementing the 2K and 8K modes that are as well available. Also all the modulation formats, QPSK, 16QAM and 64QAM with nonhierarchical or hierarchical modes, are possible to use for DVB-H. Third, a new way of using the symbol interleaver of DVB-T has been defined.

For 2K and 4K modes, the operator may select (instead of native interleaver that interleaves the bits over one OFDM symbol) the option of an in-depth interleaver that interleaves the bits over four or two OFDM symbols, respectively. This approach brings the basic tolerance to impulse noise of these modes up to the level attainable with the 8K mode and also improves the robustness in mobile environment. Finally, the fourth addition to DVB-T physical layer is the 5-MHz channel bandwidth to be used in nonbroadcast bands. This is of interest, e.g., in the United States, where a network at about 1.7 GHz is running using DVB-H with a 5-MHz channel.

The conceptual structure of DVB-H user equipment includes a DVB-H receiver (a DVB-T demodulator, a time-slicing module, and an optional MPE-FEC module) and a DVB-H terminal. The DVB-T demodulator recovers the MPEG-2 transport stream (TS) packets from the received DVB-T RF signal. It offers three transmission modes: 8K, 4K, and 2K with the corresponding signaling. The time-slicing module controls the receiver to decode the wanted service and shut off during the other service bits. It aims to reduce receiver power consumption while also enabling a smooth and seamless frequency handover.

4k Mode And In-Depth Interleavers

The objective of the 4K mode is to improve network planning flexibility by trading off mobility and SFN size. To further improve robustness of the DVB-H 2K and 4K modes in a mobile environment and impulse noise reception conditions, an in-depth symbol interleaver has also been added to the standard.

The additional 4K transmission mode is a scaled set of the parameters defined for the 2K and 8K transmission modes. It aims to offer an additional tradeoff between SFN cell size and mobile reception performance, providing an additional degree of flexibility for network planning. The operator of a dedicated DVB-H network can then select one of the three FFT sizes that best responds to the actual needs.

Terms of the tradeoff can be expressed as follows.

— The DVB-T 8K mode can be used both for single-transmitter operation [multifrequency networks (MFNs)]

— Useful Net Bitrates (Mb/s) for Nonhierarchical Systems in 8-MHz Channels With MPE-FEC Code Rate

— Full Multiplex Assumed to be DVB-H and for small, medium, and large SFNs. It provides a Doppler tolerance allowing for high-speed reception.

— The DVB-T 4K mode can be used both for single-transmitter operation and for small and medium SFNs. It provides a Doppler tolerance allowing for very high speed reception.

— The DVB-T 2K mode is suitable for single-transmitter operation and for small SFNs with limited transmitter distances. It provides a Doppler tolerance allowing for extremely high-speed reception.

For 2K and 4K modes, the in-depth interleavers increase the flexibility of the symbol interleaving, by decoupling the choice of the inner interleaver from the transmission mode used. This flexibility allows a 2K or 4K signal to take benefit of the memory of the 8K symbol interleaver to effectively quadruple (for 2K) or double (for 4K) the symbol interleaver depth to improve reception in fading channels. This provides also an extra level of protection against short noise impulses caused by, e.g., ignition interference and interference from various electrical appliances.

Time Slicing

The standard DVB way of carrying IP datagrams in an MPEG-2 TS is to use multiprotocol encapsulation (MPE). With MPE each IP datagram is encapsulated into one MPE section. A stream of MPE sections are then put into an elementary stream (ES), i.e., a stream of MPEG-2 TS packets with a particular program identifier (PID). Each MPE section has a 12-B header, a 4-B cyclic redundancy check (CRC-32) tail and a payload length, which is identical to the length of the IP datagram, which is carried by the MPE section. A typical situation for future handheld DVB-H devices may be to receive audio/video services transmitted over IP on ESs having a fairly low bitrate, probably in the order of 250 kb/s. The MPEG-2 TS may, however, have a bitrate of e.g., 10 Mb/s. The particular ES of interest thus occupies only a fraction (in this example, 2.5%) of the total MPEG-2 TS bitrate. In order to drastically reduce power consumption, one would ideally like the receiver to demodulate and decode only the 2.5% portion of interest, and not the full MPEG-2 TS. With time slicing this is possible, since the MPE sections of a particular ES are sent in high bitrate bursts instead of with a constant low bitrate. During the time between the bursts-the off-time-no sections of the particular ES are transmitted. This allows the receiver to power off completely during off-time.

During off time bursts from other time sliced ESs are typically transmitted. The peak bitrate of the bursts may potentially be the full MPEG-

2 TS bitrate, but could also be any lower peak value allocated for the ES. If the value is lower than the peak bitrate, the MPEG-2 TS packets of a particular burst may be interleaved with MPEG-2 TS packets belonging to other ESs (DVB-H or other, e.g., SI or MPEG-2 audio/video). A variable-bit-rate coded video stream could therefore use a variable burst size and/or a variable time between bursts. It should be noted that one burst could contain several services, which would then share PID but could e.g., be discriminated by different IP addresses.

If the average bitrate of the ES is 500 kb/s, the peak bitrate is 10 Mb/s and the burst size is 2 Mb (maximum allowed value), the burst time becomes 200 ms, and the burst cycle time 4s. The receiver, however, has to wake up a little bit before the burst to synchronise and be prepared to receive the sections. It is probable that the actual parameters used for Time Slicing will be a compromise between power consumption and other factors, such as service access time and RF performance.

MPE-FEC

With MPE-FEC the IP datagrams of each time sliced burst are protected by Reed-Solomon parity data (RS data), calculated from the IP datagrams of the burst. For the calculation of the RS data an MPE-FEC frame is used. The MPE-FEC frame consists of an application data table (ADT), which hosts the IP datagrams (and possible padding), and an RS data table, which hosts the RS data.

The number of rows in the MPE-FEC frame is signaled in the service information (SI) and may take any of the values 256, 512, 768, or 1024. The number of columns is 191 for the ADT and 64 for the RS data table. The IP datagrams of a particular burst are introduced vertically column-by-column in the ADT, starting in the upper left corner. If an IP datagram does not end exactly at the bottom of a column, the remaining bytes continue from the top of the next column. If the IP datagrams do not exactly fill the ADT, the remaining byte positions are padded with zeros. On each row the 64 parity bytes of the RS data table are then calculated from the 191 IP datagram bytes (and padding bytes, if applicable) of the same row, using the Reed-Solomon code RS(255 191). This provides a large virtual time interleaving, since all RS data bytes are calculated from IP datagrams distributed all over the burst.

The receiver checks the CRC-32 of all received sections of the selected ES. As pointed out above, the CRC-32 normally enables detection of all erroneous sections, which may then be discarded by the receiver. In this way only fully correct sections are passed to the MPE-FEC decoding. Each correctly received IP datagram or RS data column can then be introduced at the correct place in the MPE-FEC frame with the help of the start address of each section. If there are transmission errors, there will be some remaining gaps within the MPE-FEC frame, corresponding to lost sections. The receiver will treat all introduced bytes as "reliable" and all other byte positions as "unreliable." On each row of the MPE-FEC frame it is therefore known exactly which byte positions are correct ("reliable") and which are missing ("unreliable"). The receiver may therefore perform erasure-based decoding of the RS(255 191) code, which allows correction of twice the number of byte errors, which in our case means up to 64 per row. Assuming e.g., exactly one IP datagram per column this corresponds to an error-correction capability of up to 64 lost columns per frame, i.e., every fourth section is lost. Assuming further a 10% section loss probability, the resulting ratio of uncorrected frames after MPE-FEC decoding becomes 10^{-12}.

This powerful error correcting capability, together with the virtual time interleaving, allows a large reduction in required C/N on mobile channels. Measurements show that the resulting C/N performance is similar to what can be achieved using antenna diversity, although it is recognised that in the case of MPE-FEC there is also a penalty in terms of a reduced throughput, due to the overhead introduced by the MPE-FEC sections. However, using a weaker DVB-T convolutional code rate can compensate for this-when code rate 2/3 is used together with MPE-FEC (code rate ¾) the performance is far better than convolutional code rate ½ without MPE-FEC, even though the IP throughput is the same.

In case theADTis not completely filled with IP datagrams, the remaining part will be padded with zeros. This padding is only used for the calculation of the RS data and not transmitted. In the header of the MPE-FEC sections, it is possible to signal the number of complete padding columns. In the receiver such complete padding columns can be reintroduced and be marked as "reliable," since the content is known. Use of padding columns is in effect a shortening of the RS code, which lowers the effective code rate and improves the error correction capability somewhat, but also introduces a larger percentage overhead for the RS data. Puncturing some of the RS columns can compensate for this. Puncturing simply means that some of the last RS columns are not transmitted and this has the effect of weakening the code (i.e., higher effective code rate) and reducing the RS data overhead. The shortening and puncturing operations can be done independently of each other and may be done dynamically, i.e., different shortening and/or puncturing on consecutive MPE-FEC frames.

A reduction of the burst/frame size from the maximum value can be done in two different ways, or even combined. The first variant is to decrease the number of rows from 1024 to 768, 512, or 256. Number of rows is a quasi-static parameter, signaled by SI, and may not vary dynamically. The second variant is to introduce padding columns and puncturing. The number of padding columns may dynamically vary between 0 and 190. The corresponding puncturing range is 0-63 punctured columns.

From a coding performance point of view, the two methods are roughly equivalent. The larger the effective MPE-FEC frame, the more effective becomes the MPE-FEC scheme. Halving the frame size corresponds to halving the interleaving depth. For best mobile performance, the largest frame size may be the fittest option.

Handover Considerations

DVB-H supports very efficient handover behavior including seamless handover. This is due to the existence of the off periods in time slicing, where the receiver may scan other frequencies in order to find the best potential alternative frequency, or actually execute the handover. It should be emphasised that the possibility of "silently" evaluating alternative frequencies, without disturbing the ongoing reception of the service, is a very important feature of the DVB-H system.

If the same TS is available in a number of adjacent cells, the transmission of the TS should preferably be time synchronised. This is in principle straightforward to achieve, since the same methods could be used as in SFNs and the required time accuracy is much less strict than in the SFN case. If the transmissions of the TS on different frequencies are time synchronised, a receiver will receive the next burst at the time indicated by delta_t also on any new frequency carrying this TS. Since the TS is the same also, the content of the bursts are the same, which means that the handover will naturally be seamless.

DVB-H Complexity

The DVB-H complexity is more related to the overall transmission system than to its individual techniques used to provide efficient delivery to handheld terminals. This suggested to the DVB-H ad hoc group of the DVB Technical Module to organise a validation exercise in order to capture possible standards inaccuracies, to help early implementers and to estimate the DVB-H transmission system performance.

In October 2004, a DVB-H test session involving up to 25 equipments and 12 companies has been performed in the laboratory of T-Systems in Berlin, Germany. In December 2004, DVB-H field trials have been performed using the facilities set up by Télédiffusion de France in Metz in order to verify the laboratory results. Major findings are reported hereafter.

The laboratory session checked interoperability of numerous equipments, including full DVB-H receivers prototyped with large-sized set of field programmable gate arrays (FPGAs). Full interoperability between network equipment and receivers has been stated, in all possible transmission modes (2K/4K/8K; all coded constellations), channel bandwidths (5/6/7/8 MHz) and network operation (MFN/SFN, hierarchical/ regular transmissions).

1) *Laboratory Test Methodology*: To evaluate DVB-H performances in the laboratory and in the field (i.e., to determine the "C/N versus Doppler" curve), the various parameters of the transmission systems have been selected in order to obtain figures in the most probable or the most demanding modes offered by the DVB-H, which also constitute the worst cases for the receivers.

    a) *Physical layer*: The DVB-T physical layer offers a wide flexibility to trade off transmitted bitrate against signal robustness. The flexibility has been enlarged with DVB-H, bringing an additional dimension to the tradeoff: transmission cell size versus maximum receiving speed.

       All tests have been performed using the "8K GI ¼" transmission frame structure, which constitutes the worst transmission scheme for the receivers from the speed point of view. Effectively, the 8K mode implements the smallest ICS and thus offers the smallest room for Doppler frequency shifts. In addition, even if the longest guard interval (1/4) allows one to maximise the transmission cell (i.e., largest room for delayed echoes) it leads to a longer symbol length decreasing tolerance to mobility.

The range of coded constellation has been selected to provide various DVB-H transmission capabilities, thus to explore the tridimensional tradeoff of bitrate versus robustness versus speed. The objective of this selection of transmission modes is to compare reception performances in DVB-T like (i.e., FER criteria) and DVB-H (i.e., MFER criteria) situations.

b) *Data layer*: The MPE-FEC protection scheme applied at the link layer in DVB-H, allows for producing various time-slice burst shapes, characterised, e.g., by the FEC coding rate and the absolute burst durations. For all tests, the peak TS bitrate for DVB-H services has been limited to a constant bitrate of 4 Mb/s, this size being compatible with all bitrate made available by the physical layer and moreover corresponding roughly to the average bitrate of one regular standard definition TV program. Then, for the purpose of the performance exploration tests, three sets of burst shapes have been defined in order to explore the influences of DVB-H versus DVB-T, MPE-FEC coding rates and absolute burst durations, respectively.

2) *Laboratory Test Results*: Numerous results have been obtained from the large-scale laboratory test campaign performed by the DVB-H standardisation members. The main results are presented hereafter. The colors indicate the two different prototype receivers in test.

a) *DVB-T Versus DVB-H*: For this assessment, using MPE-FEC ¾ service bursts, the C/N versus Doppler characteristic of two receivers has been established, for QPSK and 16QAM, using coding rates ½ and 2/3.

b) *MPE-FEC coding rate influence*: To study the effects of the MPE-FEC coding rate, the weak coded constellation (i.e., 16QAM 2/3) has been used and the various MPE-FEC coding rate. The "zoom" presented in the second graph highlights the tremendous effect of the MPE-FEC on the C/N (i.e., 5-6 dB). In pedestrian situations (below 10 Hz) the progressive effect of the virtual time interleaver can be observed, which gradually allows to reach the improved C/N. In mobile situations, the C/N gain is already effective with the lowest coding rate 7/8 (i.e., 12.5% overhead) and it nicely increases proportionally with larger coding rates, to reach up to 9 dB gain for coding rate ½ (i.e., 50% overhead). For all coding rates, the maximum speed remains outstandingly around a Doppler frequency of 120 Hz which corresponds to a speed range of 160 km/h @ 800 MHz (upper part of Band V) to 650 km/h@200 MHz (lower part of Band III).

c) *Transmission mode influence*: With the DVB-H extension, theDVB-T standard allows the use of three transmission modes involving 2K, 4K, or 8K subcarriers. These three modes allow one to broadcast strictly the same bitrate range but, due to the orthogonal organisation of the frequency division multiplex (i.e., OFDM), provide three tradeoffs between ICS (i.e., room for Doppler spread) and guard interval duration.

3) *Field Trials Results*: In order to verify on the fields the DVB-H performances, a 600-W ERP transmitter using QPSK ½ and 16QAM 2/3 constellations in 8K with guard interval ¼, has been used to cover the city of Metz with the same DVB-H services organisation as the ones experienced in the laboratory.

A wide range of field measurements has been done in various receiving situation: pedestrian outdoor (in city downtown), mobile (in car traveling the city center and the highway in suburb), and pedestrian indoor (within the research center of Télédiffusion de France). Each field trial session captured up to 3000 measurement points, sampling the experienced C/N and received RF power level every second while assessing the FER and MFER criteria. The achieved results do give indications on the MPE-FEC improvements, which were in line with the laboratory measurements. Unfortunately, in the field, receivers suffer simultaneously from slow shadowing fading (produced by the environment) and fast Rayleigh fading (coming from the mobile channel); accordingly, field trial results cannot be straightforwardly compared with the laboratory measurements.

Dvb-H Networks

IPDC-System

A typical application for DVB-H is IP datacasting service to handheld terminals like mobile phones. First the service system is used to produce the various IP streams (like video streams) to the network. They are then distributed over the multicast intranet to the IP encapsulators, which will output the DVB-H TS with time slicing and MPE-FEC included. This TS is then distributed to the DVB-T/H transmitters of the broadcasting network. The IP Datacast (IPDC) system may include other functions via cellular networks like General Packet Radio Service (GPRS) or Universal Mobile Tele-communications System (UMTS).

Broadcasting Spectrum

DVB-H is intended to use the same broadcasting spectrum, which DVB-T is currently using. The physical layer of DVB-H is in fact DVB-T and therefore there is a full spectrum compatibility with other DVB-T services. DVB-H can be introduced either in a dedicated DVB-H network or by sharing an existing DVB-T multiplex between DVB-H and DVB-T services. When the final selection of the DVB-H concept was made, the capability to share a multiplex with DVB-T was indeed one of the decisive factors, as it was seen that this would enhance the commercial introduction possibilities of the service in the crowded UHF broadcasting spectrum. Technically almost any DVB-T frequency allotment or assignment can be used also for DVB-H; the only limitations come from interoperability with GSM900 cellular transmitter in the DVB-H terminal. If simultaneous operation is required, the frequencies below about 700-750 MHz are favored.

For broadcasters DVB-H can be seen just as a new means to provide broadcast services for a new, interesting group of customers, namely, the mobile phone users. If this is seen as interesting enough, spectrum will be available. It is in any case expected that the situation will be more relaxed after the analog TV services will start to close. It should also be noted that DVB-H is very spectrum efficient when compared with the traditional TV-services. One 8-MHz channel can deliver 30-50 video streaming services to the small screen terminals. This is ten times more than standard-definition TV (SDTV) with MPEG-2 or 20 times more than high-definition TV (HDTV) with AVC.

Sharing with DVB-T

There a network of DVB-T transmitters is serving both DVB-H and DVB-T terminals. The existing DVB-T network has to be, however, designed for portable indoor reception so that it can provide high enough field strength for the hand-held terminals inside the wanted service area. The only required modification in the transmitters is an update so that the DVB-H signaling bits and Cell ID bits are added to the TPS information of the transmitter.The actual sharing is done at the multiplex level. DVB-H offers a full flexibility to select the wanted portion of the multiplex to DVB-H services. The key DVB-H component in the network is the IP-encapsulator, where the MPE of IP data, time slicing, and MPE-FEC are implemented. Another possibility to share the network is to use the DVB-T hierarchical modulation. In that case the MPEG-2 and DVB-H IP services will have their own independent TS inputs in the DVB-T transmitters. The DVB-H services would use the high-priority part, which would offer increased robustness over the low-priority input, which is then used for the normal digital TV services.

Dedicated DVB-H Networks

When a full multiplex can be reserved for DVB-H, the freedom in planning is increased. If needed, now it is possible to select the new 4k mode or in-depth interleavers introduced in the latest DVB-T standard for DVB-H. A typical network is composed of several SFN areas, each using its own frequency allotment. The maximum size of one SFN area depends on the FFT size, guard interval, and geographical properties in the network, but can typically be in the order of tens of kilometers. Each SFN area has probably several GPS-synchronized transmitters supported by a number of on-channel repeaters to cover some smaller holes. As the required field strength in a DVB-H network is fairly high and the allowed total interfering power from an allotment is limited by the coordinated plan, the number of synchronised main transmitters should be higher and the transmitter powers and antenna heights lower than in a traditional DVB-T network. The network can be called dense SFN. Obviously the cost of the network is higher than in conventional DVB-T network, but also the number of services in one multiplex is ten times higher.

Pilot Networks

Technical trials and pilot projects have been two important elements in the development of DVB-H network concepts. They are aimed at speeding up the verification process for the standards and at testing the technical feasibility of various network equipment and terminals. More importantly, because of these pilots and trials, valuable experience has been gained regarding how the end users are adopting the new services and how they are consuming them. The pilots also play a role in the ongoing spectrum planning process by demonstrating the importance of hand held reception for the Regional Radio Conference. DVB-H pilot networks have been operational in Berlin, Germany; Helsinki, Finland; Turku, Finland; Pittsburgh, PA; and Oxford, U.K. Several others are in the planning stage at the time of this writing. Currently there already exist several DVB-H chips available on the market and several others have been announced. Prototype receivers for the pilots and H-transmitter equipment have existed already over a year.

Streaming Media

Streaming media started with the Internet's first streaming player, RealAudio. In April 1995, it allowed listeners to hear audio as it was being downloaded. The first Internet streaming video player was Xing Technologies' StreamWorks, released in August 1995. It was based upon Motion Picture Expert Group (MPEG) compression and provided jerky "talking heads" images the size of a postage stamp. This was followed shortly by VDOLive from VDOnet Corp. In early 1997 Progressive Networks, renamed RealNetworks, released RealVideo along with an all-in-one audio-video player called RealPlayer.

As the use of streaming media has increased, competition for customers in the streaming media market has intensified. While RealNetworks has emerged as the clear leader as of 1999, rapid changes in compression-decompression (codec) standards offers many new challengers. Increasingly, however, the question is asked, How do Microsoft's Windows Media and other formats stack up against the RealNetworks?

Microsoft entered into the streaming video market in 1997 with its buyout of WebTV Networks and Vxtreme. Microsoft introduced its Active Streaming Format in conjunction with the developing MPEG-4 standard. This protocol provides a standard method of synchronising audio, video, and multimedia. Competition between ASF and RealNetworks' G2 emerged in 1999, as the World Wide Web Consortium (W3C) endorsed Synchronised Multimedia Integration Language. SMIL provides a text-based tag markup format for streaming multimedia, freeing developers from proprietary formats and enabling multiple vendors to supply software tools. Other groups developed open standards with Java-based applets that didn't require preinstalled players in order to stream video.

Macromedia's Shockwave and Flash protocols first produced streaming animation. Authoring platforms for real-time delivery of animation during streaming videos have become available. They allow multimedia-style animation and interactive controls to be linked with broadcast-style audio and video. Regardless of which vendor you choose, the equipment and software used in multimedia production is often on the cutting edge and not as fully developed as products in the more established computer desktop applications. As a result, there are often compatibility issues that must be resolved in making a set of software and hardware choices to complement your production system.

The actual making of the multimedia content involves the following five basic steps:

— Preparing the content source material

— Capturing the audio/video using a computer with a video capture card

— Editing the video and saving the large uncompressed file

— Compressing the video

— Delivering the movie content over the Web

Each of these steps can be optimised toward improving the final client video. For example, optimising computer capture hardware requires a balanced understanding of data-flow versus choke points within the PC capture process. A high speed Pentium III, with 256MB RAM, an 8.4GB (8 millisecond) hard drive, and wide-SCSI-3 bus can demonstrate up to 40Mbps throughput while capturing video. Unfortunately, many low-to-medium-priced capture cards provide a throughput of only 2 to 5Mbps, producing a limiting choke point in your systems.

But even after heroic efforts on your part in optimising the source video, the hardware and software, and the editing and compression process, there remains a significant barrier to delivering your video over the Web. This is the "last mile" connection to the client.

The bandwidth of Internet communications has been steadily increasing due to the overall pressures to improve performance from users. The important point is that the infrastructure provided by the Internet has become widespread and has developed enough performance to allow rapid transmission of large volumes of data. Now it is becoming ready for video.

The problem with video, however, has been trying to push it over digital networks where it clogs and chokes the critical connections. The arrival of data compression has reduced the problem of transmitting video data to more manageable levels. The technology has only recently reached the point where video can be digitised and compressed to levels that allow reasonable quality of appearance following distribution over digital networks

Yogi Berra once said, "Predictions can be tricky, especially when you're talking about the future." And looking forward is certainly more perilous than using hindsight to review history. However, the future of rapidly converging technology is not so complex and uncertain that a few reasonable predictions about certain aspects of streaming video as well as the future of the Internet can't be discerned.

Electronic Video, or "e-Video," includes all audio/video clips that are distributed and played over the Internet, either by direct download or streaming video. And it is streaming video that is the nexus of technology convergence because it is the improvement in bandwidth to deliver video that will prove decisive in reconciling competing technology standards. As this last stumbling block of bandwidth limitation is finally overcome, the television, cable, data, and telecommunication technologies will converge toward a compatible and coherent industry standard based on a one-to-one customised Internet commerce model.

Up to this point, video has involved moving very large files (3-40Mbps), and delivering such large data rates on the Internet seemed prohibitive. Consider that to expand the Internet bandwidth a factor of 10 times its current backbone would cost additional billions of dollars for construction of fiber, copper, or satellite equipment. Now consider the relatively small cost of an equivalent expansion of bandwidth improvement produced by software changes in data compression or by equipment upgrades, such as, optical multiplexing. The ideal vision for broadband may be an end-to-end optical fiber network with fiber direct to the home. But this expensive and long-term option may be preempted by a combination of a near term breakthrough in compression technology and/or less expensive optical wave division multiplexing. Obviously, the data compression of streaming video compression-decompression (codec) standards will play a critical role in the form of required bandwidth reduction. This in turn will contribute to technology convergence. Streaming Media is media (audio, video, or graphics) that is delivered as a stream of data, and played as it is received. It allows you to view large data files without long delays and minimal data loss as well as to view live events in real time.

Process of Streaming

The process of streaming starts when a media file is broken into smaller pieces so it can be transferred and played as each of the pieces is received, rather than waiting for the whole file to be transferred before playback starts. How quickly you can receive files is mostly a matter of your internet bandwidth. One of the features of RealPlayer is that it can select a data stream that best matches your available bandwidth (some media is streamed at more than one bandwidth) so the media stream provided matches the transfer/download speed available to you.

RealPlayer can also display media created in SMIL (Synchronised Multimedia Integration Language) protocol, which is used to better optimise the bandwidth of a presentation. SMIL presentations send different streams for each of the components of a presentation. Each stream has a different optimum bit-rate associated with it. The result is that a complex presentation can be streamed with a much lower bandwidth than if the whole presentation was limited to the format and bandwidth of the largest media type.

Bandwidth

The property that most affects your experience playing any type of Streaming Media over the Internet is bandwidth. Usually this means the maximum speed (Kbps) of your Internet connection, but it can also refer to capacity of the media server (how many data streams the server can provide), as well as other network constraints. If RealPlayer had to download data faster than your connection can handle, such as viewing a 256Kbps stream over a 56Kbps connection (you can see the bandwidth of any stream on your Status Display), the presentation would have to regularly pause to let the system catch up.

To avoid this, a media provider can stream RealAudio and Real Video in multiple bandwidths at the same time, such as at 56Kbps and at 256Kbps. RealPlayer will choose the data stream with a bandwidth that best matches your Preferences. Of course a narrower, or lower bandwidth, data stream will be of lower quality, but it is less likely to be interrupted than a wider data stream.

Buffering

When media is being streamed, the bandwidth does not always remain constant. Often it will fall below what is required to stream the presentation smoothly. To avoid pauses due to delays or slow transmissions, RealPlayer will cache, or buffer, a portion of the media stream before beginning to play it. (This is indicated by "Loading xx%" appearing in the Status Display when you start playing a clip.) When the bandwidth through your connection is low, or data drops, RealPlayer takes data from the buffer. When bandwidth returns to normal, RealPlayer puts data into the buffer until the cache is refilled. When you attempt to view a high-bandwidth clip over a low-bandwidth connection, RealPlayer will attempt to create as large a buffer as possible before beginning playback.

Streaming Media vs. Recorded Media

Generally speaking, Streaming Media refers to media that is being presented on the Internet. The data stream originates on the Internet, is transferred by modem/data-line to your computer, is decoded by a Player, and is then viewed by a consumer. Recorded Media refers to data files that are directly accessible from your computer (on a hard drive or network drive) such as audio CD tracks on a CD, or .RM or .MP3 files.

On Demand vs. Live Steaming Media

On Demand Media: A media file that is available on the Internet and is streamed to your computer. Typically it is an audio or video clip that you can select and listen to from start to finish.

Live Streaming Media: An audio or video stream that is being datacast live, and is available continuously. Typically these are Internet Radio or TV stations.

Internet Television

Internet television is the digital distribution of television content via the Internet. It should not be confused with Web television - short programs or videos created by a wide variety of companies and individuals, or Internet protocol television (IPTV) - an emerging internet technology standard for use by television broadcasters. Some Internet television is known as catch-up TV. Internet Television is a general term that covers the delivery of television shows and other video content over the internet by video streaming technology, typically by major traditional television broadcasters. It does not describe a technology used to deliver content (see Internet protocol television). Internet television has become very popular through services such as RTÉ Player in Ireland; BBC iPlayer, 4oD, ITV Player (also STV Player and UTV Player) and Demand Five in the United Kingdom; Hulu in the United States; Nederland 24 in the Netherlands; ABC iview and Australia Live TV in Australia; Tivibu in Turkey. See List of Internet television providers.

Internet television allows the users to choose the content or the television show they want to watch from an archive of content or from a channel directory. The two forms of viewing Internet television are streaming the content directly to a media player or simply downloading the media to the user's computer. With the "TV on Demand" market growing, these on-demand websites or applications are essential for major television broadcasters. For example, the BBC iPlayer brings in users which stream more than one million videos per week, with one of the BBC's headline shows The Apprentice taking over three percent to five percent of the UK's internet traffic due to people watching the first episode on the BBC iPlayer. Availability of online TV content continues to grow. As an example, in Canada as of May 2011 there were more than 600 TV shows available for free streaming, including several major titles like Survivor and The Daily Show with Jon Stewart.

Every night the use of on-demand television peaks at around 10 pm. Most providers of the service provide several different formats and quality controls so that the service can be viewed on many different devices. Some services now offer a HD service along side their SD, streaming is the same but offers the quality of HD to the device being used, as long as it is using a HD screen. During Peak times the BBC iPlayer transmits 12 GB (gigabytes) of information per second. Over the course of a month the iPlayer sends 7 PB (petabytes) of information.

Before 2006, most catch-up services used peer-to-peer (P2P) networking, in which users downloaded an application and data would be shared between the users rather than the service provider giving the now more commonly used streaming method. Now most service providers have moved away from the P2P systems and are now using the streaming media. The old P2P service was selected because the existing infrastructure could not handle the bandwidth necessary for centralized streaming distribution. Some consumers didn't like their upload bandwidth being consumed by their video player, which partially motivated the rollout of centralized streaming distribution.

Launching in March 2012 in New York City, Aereo streams network TV to customers over the internet. Broadcasters filed lawsuits against Aereo which Aereo captured broadcast signals and streaming the content to Aereo's costumers without paying broadcasters. In mid-July 2012, a federal judge sided with the Aereo start-up. Aereo planned to expand it to every major metropolitan area by the end of 2013.

Market Competitors

Many providers of internet-television services exist including conventional television stations that have taken advantage of the internet as a way to continue showing television shows after they have been broadcast often advertised as "on-demand" and "catch-up" services. Today, almost every major broadcaster around the world is operating an internet-television platform. Examples include the BBC, which introduced the BBC iPlayer on 25 June 2008 as an extension to its "RadioPlayer" and already existing streamed video-clip content, and Channel 4 that launched 4oD ("4 on Demand") in November 2006 allowing users to watch recently shown content. Most internet-television services allow users to view content free of charge; however, some content is for a fee.

Control

Controlling content on the Internet presents a challenge for most providers; to try to ensure that a user is allowed to view content such as content with age certificates, providers use methods such as parental controls that allows restrictions to be placed upon the use and access of certificated material. The BBC iPlayer makes use of a parental control system giving parents the option to "lock" content, meaning that a password would have to be used to access it. Flagging systems can be used to warn a user that content may be certified or that it is intended for viewing post-watershed. Honor systems are also used where users are asked for their dates of birth or age to verify if they are able to view certain content.

Archives

An archive is a collection of information and media much like a library or interactive-storage facility. It is a necessity for an on-demand media service to maintain archives so that users can watch content that has already been aired on standard-broadcast television. However, these archives can vary from a few weeks to months to years, depending on the curator and the type of content.For example, the BBC iPlayer's shows are in general available for up to seven days after their original broadcast. This so called "seven-day catch-up" model seems to become an industry standard for internet-television services in many countries around the world. However, some shows may only be available for shorter periods. Others, such as the BBC's Panorama, may be available for an extended period because of the shows documentary nature or its popularity.

In contrast, 4oD channel 4's on-demand service offers many of its television shows that were originally aired years ago. An example of this is the comedy The IT Crowd where users can view the full series on the internet player. The same is true for other hit channel 4 comedies such as The Inbetweeners and Black Books.

Having an extensive archive, however, can bring problems along with benefits. Large archives are expensive to maintain, server farms and mass storage is needed along with ample bandwidth to transmit it all. Vast archives can be hard to catalogue and sort so that it is accessible to users.

The benefits in most cases outweigh these problems. This is because large archives bring in far more users who, in turn, watch more media, leading to a wider audience base and more advertising revenue. Large archives will also mean the user will spend more time on that website rather than a competitors, leading to starvation of demand for the competitors.

Broadcasting Rights

Broadcasting rights vary from country to country and even within provinces of countries. These rights govern the distribution of copyrighted content and media and allow the sole distribution of that content at any one time.

An example of content only being aired in certain countries is BBC iPlayer. The BBC checks a user's IP address to make sure that only users located in the UK can stream content from the BBC. The BBC only allows free use of their product for users within the UK as those users have paid for a television license that funds part of the BBC. This IP address check is not foolproof as the user may be accessing the BBC website through a VPN.

Broadcasting rights can also be restricted to allowing a broadcaster rights to distribute that content for a limited time. Channel 4's online service 4oD can only stream shows created in the US by companies such as HBO for thirty days after they are aired on one of the Channel 4 group channels. This is to boost DVD sales for the companies who produce that media.Some companies pay very large amounts for broadcasting rights with sports and US sitcoms usually fetching the highest price from UK-based broadcasters.

Profits and Costs

With the exception of Internet-connectivity costs many online-television channels or sites are free. These sites maintain this free-television policy through the use of video advertising, short commercials and banner advertisements may show up before a video is played. An example of this is on the abc.com catch-up website; in place of the advertisement breaks on normal television, a short thirty-second advertisement is played.

Technologies Used for Internet Television

The Hybrid Broadcast Broadband TV (HbbTV) consortium of industry companies (such as SES, Humax, Philips, and ANT Software) is currently promoting and establishing an open European standard (called HbbTV) for hybrid set-top boxes for the reception of broadcast and broadband digital television and multimedia applications with a single-user interface.

Current providers of internet television use various technologies to provide a service such as peer-to-peer (P2P) technologies, VoD systems, and live streaming. BBC iPlayer makes use of the Adobe Flash Player to provide streaming-video clips and other software provided by Adobe for its download service. CNBC, Bloomberg Television and Showtime use live-streaming services from BitGravity to stream live television to paid subscribers using a standard http protocol. DRM (digital rights management) software is also incorporated into many internet-television services. Sky Go has software that is provided by Microsoft to prevent content being copied. Internet television is also cross platform, the Sky Player service has been expanded to the Xbox 360 on October 27 and to Windows Media Center and then to Windows 7 PCs on November 19.

The BBC iPlayer is also available through Virgin Media's on-demand service and other platforms such as FetchTV and games consoles including the Wii and the PlayStation 3. Other Internet-television platforms include mobile platforms such as the iPhone and iPod Touch, Nokia N96, Sony Ericsson C905 and many other mobile devices.

Samsung TV has also announced their plans to provide streaming options including 3D Video on Demand through their Explore 3D service.

Website vs. Applications

The main problem with on-demand video services that are applications on desktop computers is getting users to download them and register. It is far easier for a user to simply log onto a webpage without registering than to have to spend time registering and downloading often large applications.However, applications are more powerful in that they can manage the downloading of content far better and the content they access can usually be watched offline for thirty days after downloading.

Stream Quality

Stream quality refers to the quality of the image and audio transferred from the servers of the distributor to the user's home screen. Higher-quality video such as video in high definition (720p+) requires higher bandwidth and faster connection speeds. The generally accepted kbit/s download rate needed to stream high-definition video that has been encoded with H.264 is 3500 kbit/s, whereas standard-definition television can range from 500 to 1500 kbit/s depending on the resolution on screen.

In the UK, the BBC iPlayer deals with the largest amount of traffic yet it offers HD content along with SD content. As more people get broadband connections which can deal with streaming HD video over the internet, the BBC iPlayer has tried to keep up with demand and pace. However, as streaming HD video takes around 1.5 gb of data per hour of video the BBC has had to invest a lot of money collected from License Fee payers to implement this on such a large scale.

For users which do not have the bandwidth to stream HD video or even high-SD video which requires 1500 kbit/s, the BBC iPlayer offers lower bitrate streams which in turn lead to lower video quality. This makes use of an adaptive bitrate stream so that if the user's bandwidth suddenly drops, iPlayer will lower its streaming rate to compensate.

Although competitors in the UK such as 4oD, ITV Player and Demand Five have not yet offered HD streaming, the technology to support it is fairly new and widespread HD streaming is not an impossibility. The availability of Channel 4 and Five content on YouTube is predicted to prove incredibly popular as series such as Skins, Green Wing, The X Factor and others become available in a simple, straightforward format on a website which already attracts millions of people every day.

References

Cianci, Philip J. *High Definition Television.* NC, USA: McFarland. pp. 1-25. 2012.

Digital video broadcasting (DVB), *DVB mega-frame for single frequency network (SFN) synchronization*, ETSI TS 101 191 V1.4.1, European Telecommunications Standards Institute, 2004-06.

Hart, Jeffrey A., *Television, technology, and competition : HDTV and digital TV in the United States, Western Europe, and Japan, New York :* Cambridge University Press, 2004.

Joel Brinkley, *Defining Vision: The Battle for the Future of Television*, New York: Harcourt Brace, 1997.

Kruger, L. G. *Digital Television: An Overview*. Hauppauge, New York: Nova Publishers. 2001

Ong, C. Y., Song, J., Pan, C., & Li, Y.(2010, May). Technology and Standards of Digital Television Terrestrial Multimedia Broadcasting, *Communications Magazine,* IEEE , 48(5),119-127

Reimers U., *DVB—The Family of International Standards for Digital Video Broadcasting*, 2nd ed. Berlin, Germany: Springer, 2005.

Setton, E.[Eric], Girod, B.[Bernd], "Rate-Distortion Analysis and Streaming of SP and SI Frames", *CirSysVideo*(16), No. 6, June 2006.

Bibliography

Aitkin Hugh G. J. *The Continuous Wave: Technology and the American Radio, 1900-1932*. Princeton University Press, 1985.

Alan Taylor, *We, the Media: Pedagogic Intrusions into US Mainstream Film and Television News Broadcasting Rhetoric*, Peter Lang, 2005.

Albert Abramson, *The History of Television, 1942 to 2000*, Jefferson, NC, and London, McFarland, 2003.

Beretta E. Smith-Shomade, *Shaded Lives: African-American Women and Television*, Rutgers University Press, 2002.

Briggs Asa. *The History of Broadcasting in the United Kingdom*, Oxford University Press, 1961.

Ceylon, Radio. - *Standards of Broadcasting Practice* - Commercial Broadcasting Division. - Radio Ceylon, 1950.

Cianci, Philip J. *High Definition Television.* NC, USA: McFarland. pp. 1-25. 2012.

Crisell, Andrew *An Introductory History of British Broadcasting.* 2nd ed. London: Routledge. 2002.

David E. Fisher and Marshall J. Fisher, *Tube: the Invention of Television*, Counterpoint, Washington, DC, 1996.

Digital video broadcasting (DVB), *DVB mega-frame for single frequency network (SFN) synchronization*, ETSI TS 101 191 V1.4.1, European Telecommunications Standards Institute, 2004-06.

Douglas B. Craig. *Fireside Politics: Radio and Political Culture in the United States, 1920-1940*, 2005.

Dunaway, David *Community Media in the Information Age: Perspectives and Prospect,* Cresskill, NJ: Hampton Press. 2002.

Evan I. Schwartz, *The Last Lone Inventor: A Tale of Genius, Deceit, and the Birth of Television*, New York, Harper Paperbacks, 2003.

Ewbank Henry and Lawton Sherman P. *Broadcasting: Radio and Television*, Harper & Brothers, 1952.

Girard, Bruce (ed). ·*A Passion for Radio: Radio waves and community*. Black Rose Books. 1993.

Gwenyth L. Jackaway; *Media at War: Radio's Challenge to the Newspapers, 1924-1939* Praeger Publishers, 1995.

Hart, Jeffrey A., *Television, technology, and competition : HDTV and digital TV in the United States, Western Europe, and Japan, New York :* Cambridge University Press, 2004.

Hendy, David, *Radio in the Global Age*, Cambridge: Polity Press, 2000.

Hoeg, Wolfgang; Lauterbach, Thomas. *Digital audio broadcasting: principles and applications of DAB, DAB+ and DMB.* Wiley, 2009.

Jacques Derrida and Bernard Stiegler, *Echographies of Television*, Polity Press, 2002.

Jankowski, Nicholas W.; Prehn, Ole. eds. *Community Media in the Information Age: Perspectives and Prospects.* Cresskill, NJ: Hampton Press.2001.

Jerry Mander, *Four Arguments for the Elimination of Television*, Perennial, 1978.

Jesse Walker, *Rebels on the Air: An Alternative History of Radio in America.* New York University Press, 2001.

Joel Brinkley, *Defining Vision: The Battle for the Future of Television*, New York: Harcourt Brace, 1997.

John Dunning, *On The Air: The Encyclopedia of Old-Time Radio*, Oxford University Press, 1998. ISBN 0-19-507678-8

Kahn Frank J., ed. *Documents of American Broadcasting,* fourth edition, Prentice-Hall, Inc., 1984.

Kapoor, D N., *Broadcast Journalism.* Mohit Pubications, 2006.

Kruger, L. G. *Digital Television: An Overview*. Hauppauge, New York: Nova Publishers. 2001

Kumar, K. *Mass Communications in India.* Mumbai: Jaico Publishing. 2007.

Lazarsfeld Paul F. *The People Look at Radio*, University of North Carolina Press, 1946.

Maclaurin W. Rupert. *Invention and Innovation in the Radio Industry.* The Macmillan Company, 1949.

Michael Roberts. "Digital Dilemma: Will new royalty fees kill Web radio?". *Westword.* Retrieved 2010-03-14.

Ong, C. Y., Song, J., Pan, C., & Li, Y.(2010, May). Technology and Standards of Digital Television Terrestrial Multimedia Broadcasting, *Communications Magazine,* IEEE , 48(5),119-127

Priestman, Chris, *Web Radio: Radio Production for Internet Streaming*, Melbourne: Focal Press, 2002.

Reid, Alasdair, "Radio's Digital Challenge," *Campaign*, 14 November, 2003.

Reimers U., *DVB—The Family of International Standards for Digital Video Broadcasting*, 2nd ed. Berlin, Germany: Springer, 2005.

Rosen Philip T. *The Modern Stentors; Radio Broadcasting and the Federal Government 1920-1934*, Greenwood Press, 1980.

Scannell, Paddy, and Cardiff, David. *A Social History of British Broadcasting, Volume One, 1922-1939*, Basil Blackwell, 1991.

Setton, E.[Eric], Girod, B.[Bernd], "Rate-Distortion Analysis and Streaming of SP and SI Frames", *CirSysVideo*(16), No. 6, June 2006.

Singhal, A. and E.M. Rogers. *The Emerging Information Revolution In India.* New Delhi: Sage 1988.

Spurgeon, Christina L. and McCarthy, Joanna. "Mobilising the Community Radio Audience". *3CMedia: Journal of Community, Citizen's and Third Sector Media and Communication*, 1 (February), pp. 1-13. 2005.

Sterling Christopher, and Kittross John M. *Stay Tuned: A Concise History of American Broadcasting*, Wadsworth, 1978.

Tim Crook; *International Radio Journalism: History, Theory and Practice* Routledge, 1998.

UNESCO. *How to Do Community Radio: A Primer*. UNESCO. 2004.

Vinod Pavarala and Kanchan K. Malik. *Other Voices: The Struggle for Community Radio in India.* Sage Publications India Pvt. Ltd. , New Delhi, India , 2007.

Wavell, Stuart. - *The Art of Radio* - Training Manual written by the Director Training of the CBC. - Ceylon Broadcasting Corporation, 1969.

White Llewellyn. *The American Radio*, University of Chicago Press, 1947.